Teaching Multilingual Students Through Culture and Language

This book serves as a professional development guide designed for elementary school teachers to help them center multilingual and bilingual students' language and culture in the classroom by recognizing and harnessing their students' assets through semiotics and self-discovery. Its purpose is to promote compassionate education, fostering empathy and connection to students' identities in response to the known problem of student disengagement and the challenges in teaching reading and writing.

The guide showcases planned and tested modules to facilitate student success in diverse learning environments, and each module includes resources, sample lesson plans, and hands-on experiences designed to help students find joy in learning. Emphasizing strategies intended for learners with varied abilities and interests, this book focuses on students' identities and cultures as they are related to race, language, heritage, and semiotics. It is an ideal resource for in-service elementary school teachers interested in incorporating culturally responsive teaching practices into their classrooms, as well as for preservice teachers who want to focus on students' cultures, languages, and assets. Teachers, students, and the student community share the joy of knowledge together through this guide.

Tala Michelle Karkar-Esperat is Assistant Professor of Curriculum and Instruction in the College of Education and Technology at Eastern New Mexico University. Her research is focused on preservice teachers' literacies, online literacies, coaching of teachers, and pedagogical literacy practices through multiliteracies, new literacies, and semiotics.

Also Available from Routledge Eye On Education
(www.routledge.com/eyeoneducation)

An Educator's Guide to Dual Language Instruction:
Increasing Achievement and Global Competence, K–12,
2nd edition
Gayle Westerberg and Leslie Davison

Building Proficiency for World Language Learners: 100+
High-Interest Activities
Janina Klimas

Learning and Leading for Transdisciplinary Literacy through
Multi-Tiered Systems of Support
Mary E. Little and Enrique A. Puig

Teaching World Languages with the Five Senses:
Practical Strategies and Ideas for Hands-On Learning
Elizabeth Porter

Sentence Strategies for Multilingual Learners:
Advancing Academic Literacy through Combinations
Nell Scharff Panero and Joanna Yip

Going Global in the World Language Classroom:
Ideas, Strategies, and Resources for Teaching and Learning
With the World
Erin Austin

Accelerating Newcomer Literacy:
An Integrated Writing Process Playbook for English Learners
Eugenia Krimmel

Teaching Multilingual Students Through Culture and Language

An Elementary Teacher's Guide to Self-Discovery Using Semiotics

Tala Michelle Karkar-Esperat

Routledge
Taylor & Francis Group

NEW YORK AND LONDON

Designed cover image: © Getty Images

First published 2026
by Routledge
605 Third Avenue, New York, NY 10158

and by Routledge
4 Park Square, Milton Park, Abingdon, Oxon, OX14 4RN

Routledge is an imprint of the Taylor & Francis Group, an informa business

© 2026 Taylor & Francis

The right of Tala Michelle Karkar-Esperat to be identified as author of this work has been asserted in accordance with sections 77 and 78 of the Copyright, Designs and Patents Act 1988.

All rights reserved. No part of this book may be reprinted or reproduced or utilised in any form or by any electronic, mechanical, or other means, now known or hereafter invented, including photocopying and recording, or in any information storage or retrieval system, without permission in writing from the publishers.

For Product Safety Concerns and Information please contact our EU representative GPSR@taylorandfrancis.com. Taylor & Francis Verlag GmbH, Kaufingerstraße 24, 80331 München, Germany.

Trademark notice: Product or corporate names may be trademarks or registered trademarks, and are used only for identification and explanation without intent to infringe.

ISBN: 978-1-041-06694-1 (hbk)
ISBN: 978-1-041-06692-7 (pbk)
ISBN: 978-1-003-63667-0 (ebk)

DOI: 10.4324/9781003636670

Access the Support Material: www.routledge.com/9781041066927

Typeset in Palatino
by SPi Technologies India Pvt Ltd (Straive)

To my guardian angel parents, my teachers, and former educators, Aida and Michael Karkar, who instilled in me the values of perseverance, integrity, hard work, and compassion.

To Uncle Jack (Yacoub) Karkar, I called you my second father and your students called you Professor Karkar. Thank you for being the cornerstone of my education journey. Your wisdom, inspiration, and kindness are imprinted in this guide.

To my mentor, Dr. Pamela Mason, thank you for your guidance, support, and assistance in embracing my voice as a teacher educator.

To Will Cass, my friend and neighbor, who always reminded me to find joy in everything I do. Thank you for your boundless motivation.

To my community—my siblings, my uncle, Dr. Maurice Karkar colleagues, friends, nephews and nieces, current and former students— thank you for your inspiration.

To my lifelong best friends, my triplet brother and sister, Tariq M. Karkar and Diala M. Karkar Hazboun, you are my force, lifelong partners, and guiding lights. I am deeply grateful for your unconditional love, support, and motivation.

To my extended parents, Dr. Christina Roble Esperat and Oswaldo Esperat, thank you for your constant support and love, which helped me stay focused.

To my husband, my best friend, and my better half, Dominic Roble Esperat, thank you for everything you do for us. Your love and support shine through this work.

Support Material

This book contains additional materials that are available on our website as free downloads, so you can easily print and reproduce them for classroom use. You can access them by visiting the book product page: www.routledge.com/9781041066927 (or search for the book title on routledge.com). Click on the tab that says "Support Material" and select the files. They will begin downloading to your computer.

Contents

Meet the Author viii
Foreword x
Acknowledgments xiii
Preface xv

1 A New Day for Education: A Guide Toward
   Self-Discovery 1

2 Self-Discovery Through the Linguistic Mode:
   Idioms, Identity Text, and Storytelling. 22

3 Self-Discovery Through the Visual Mode: Examining
   Customs and Traditions and Visual Knowledge 71

4 Self-Discovery Through the Audio Mode:
   Examining Language Using Music Genres -
   Mariachi, Hip-Hop, Folk Music. 117

5 Self-Discovery Through the Spatial Mode:
   Connecting Local to Global 171

6 Self-Discovery Through the Gestural Mode:
   Examining Gestures in the Classroom 203

7 Self-Discovery Through the Synesthesia Mode:
   Examining Culture Through Local Historical Figures. . . . 232

Postscript 259

Meet the Author

Tala Michelle Karkar-Esperat is a teacher educator, research scholar, and curriculum designer. Tala serves as an assistant professor in the Department of Curriculum and Instruction at Eastern New Mexico University. In her role as the professional development site coordinator, she works with inservice teachers on empowering their practice using the *community engaged partnership model*. This model aims to bridge that gap between theory and practice, integrating professional learning communities, content knowledge, pedagogical knowledge, and face to face visual support.

Tala started her international educational career early in her life. She grew up in a household where education was a way of life. Her mother was a dedicated schoolteacher and her father was a committed athletic coach. From watching them guide, inspire and uplift their students, Tala developed a deep passion for teaching early on, recognizing the powerful impact educators can have on the lives of others. She aspires to continue her parents' legacy. Her joy is preparing preservice teachers to be impactful educators.

Tala's research is focused on improving the scholarship of preservice and inservice teachers. She has studied the use of both teacher pedagogical content knowledge of multiliteracies, new literacies, and traditional literacies in the classroom. Her classroom and curriculum vision started with developing the Pedagogical Holistic Model of New Literacies, followed by the Pedagogical Content Knowledge of Multiliteracies (PCKM) Survey Instrument. Her work in the classroom and preparing preservice teachers inspired her to change the dynamics and direction by proposing the *Raciosemiotic Architecture Framework*® and the *MultiSemiotic Architecture Framework*® for bilingual and multilingual students to encourage transparency in the classroom. She contributed to the development of the *Transmultiliteracies Sustaining Pedagogy* approach, an interdisciplinary pedagogical approach of using multiliteracies across curriculum drawing on monolingual, bilingual, and multilingual learner assets. She also focuses on exploring best online teaching and learning practices through the *"interactive online teaching model"* and *"triple A"* concept that she developed to build a collaborative online community informed by the concept of love. Her original work aims to humanize education and advocate for meeting all diverse students' needs in the classroom.

Foreword

Last quarter, as I taught a course on culturally responsive assessment in the elementary teacher education program at my university, several issues arose repeatedly for me in relation to the goals of the course: (1) How can I support my teacher candidates in drawing from the rich cultural and linguistic funds of knowledge (Moll et al., 1992) that students bring to the classroom from their families and communities? (2) How can the teacher candidates in the room help their students connect learning to the world around them in ways that help students read both the word and the world (Freire, 1985)? (3) How do we bridge theory and practice in truly authentic ways, providing examples for teacher candidates who might not have experiences of authentic instruction to draw from? My questions led me to extensive self-reflection and a search for resources that might scaffold the complexity of teaching in culturally and linguistically diverse classrooms for the teacher candidates in my classroom.

This book, *Teaching Multilingual Students Through Culture and Language: An Elementary Teacher's Guide to Self-Discovery Using Semiotics* by Dr. Tala Karkar-Esperat offers an invaluable resource to teachers and teacher candidates teaching literacy and language in elementary school classrooms, particularly in diverse setting with multilingual learners. It is, in fact, the book I didn't know that I needed to help answer the questions I had throughout the term.

Teaching Multilingual Students Through Culture and Language helps teachers to draw from the rich assets of culture and language that students bring into the classroom while also supporting teachers to develop as reflective practitioners. Each chapter blends research with hands-on tools, including lesson plans with embedded strategies, to support students in their academic growth and teachers to discover ways that they can use multiple modalities. Through these strategies, teachers will learn to engage students, and to help them read both the word and the world around them. Dr. Karkar-Esperat draws from her own experiences as a former classroom teacher and a current teacher educator, adopting an approachable tone, to draw readers in, inviting them on a journey of self-discovery across multiple modalities to make meaning for themselves and support students as meaning makers (the heart of semiotics).

Dr. Karkar-Esperat's chapters take teachers through a journey across modalities, conceptualizing literacies broadly and positioning students and teachers as active meaning makers, using multiple tools of inquiry to support their learning and meaning making. Each chapter affirms students' humanity, their identities, and the many ways that they can make meaning in a 21st-century world. The lesson plans that she offers use literacy-based and multimodal strategies and state content standards, include language objectives and clear guiding questions, and offer resources that can be used or adapted based on individual teacher contexts. In addition to broad notions of literacy, *Teaching Multilingual Students Through Culture and Language* integrates opportunities for students to connect their classroom learning to their home spaces, their local/state contexts, and global contexts, using linguistic, visual, audio, spatial, and gestural modes.

Given the increasingly scripted nature of curricula, Dr. Karkar-Esperat's framework offers teachers ways to think beyond the curriculum guides they may be given, to enhance authentic learning opportunities for students. By anchoring the text in research as well as professional and content standards, the ideas in the book show respect for teacher professionalism while also providing valuable resources and models that can help teachers not to have to fully reinvent the wheel, a necessity given the many demands that teachers must navigate to support student learning. The book has a broad audience and can be used by more veteran teachers to support their reflective practice, new teachers entering the field and seeking guidance in adapting curriculum, and teacher educators looking to support teacher candidates to consider how to teach multilingual learners in ways that are asset-based, responsive, and affirming, building from the knowledge they bring into schools, and helping them to grow.

I am deeply grateful to learn from Dr. Karkar-Esperat and to be able to use her work as a resource for teacher candidates with whom I work. Her frameworks and approaches bring multi-leveled, layered ways of supporting more equitable, inclusive literacy education, simultaneously meeting all students (particularly multilingual and culturally diverse students) where they are at and helping them to grow. I hope that as you, the reader, engage with your own journey of self-discovery through this text, you see the brilliance of your own identities expressed in the multiple modes throughout this book. We teach who we are, and as educators committed to our own ongoing learning and development across modes, we can also teach our students the importance of self-discovery across their educational journeys.

Dr. Betina Hsieh
Endowed Professor of Teacher Education
University of Washington (Seattle)

References

Freire, P. (1985). Reading the world and reading the word: An interview with Paulo Freire. *Language Arts*, *62*(1), 15–21.

Moll, L. C., Amanti, C., Neff, D., & Gonzalez, N. (1992). Funds of knowledge for teaching: Using a qualitative approach to connect homes and classrooms. *Theory Into Practice*, *31*(2), 133–141.

Acknowledgments

This book includes theoretical frameworks that I developed in 2021–2023.

I want to thank and give recognition to the following:

The reviewers and editors who believed in this work and provided critical feedback, which enhanced the presentation of these frameworks.

My mentor, Dr. Pamela Mason, who has been a great role model for professionalism. Gave me feedback and confidence that encouraged me to continue working on my modules. Her guidance and expertise helped me embrace my teacher education voice and passion for curriculum development.

My wonderful neighbour, and friend, William Cass, for always being ready to engage with my ideas, giving me support, inspiration, and the courage to explore new avenues through joy and my own self-discovery.

Maria Linda Roble, Ellen Morgan, and Dr. Sipra N. Eko for always being ready to listen to my ideas and for their encouragement and guidance.

To all my teachers, instructors, professors, and uncle Jack (Yacoub), Professor Karkar, who have been part of my education journey.

My parents, Aida and Michael Karkar, who were my first teachers and role models. They instilled in me a love for learning and teaching and essential principles such as integrity, perseverance, and dignity. Their legacy continues in this work.

The Roswell Independent School District, headed by the superintendent, Mr. Brian Luck, and the assistant superintendent, Mrs. Mireya Trujillo. This work wouldn't have come to fruition without their support. I am forever grateful for believing in this work and supporting teachers' participation in learning and implementing these modules.

The Roswell Independent School District teachers who participated in this project. I appreciate your enthusiasm and zeal to be part of this project and the encouragement to publish this plan to guide other teachers.

My Eastern New Mexico University family, which includes administration, colleagues, staff, and students who have been my cheerleaders and exemplary supporters.

My lifelong friends and colleagues, especially, Dr. Stephanie Reid, Dana Abu Lail, Jumana Salfiti Sakakini, Elias Halabi, and Dr. Brady Nash, for always checking on me and sharing their love and support.

My family, my siblings, and my in-laws. You continue to be my guiding star.

My triplet siblings, Tariq M. Karkar and Diala M. Karkar-Hazboun; I am beyond blessed to have started my life journey with you, with your unique joy, compassion, and empathy.

To my little teaching and research companions, Oscar Stark and Molly Sophia Esperat for the companionship and joy they bring to my life.

Finally, my amazing husband, Dominic R. Esperat, you are my rock, my rod, and my staff. You are my good shepherd, and you comfort me always.

All of you have been my inspiration to help me find my own self-discovery.

Love,
Tala Michelle Karkar-Esperat

Preface

My Story of the Raciosemiotic Architecture Framework

In early 2021, I was asked to expand on the Pedagogical Holistic Model of New Literacies, which I had developed in 2019, and to add a semiotic lens to the work. I was not ready at that point; my father had passed away in January 2021, and I was still mourning the loss. As I realized that both of my parents had left this world, I was lonely, and I had lost my source of inspiration, strength, and joy. With their loss, I felt rootless, and I pondered the purpose of my life. When I eventually found my way back to working on the raciosemiotic framework, it was a way to honor my parent's legacy, which is to advocate for students, especially for those who are underrepresented and underserved, through creating authentic classroom experiences.

After reading about semiotics, I was fascinated with the power of symbols and signs to create new views of reality and the ability of semiotics to connect with language through symbols. I also was inspired by Krystal Smalls's work and how she engaged with the racial semiotics, which, she explains, "demands attention to the ways signs and sign relations interpellat[e] racialized bodies, subjects, and subjectivities" (2020, p. 10). I was moved by April Baker-Bell's (2020) work, which emphasized that classrooms lack ways to recognize students' identities. The Raciosemiotic Architecture Framework invites teachers to be transparent in their practice by acknowledging students' identities in the classroom using the pedagogical holistic model of new literacies (multiliteracies and new literacies) and language and semiotics drawing from students' race and culture.

During COVID-19 pandemic, I was working on this theme. One day, I was walking in Roswell in the Ceilo Grande Park with my dog Oscar, admiring nature and mountain scenery. It gave me the idea to use architecture, thinking about students being the architects of their own learning. "I found it! I'm calling it the raciosemiotic architecture framework." I wanted to use race to refer to bilingual and multilingual students and that semiotics were the modes of communication with languages. The raciosemiotic architecture become the symbol for the framework that inspired me to build a curriculum to achieve my goal. I completed writing this manuscript in fall 2021, and it was later published in the Semiotics Society of America yearbook.

Race has many definitions, but the one I chose to use describes my framework as "multiethnic, bi/multilingual learners who speak varying languages, using various signs of meaning to create an understanding of cultures, history, and language for lesser served groups" (Karkar-Esperat, 2023, p. 40). The raciosemiotic framework "fosters a culture of love, dignity, and cultural awareness in the classroom, tapping on various modalities, and prompts teachers to modify their instruction based on their students' identities" (Karkar-Esperat, 2023, p. 47).

Today, I want anyone who refers to the raciosemiotic architecture to attach it to empathy, compassion, and positivity. I found my own self-discovery in these frameworks, and teachers, guardians, and students who use this guide may also discover their own identities.

The Guide

This book guides teachers in becoming compassionate educators. It teaches them strategies by providing examples of lessons that connect with students and support bilingual and multilingual learners.

The modules are divided into modalities: visual, audio, linguistic, spatial, gestural, and synesthesia. This book supports joy, love, compassion, and self-discovery in education, viewing student differences as assets. Educators are guided to facilitate students' self-discovery, nurturing their growth while advancing and sharing their cultural understanding in a multilingual classroom. It explains the interdisciplinary, multiliteracies pedagogical approaches used in planning curricula to connect students' identities to learning to ensure student success.

The frameworks used in this book—the MultiSemiotic architecture framework, the raciosemiotic architecture framework, and the transmultiliteracies sustaining pedagogy—emphasize students' roles in their learning as architects of their own experiences while teachers design their learning experiences and guide them through personal self-discovery in their learning journeys.

It is time for teachers and parents to think of teaching moments as opportunities for self-discovery and self-growth. Using this guide, we will explore resources that can connect the learning materials with students' lives. Without engagement, learning cannot occur. Our students are the future, and we must prepare them to be the best they can be.

This guide focuses on multilingual classrooms because they are often underrepresented and overlooked. Each chapter in this book voices students' needs and provides them with meaningful and lifelong experiences through language and culture. This guide can be used as supplementary materials and can aid in developing unit plans, lesson plans, and professional development plans.

This guide is not just a theoretical resource. It is planned to be a practical tool that enhances teachers' creativity in the classroom. Through this guide, teachers, students, and the students' community can share the joy of knowledge.

Going through this guide will be a pleasure, a walk in the park. Take my hand; let us begin our journey together.

References

Baker-Bell, A. (2020). Dismantling anti-Black linguistic racism in English language arts classrooms: Toward an anti-racist Black language pedagogy. *Theory Into Practice*, *59*(1), 8–21. https://doi.org/10.1080/00405841.2019.1665415

Karkar-Esperat, T. (2023). Transparency in the Classroom: The Raciosemiotic Architecture Framework for Multilingual Learners. Semiotics Society of America 2023 Yearbook.

Smalls, K. A. (2020). Race, signs, and the body: Towards a theory of racial semiotics. In H. S. Alim (Ed.), *The Oxford handbook of language and race*. Oxford University Press. https://doi.org/10.1093/oxfordhb/9780190845995.013.15

1

A New Day for Education

A Guide Toward Self-Discovery

Dear Literacy Teacher,

Many of you, as educators, will face the challenge of engaging students with a prescribed curriculum. You understand that the heart of learning is motivating students. However, with your demanding schedules, finding supplementary materials to help students connect with the curriculum can seem daunting, though you know that incorporating elements from students' cultures and backgrounds into your teaching is highly effective. Doing so creates a more relatable and inspiring learning environment that resonates deeply with your students.

The New Day for Education guide focuses on self-discovery by fostering respect for students' learning and for students sharing their own cultures and other cultures, integrating students in the curriculum using three distinct approaches. Using the transmultiliteracies sustaining pedagogy, the raciosemiotic architecture framework, and the MultiSemiotic architecture framework to generate warmth in learning (explained later), this approach teaches students fairness, sharing, and productive citizenship. This book is a collection of strategies and lesson examples to guide the teacher in connecting students' local experiences to life experiences. These lesson examples can be used as a supplement to any curriculum. My own personal experiences as both an elementary teacher and a teacher educator guided the design of the lessons, and they have been tested with in-service teachers. This approach should also be a success for you. Let's give it a try!

Here's what some other teachers have said after completing the modules:

> This has been a great, informative, and interesting semester. The modules were very interesting to learn more in depth about. There were some things that I already implemented in the classroom but these modules allowed me to learn the importance and read about studies that have been done on different things. I enjoyed learning about hip hop culture and the different genres. I enjoyed the materials on how to implement the various areas into the classroom and look forward to including them in my classroom next year. I look forward to learning more about my students through family trees, songs, traditions, and interviews. The modules on identity were very informative and I was happy to learn how everything ties into a person's identity, culture, environment, etc.
>
> These modules are important because they provide you with new insight and learning. I would definitely recommend these modules to fellow teachers. I think tenured teachers could benefit from these because it has been a while since we have been in college. We get busy in our day to day and do not always pay attention to the important things like multiple modalities and various ways that students learn. I would tell them that this course provided me with new resources and helped me gain back my confidence.
>
> With my students, I can say that the level of student interest was much higher when lessons using information from the modules were used. There was a consistent use of idioms and figurative language used in my students' writing or in our conversations, a consistent reference to what was learned in the historical museum, the usage of maps (US and world map) for personal use, sharing of photos and stories of family and traditions and family history.

In both language arts and social studies, the modules helped me be creative with the way the content was presented to my students. My students were allowed to be creative and to think 'outside of the box.' They were allowed to bring in their own personal experiences, family history, traditions, language, photos, and so on to be used as part of their academic learning. I was able to break down the content and emphasize the needs of my students, being able to use their background and personal experience in the classroom, making their learning more personal and purposeful. The content of the modules, in general, helped me to bridge what the curriculum and what my students' needs were.

Why Do We Need this Approach?

This book is intended for you, literacy teachers, as a new approach to teaching and learning.

Many first-time educators and experienced educators need help in addressing the needs of bilingual and multilingual students. They often feel disconnected from their students and doubt their ability to make a meaningful impact on their lives. The pressure to adhere to the curriculum and help students pass exams can be overwhelming, leading some to consider dropping out due to feelings of helplessness, exhaustion, and lack of success caused by interactions with parents and students.

Teaching must be infused with love and creativity for it to be sustained with compassion. Educators must leverage their strengths just as they recognize and utilize their students' strengths. This book serves as an inspiration to empower your teaching methods with robust content knowledge and effective teaching strategies.

The goal of learning should be to help students become independent, lifelong lovers of learning. Students need opportunities and resources that allow them to connect with the material on both personal and academic levels. While the prescribed curriculum aims to cover state standards and ensure students pass their state exams, it is also essential to provide students with a space to learn, grow, and discover their interests alongside the curriculum. Teachers will discover the needs of their students with flexibility rather than by strictly following a script.

Teaching has progressed from the No Child Left Behind (NCLB) Act of 2001 toward a more inclusive education system. The aim was to close achievement gaps and ensure all students receive a high-quality education. NCLB required states to develop standardized tests to hold schools accountable for students' progress based on curriculum benchmarks. This has led to an excessive focus on standardized testing, with teachers required to "teach to the test" by concentrating on the skills and materials that would be tested.

In response to concerns about overemphasizing testing, the Every Student Succeeds Act (ESSA) was signed into law in 2015. ESSA included provisions from the Individuals with Disabilities Education Act to provide more equitable access to education for all students, including those with disabilities and diverse needs. Teachers are now required to use differentiated instruction to accommodate all students' learning styles and abilities. This shift also encouraged collaboration between special education and general education teachers to better identify students' needs. Ongoing professional development became essential for teachers to stay informed about best practices in inclusive education. These initiatives have pushed for more equitable and inclusive education. Still, students struggle with testing and staying engaged in the classroom.

There is a need for a foundational practical approach for connecting knowledge to student self-discovery. The goal of this guide is to provide the literacy teacher, who could have a variety of their own life experiences, with ways of creating innovative, critical, and practical experiences that stem from students' identities and experiences.

What Are the Approaches that Facilitate Self-discovery?

Transmultiliteracies Sustaining Pedagogy Approach

Teachers can facilitate students' self-discovery by helping them deeply connect with their own identities, cultures, languages, backgrounds, and interests. Teachers can employ the various practical approaches that this guide presents and that are demonstrated in the lessons provided. The first approach is the transmultiliteracies sustaining pedagogy approach (Karkar-Esperat & Stickley, 2024), which is a transdisciplinary approach to using multiple forms of literacy, or multiliteracies, across curricula. It encourages teachers to "use different modalities to nurture student learning experiences as students continue to create their literate identity" (Karkar-Esperat & Stickley, 2024, p. 2590).

This approach is practical and is used by instructors who teach different subjects in the same grade level to curriculum map the standards across disciplines to create unit plans and thematic units, choose mentor texts, create text sets, and teach academic vocabulary. The approach exposes students to different modalities simultaneously in various classes in a way that transcends cultural, linguistic, racial, and historical topics. This approach allows students to connect with the material and bolster their engagement, acknowledging their various learning styles. It also helps in scaffolding by implementing the learned material in different contexts, and students are given ample opportunities to use various reading comprehension strategies such as metacognition, questioning, and activating their schema. By adopting transmultiliteracies, teachers can achieve a shared understanding with their students for making instructional and curricular decisions that leverage multiliteracies to meet the diverse needs of today's students, ultimately fostering equal access to materials to ensure social justice in the classroom.

This approach, as presented in this guide, shows teacher educators how to inspire students to construct meaning through various modalities and to develop higher-order thinking skills, such as analyzing, synthesizing, and critiquing texts (Leu et al., 2004). This approach is foundational for the language arts and social studies examples in this guide, aiming to connect with students' identities. The lesson examples provided reflect this approach as they enable teachers to use multimodal meaning strategies in elementary classrooms, assisting teachers in making curricular and instructional decisions to meet student needs.

Frameworks That Informed This Guide
The Pedagogical Holistic Model of New Literacies

As teachers you learned about educational theories, and you have heard the phrase "connecting theory to practice." How can we do that? Well, let's start by discussing constructivism in relation to our teaching. Constructivism promotes collaboration and exploration, encouraging students to investigate information using diverse resources and engage in readings, discussions, and social activities to build on collective knowledge (Vygotsky, 2005). As teachers, we need to support our students to co-construct knowledge through constructivism. This guide draws on the Pedagogical Holistic Model of New Literacies, which is rooted in constructivism (Vygotsky, 2005) and new literacies theories (which refers to using technologies; Leu et al., 2017).

In particular, this theory and framework guided the development of the raciosemiotic Architecture framework and the MultiSemiotic architecture framework, which are the other two approaches this guide is based on. The raciosemiotic architecture framework (Karkar-Esperat, 2023a) and the MultiSemiotic architecture framework (Karkar-Esperat, 2025) emphasize that students construct meaning through various modes (linguistic, visual, audio, spatial, and gestural) and various approaches to literacy (didactic, authentic, critical, and functional). Teachers facilitate learning by providing resources and guidance, supporting active engagement in making meaning using this model (Au, 1998; Figure 1.1).

The Pedagogical Holistic Model of New Literacies (Karkar-Esperat, 2019) aids teachers in differentiating instruction using multiliteracies—different modalities and literacy approaches. Integrating new literacies (technologies) and various modes of literacy offers a comprehensive and mindful instructional approach. According to the New London Group (1996), these modes include linguistic (text-based meaning), audio (sound effects), visual (images and mental visuals), spatial (spatial communication), and gestural (bodily movement), as well as synesthesia (a switch between different modes, such as using visuals, sound effects, language, or body language, to demonstrate concepts learned individually or in a group). Teachers are encouraged to

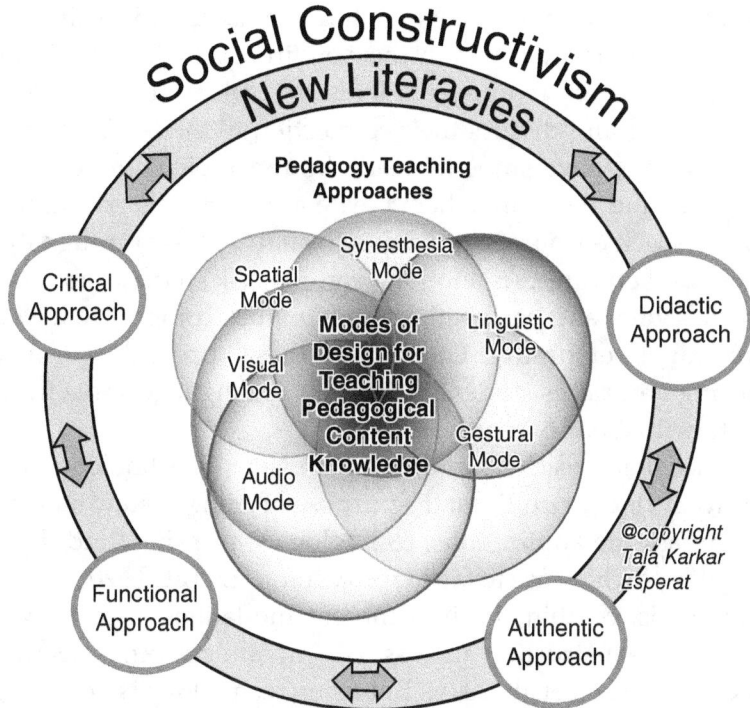

FIGURE 1.1 The Pedagogical Holistic Model of New Literacies
Source: This model was produced in a dissertation by Karkar-Esperat, (2019, p. 63).

employ diverse literacy approaches to connect learning to students' identities.

Approaches to Literacy

I plan to explain the literacy approaches that will guide you in understanding the goal of using them. The authentic, functional, and critical literacy approaches are student-centered, while the didactic approach is teacher-centered (Kalantzis & Cope, 2008). For instance, the didactic approach involves direct instruction and curriculum creation by teachers. When teachers rely heavily on it, the students' engagement declines. In the authentic literacy approach, students learn by doing and taking ownership of their learning. Think about teaching students about citizenship and having them apply it within their environment. The functional literacy approach requires students to explain how text delivers meaning and discuss their connection to the text's purpose. For example, have students read about a topic using different resources and then have them create a poster. This critical literacy approach encourages students to analyze texts through their values and cultures. As another example, ask students about the author's voice and perspective and how they compare to the student's own perspective. Utilizing all these approaches deepens learning and raises student awareness of language's role in text and how to identify representation.

Since many teachers may want to use new technology in the classroom, let's learn about the purpose of using it. New literacies encompass the applications, technologies, websites, and digital tools that teachers use to facilitate learning (Leu et al., 2004, 2017). These tools, combined with different modalities, help teachers differentiate instruction and assessment and customize learning experiences (Leu et al., 2004). But using technology is not limited to the applications teacher use. New literacies, which is technologies, involve the skills, strategies, and dispositions necessary for adapting to evolving technologies that impact our personal and professional life (Leu et al., 2004). They enable students to use higher-order skills like synthesizing, analyzing, evaluating, and communicating (Leu et al., 2017). The pedagogical holistic model of new literacies (Karkar-Esperat, 2019) reminds the literacy teacher to use a variety of literacy approaches and modalities in teaching to foster self-discovery. This holistic model encourages teachers to be reflective, intentional, and flexible, refining their practice through various approaches, modalities, and technologies. Consequently, it supports the integration of multiple modalities into teaching while acknowledging each modality's impact on learning.

Teachers of compassion do not impose specific values, views, or agendas on students. Instead, they guide students to explore topics that ignite their curiosity and help them discover themselves as lifelong learners. They reject the notion that any one race or cultural background is superior or inferior, embracing a multiethnic perspective through a pedagogy of compassionate love, supporting students in finding their own paths and identities.

The Raciosemiotic Architecture Framework®

The raciosemiotic architecture framework (Karkar-Esperat, 2023a) is the next approach used in the book that encourages transparency in creating teaching and learning experiences for students by being mindful and intentional to achieve equal access to resources. Students and teachers are architects of their learning process, which creates opportunities for students to shape their learning experiences, engaging with diverse modalities that resonate with them. The raciosemiotic architecture framework amplifies the needs and identities of students, providing a comprehensive approach that helps teachers tap into students' assets. "It aims to ensure teachers use a variety of pedagogical practices, engage students' background knowledge, and are purposeful about achieving education justice for students in classrooms" (Karkar-Esperat, 2023a, p. 47) by being transparent in using linguistic equity and multiliteracies centered on love, compassion, dignity, and joy. "Joy is the product of cultivating love, dignity, and compassion in the classroom" (Karkar-Esperat, 2023a, p. 40). This framework encourages teachers to adapt their instruction based on their students' identities as teachers acknowledge students' experiences and build on their strengths. The framework offers teachers strategies to accommodate diverse abilities. The raciosemiotic architecture framework (see Figure 1.2) encourages teachers to be mindful in their practice by acknowledging students' identities in the classroom using the pedagogical holistic model of new literacies (multiliteracies and new literacies) as well as language and semiotics that draw from each student's race and culture, and cultural context (Hodge et al., 1988). "Race" is used in this framework as an inclusive term representing all ethnicities.

This approach has been developed and implemented in conjunction with preservice and in-service teachers working with K–12 students, incorporating the raciosemiotic architecture

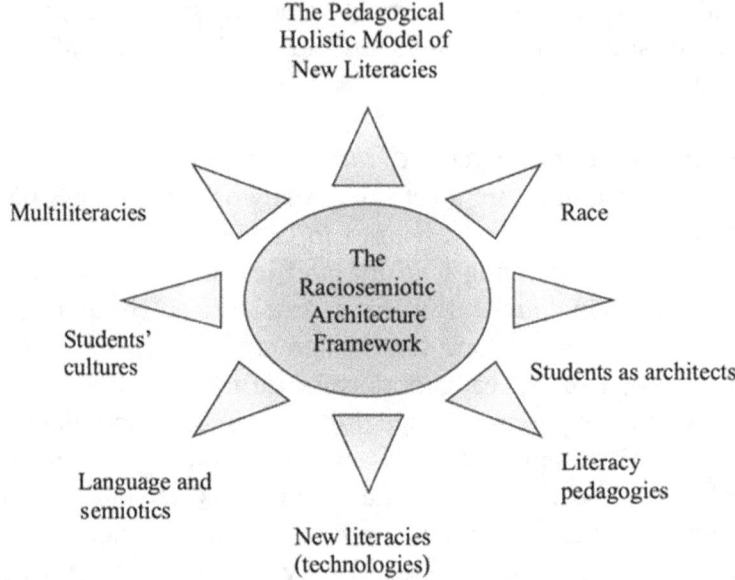

FIGURE 1.2 The Raciosemiotic Architecture Framework
Source: This model was produced by the *Semiotics Society of America 2023 Yearbook* (Karkar-Esperat, 2023a).

framework along with the MultiSemiotic architecture framework into bilingual and multilingual classrooms. The lesson examples blend elements of the raciosemiotic and MultiSemiotic frameworks with K–12 curricular standards. Each lesson provides preservice and in-service teachers with exploratory learning materials they can use with their students.

For example, Module One focuses on teaching idioms in a way that connects culture and language, integrating students' vernacular into their learning experiences. This approach values students' linguistic repertoires, allowing them to explore idioms from their household that reflect their culture. Teachers can differentiate instruction to make teaching personal and compassionate, using a holistic model that includes new literacies, language, semiotics, and differentiated strategies. These strategies involve audio and visual aids, class discussions, art and visuals, activities involving idioms in two languages, restatements, movement to clarify concepts, and online resources.

In addition to these strategies for students, the module includes ways for you to reflect on your own learning. Prompts are provided to help you complete reflective practitioner journals, and complete thought questions after each module to demonstrate your understanding. Additionally, the book provides prompts for discussions with your professional learning communities or professor to reflect on your learning experiences.

The MultiSemiotic Architecture Framework®

When I was teaching, I noticed a need to build on the raciosemiotic architecture framework (Figure 1.3) because the current

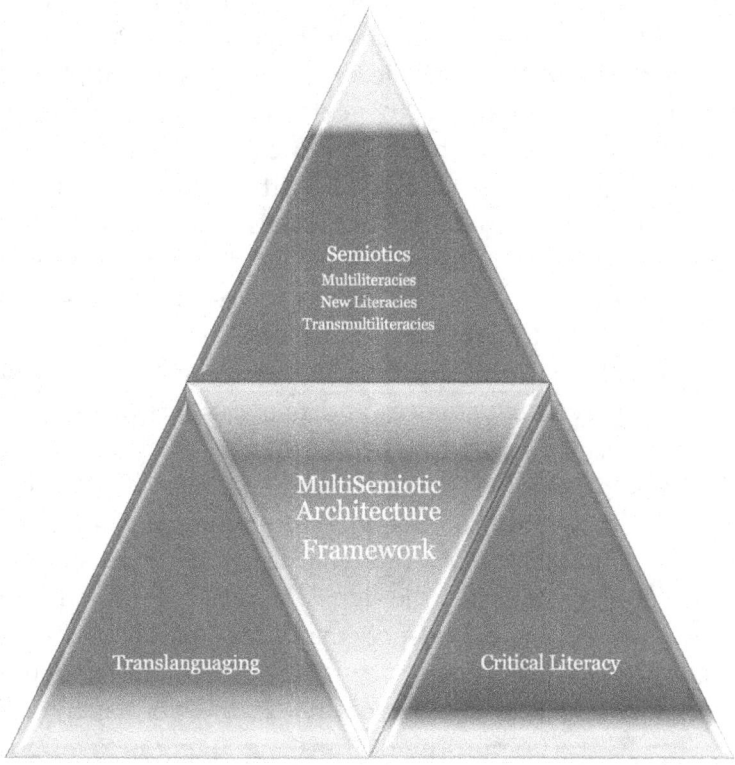

FIGURE 1.3 The MultiSemiotic Architecture Framework
Source: This model was produced by the *International Journal of Bilingual Education and Bilingualism* (Karkar-Esperat, 2025).

changes in the classroom have required teachers to be able to fluidly use student languages as assets. The MultiSemiotic architecture framework (Karkar-Esperat, 2025), which focuses on multiliteracies for multilingual learners, emphasizes students' assets through critical literacy (Bruner, 1991; Luke, 2017) and translanguaging, building on transmultiliteracies sustaining pedagogy (an inquiry-based interdisciplinary curriculum) and new literacies (new technologies) to inform teachers' knowledge.

Multiliteracies, which originated from the New London Group (1996), explains how learners develop proficiency in meaning-making through various modes, including linguistic, visual, audio, gestural, and spatial modes and multimodal designs. Teachers use multiliteracies in explaining content, differentiating strategies, and planning assessments (Cope & Kalantzis, 2015; Kalantzis & Cope, 2008, 2012; Karkar-Esperat, 2019, 2023b, 2024).

Critical literacy involves learners' success in adopting dispositions and attitudes toward texts and dialogue about texts (Luke, 2017). It fosters teachers' critical ability to participate in connecting representation, text, writing, image, and reality (Luke, 2017). This approach encourages teachers to help students analyze how language and text—including visual images and media—influence them. For instance, when instructors teach critical debates around texts, students can discover meaning through their social realities. Learners construct literacy as part of their lived experiences and make it part of their classroom culture.

Translanguaging is a "pedagogical strategy to foster language and literacy development" (Hornberger & Link, 2012, p. 242). This approach values bilingual learners' linguistic repertoires through considering the significance of the individual languages, cultures, and experiences that form their identity (García & Kleyn, 2016). Wei (2024) "view[s] the racial/ethnic identities and linguistics practices together, that is, their translanguaging being" (p. 203). The purpose of translanguaging is to empower students who might otherwise be marginalized linguistically (García, 2009). Velasco and García assert that translanguaging can "promote bilingual students' self-regulation of their entire linguistic repertoire" (2014, p. 21), which will improve their success at school (Hornberger & Link, 2012). García expanded the concept of translanguaging from a pedagogical practice (2009) with the purpose of aiding students to make sense of their bilingual world (2009, p. 4). Wei (2018) introduced the practice theory of language, which emphasizes that language processes encompass multisensory, multimodal semiotic systems that "cannot be independent of language" (p. 20).

The MultiSemiotic architecture framework aims to improve teachers' pedagogical practices to support racialized students. It provides a self-discovery approach to address students' assets, needs, and experiences by offering pedagogical opportunities for teachers, schools, parents, student communities, organizations, and school communities to consider students' abilities. This framework allows students and educators to find hope in the students' learning experiences through an opportunity lens (Souto-Manning, 2016).

The lessons provided in Chapter 4 focus on teaching mariachi music in a way that connects culture and language, integrating students' backgrounds and experiences. This example values students' culture and history. Music is a way to connect to the students' interests, form relationships, and increase their engagement in the classroom. It involves language skills—such as storytelling and tone—and helps students share their voice, culture, and language through music. Teachers use the holistic mode to present the material and differentiate instruction using new literacies, multiliteracies, semiotics, critical literacies, and language. Through mariachi music, students learn about others and themselves.

The lessons presented in this book use the three approaches of transmultiliteracies sustaining pedagogy, the raciosemiotic architecture framework, and the MultiSemiotic architecture framework to guide teachers to be transparent in the classroom by explicitly defining the modes and literacy approaches to help access learners' knowledge, cultures, and languages. The lessons aim to ensure that teaching connects to students' lives through language, culture, and race, fostering joy, compassion, and self-discovery and guiding students to be aware of their future goals and capabilities through the learning process.

Terms Used in the Book

Pedagogy: The teaching strategies and underlying beliefs in education.

Multilingual learners: "All children and youth who are, or have been, consistently exposed to multiple languages" in addition to English (World Instructional Design Accolades [WIDA], 2020, p. 11.

Translanguaging: "How multilingual learners access and use their full linguistic repertoires in communication and learning, including by using more than one language (WIDA, 2020, p. 258).

Multimodality: Engaging through varied modes of communication, including images, symbols, graphs, videos, maps, gestures, written and spoken language, facial expressions, and computer facilitated communications. (Jewitt, 2009, Kress, 2010, Kress & van Leeuwen, 2001, WIDA, 2020). Multimodal texts are used to support students in text interpretation and composition (Reid, 2020; Reid & Serafini, 2018; Reid et al., 2025; Serafini & Gee, 2017).

Linguistic repertoire: "The languages, language varieties, and registers that combine into a set of dynamic resources from which language users can draw when they communicate. A linguistic repertoire is not fixed from birth. Rather, people develop their language resources as they go through life by engaging in a variety of contexts in local and global communities (WIDA, 2020, p. 255).

The Raciosemiotic Architecture Framework: A framework that encourages transparency in the classroom for multilingual learners and aims to ensure "teachers use a variety of pedagogical practices, engage students' background knowledge, and are purposeful about achieving education justice for racialized students in classrooms by being transparent in using linguistic equity and multiliteracies in a way that is centered on love, compassion, dignity, and joy" (Karkar-Esperat, 2023a, p. 47). The raciosemiotic architecture framework "addresses linguistic injustice by incorporating the holistic pedagogical model of new literacies (including new literacies and multiliteracies), language, and semiotics (de Roock 2021; New London Group 1996) to inform teachers' knowledge in addressing racial disparities in the classroom" (Karkar-Esperat, 2023a, p. 45).

MultiSemiotic Architecture Framework: The MultiSemiotic Architecture Framework (Karkar-Esperat, 2025) "addresses linguistic injustice by incorporating translanguaging (García, 2009), critical literacy (Luke, 2017), and multiliteracies (de Roock, 2021; New London Group, 1996) and transmultiliteracies sustaining pedagogy to inform teachers' knowledge and practice." (Karkar-Esperat, 2025, p. 3)

How Is this Book Organized?

This book is organized into seven chapters.

Chapter 1: A New Day for Education: A Guide Toward Self-Discovery

Chapter 1 provides information about why there is a need for this approach, what approaches facilitate self-discovery, and how the book is organized. This guide provides examples of the use of the modules to help teachers generate ideas for specific modes using the three approaches. Chapter 1 also defines all the terminology used in each subsequent chapter.

Chapter 2: Self-Discovery Through the Linguistic Mode: Idioms, Identity Texts, and Storytelling

This chapter's focus is on the linguistic mode, using a holistic approach to refer to culture and historical words that embrace identity in connection to multilingualism and culture. The chapter includes a brief literature review that explains how the use of the raciosemiotic architecture framework, the MultiSemiotic architecture framework, and the transmultiliteracies sustaining pedagogy can be applied to self-discovery in the linguistic mode. This section will prepare the literacy teacher to implement the linguistic mode, guided by the state standards. The learning materials focus on how teachers can integrate students' vernacular into their teaching and learning experiences for their students. Exploring idioms is a way to consider students' linguistic repertoire. This explanation is followed by concrete examples using instructional materials that focus on research, vocabulary knowledge, and reading comprehension and that can be used with the students in language arts and social studies classes using mentor texts and application activities.

Chapter 3: Self-Discovery Through the Visual Mode: Examining Customs and Traditions and Visual Knowledge

This chapter uses customs, traditions, and visual knowledge to focus on the visual mode. It is divided into two sections: The first section is on customs and traditions, and the second is on visual knowledge using the MultiSemiotic architecture framework, the raciosemiotic architecture framework, and transmultiliteracies sustaining pedagogy. The chapter includes a brief literature review that explains how the three frameworks can be applied to self-discovery in the visual mode. The learning materials on customs and traditions and local arts include murals, paintings, landscapes, stories, calligraphy, and music, in addition to text, as tools to develop an understanding of culture and language. Each section will prepare the teacher to implement the visual mode, guided by the state standards. This is followed by concrete examples of activities that support student exploration of the art around them, art in their state, and world art. The instructional materials can be used with the students in language arts and social studies to produce a multimodal project such as a photo story.

Chapter 4: Self-Discovery Through the Audio Mode: Examining Language Using Music Genres

This chapter's focus is on the audio mode, using music genres. It is divided into three sections covering three popular music genres and uses the raciosemiotic architecture framework, MultiSemiotic architecture framework, and the transmultiliteracies sustaining pedagogy, whose application to self-discovery in the music mode is discussed in a literature review. Music represents national identity and social and cultural aspects of students' lives. Students will learn about mariachi, hip-hop, and folk music to develop an understanding of how music represents identity within cultures. The modules prepare the teacher to implement the music mode guided by the state standards. This module is followed by instructional materials that can be used for explaining, describing, and discussing music genres in language arts and social studies classrooms. These include research activities and multimodal production activities such as a storyline.

Chapter 5: Self-Discovery Through the Spatial Mode: Connecting Local to Global

This chapter's focus is on self-discovery through the spatial mode using the raciosemiotic architecture framework, MultiSemiotic architecture framework, and the transmultiliteracies sustaining pedagogy. A brief literature review defines spatial knowledge, which refers to connecting language to place to culture, and spatial knowledge's place in the three frameworks. Students learn about a place in connection to its history, industry, and economy using a cultural and multiliteracies lens. The learning materials connecting language to place and cultures for each section will prepare the teacher to implement the spatial mode, guided by the state standards. The explanation of the learning materials is followed by concrete examples of instructional materials for exploring the ways the place has been shaped by land, space, and culture, with language arts and social studies students using various resources and multimodal application activities such as a multimodal poster.

Chapter 6: Self-Discovery Through the Gestural Mode: Examining Gestures in the Classroom

This chapter's focus is on the gestural mode using the MultiSemiotic architecture framework and the transmultiliteracies sustaining pedagogy. Gestural knowledge in this module refers to discovery through signs, logos, ads, exercise, expression, and collaboration to support student learning. The chapter includes a brief literature review that explains how the use of the raciosemiotic architecture framework, MultiSemiotic architecture framework, and the transmultiliteracies sustaining pedagogy can be applied to self-discovery in the gestural mode. The learning materials for each of these sections will prepare the teacher to implement the gestural mode, guided by the state standards, through signs, logos, ads, and expression. The learning materials are followed by concrete examples using instructional materials (i.e., pictorial representations) that can be used with the students in language arts and social studies.

Chapter 7: Self-Discovery Through the Synesthesia Mode: Examining Culture Through Local Historical Figures

This chapter's focus is on the synesthesia mode using the MultiSemiotic architecture framework and the transmultiliteracies sustaining pedagogy. This mode includes audiovisuals, memoirs, historical and cultural documentaries, dancing, and so forth. The chapter consists of a literature review that explains how the use of the raciosemiotic architecture framework and the transmultiliteracies sustaining pedagogy, and, briefly, the MultiSemiotic architecture framework, can be applied to self-discovery in the synesthesia mode. The learning materials for each section, which include a lesson overview, learning outcomes for teachers, guiding questions, and multimodal resources, will prepare the teacher to implement the synesthesia mode through memoirs, guided by the state standards. The instructional materials follows this section, language objectives, and resources connected to history, culture, and identity, to help students understand the synesthesia mode in language arts and social studies.

References

Au, K. H. (1998). Social constructivism and the school literacy learning of students of diverse backgrounds. *Journal of literacy research*, *30*(2), 297–319.

Bruner, J. (1991). The narrative construction of reality. *Critical Inquiry*, *18*(1), 1–21.

Cope, B., & Kalantzis, M. (2015). The things you do to know: An introduction to the pedagogy of multiliteracies. In *A pedagogy of multiliteracies: Learning by design* (pp. 1–36). London: Palgrave Macmillan UK.

de Roock, R. S. (2021). On the material consequences of (digital) literacy: Digital writing with, for, and against racial capitalism. *Theory Into Practice*, *60*(2), 183–193. https://doi.org/10.1080/00405841.2020.1857128

García, O. (2009). *Bilingual education in the 21st century: Global perspectives*. Blackwell.

García, O., & Kleyn, T. (2016). *Translanguaging with multilingual students: Learning from classroom moments*. New York.

Hodge, B., Hodge, R. I. V., Hodge, R., & Kress, G. R. (1988). *Social semiotics*. Cornell University Press.

Hornberger, N. H., & Link, H. (2012). Translanguaging and transnational literacies in multilingual classrooms: A biliteracy lens. *International Journal of Bilingual Education and Bilingualism*, *15*(3), 261–278. https://doi.org/10.1080/13670050.2012.658016

Jewitt, C. (2009). *The Routledge handbook of multimodal analysis*. Routledge.

Kalantzis, M., & Cope, B. (2008). Language education and multiliteracies. In S. May, & N. H. Hornberger (Eds.), *Encyclopedia of language and education* (2nd ed., Vol. 1; 195–211).: Springer.

Kalantzis, M., & Cope, B. (2012). *Literacies*. Cambridge University Press.

Karkar-Esperat, T. (2019). Assessing preservice teachers' knowledge of new literacies [Doctoral dissertation, Texas Tech University].

Karkar-Esperat, T. (2023a). *Transparency in the classroom: The raciosemiotic architecture framework for multilingual learners*. Semiotics Society of America 2023 Yearbook.

Karkar-Esperat, T. M. (2023b). The pedagogical content knowledge of a multiliteracies survey instrument for preservice teachers that meets the needs of diverse populations. *The Teacher Educator*, *58*(4), 406–427.

Karkar-Esperat, T. M.. (2024). "Multiliteracies in Teacher Education." In George Noblit (Ed.), *Oxford Research Encyclopedia of Education*. New York: Oxford University Press. doi:10.1093/acrefore/9780190264093.013.1890

Karkar-Esperat, T. M., & Stickley, Z. L. (2024). Revisioning curriculum through the transmulitliteracies sustaining pedagogy approach.

Social Sciences & Humanities Open, 9(7), Article 100826. https://doi.org/10.1016/j.ssaho.2024.100826

Karkar-Esperat, T. M. (2025). Multiliteracies for multilingual learners: The multisemiotic architecture framework. *International Journal of Bilingual Education and Bilingualism, 28*(2), 117–134.

Kress, G., & van Leeuwen, T. (2001). *Multimodal discourse: The modes and media of contemporary communication*. London: Arnold.

Kress, G. (2010). *Multimodality: A social semiotic approach to contemporary communication*. Routledge.

Leu, D. J., Kinzer, C. K., Coiro, J., Castek, J., & Henry, L. A. (2017). New literacies: A dual-level theory of the changing nature of literacy, instruction, and assessment. *Journal of Education, 197*(2), 1–18.

Leu, D., Kinzer, C., Coiro, J., & Cammack, D. (2004). Toward a theory of new emerging from the Internet and other information and communication technologies. In R. B. Ruddell (Ed.), *Theoretical models and processes of reading* (5th ed., pp. 1570–1613). International Reading Association.

Luke, A. (2017). Commentary: On the race of teachers and students: A reflection on experience, scientific evidence, and silence. *American Educational Research Journal, 54*(1). https://doi.org/10.3102%2F0002831216679503

New London Group. (1996). A pedagogy of multiliteracies: Designing social futures. *Harvard Educational Review, 66*(1), 60–92.

Reid, S. F., & Serafini, F. (2018). More than words: An investigation of the middle-grade multimodal novel. *Journal of Children's Literature, 44*(2), 32–44.

Reid, S. F., Moses, L., & Rylak, D. (2025). "That storrey reminse you to be cefl": A multimodal analysis of a first-grader's blended genre composition. *Journal of Early Childhood Literacy*, 14687984251337368. https://doi.org/10.1177/14687984251337368

Reid, S. F. (2020). *Multimodality matters: Exploring words, images, and design features in a seventh-grade English language arts classroom* (Doctoral dissertation, Arizona State University).

Serafini, F., & Gee, E. (Eds.). (2017). *Remixing multiliteracies: Theory and practice from New London to new times*. Teachers College Press.

Souto-Manning, M. (2016). Honoring and building on the rich literacy practices of young bilingual and multilingual learners. *The Reading Teacher, 70*(3), 263–271. https://doi.org/10.1002/trtr.1518

Velasco, P., & García, O. (2014). Translanguaging and the writing of bilingual learners. *Bilingual Research Journal, 37*(1), 6–23. https://doi.org/10.1080/15235882.2014.893270

Vygotsky, L. S. (2005). *Psicología pedagógica: Un curso breve* [*Educational psychology: A brief course*]. Aique.

Wei, L. (2018). Translanguaging as a practical theory of language. *Applied Linguistics 39*(1), 9–30. https://doi.org/10.1093/applin/amx039

Wei, L. (2024). Transformative pedagogy for inclusion and social justice through translanguaging, co-learning, and transpositioning. *Language Teaching 57*(2), 203–214. https://doi.org/10.1017/S0261444823000186

WIDA. (2020). WIDA English language development standards framework, 2020 edition. Board of Regents of the University of Wisconsin System. https://wida.wisc.edu/sites/default/$les/resource/WIDAELD-Standards-Framework-2020.Pdf

2

Self-Discovery Through the Linguistic Mode

Idioms, Identity Text, and Storytelling

> **VIGNETTE**
>
> *Students have to experience the beauty of language through all kinds of communication. My first encounter with strange idioms in the United States confused me so much that my husband responded by giving me a book about idioms: "Please study these idioms so you don't feel left out. They are a part of this culture." I recognized that the idioms used in the States connected to idioms that are used in Arabic language in my country. Students struggle with language. Rather than focusing just on reading and writing, we can use language holistically, with communication being the focal point. Students can learn about communication and the enormous diversity of cultures.*
>
> *As a teacher educator, I find all languages inspiring, each having a rhythm and distinct sound connected to them. There is*

plethora of strategies to teach languages, and I encourage teachers to use idioms, identity texts, and folktales representing cultures through language. Language is ever changing and evolving, as each generation discovers. Each culture has its own collection of stories, identities, and beauty. Teachers can celebrate them in the classroom through sharing and comparing.

Teachers who implemented this chapter's content shared their thoughts; one said: "By incorporating culture and situations' nuances related to idiomatic expressions, I gained a comprehensive understanding that I could effectively communicate to my students, resulting in a more captivating and fruitful teaching experience." Another teacher added, "I can connect idioms to my student culture by introducing my students to idioms more frequently. I could also look up idioms from Mexico." A different teacher stated, "I have taught idioms and find it makes great conversational starters for students with their peers." Another teacher specified, "After looking at the resources provided, I see opportunities where I can have students dig much deeper into idioms and look at their origins and translations in other parts of the world." A teacher who studied identity acknowledged, "I've loved adding identity into my lesson. I think it made my students collaborate better and is helping them become a more cohesive bunch." A different teacher wrote, "I was able to connect to my students by understanding the deeper meaning of the word 'culture.' It goes far beyond race, ethnicity, and language. It truly has several components that make every person who they are. I think that is why it is important to understand that two people can be raised in the same home but have completely different identities." One teacher noted about learning folktales, "With going over storytelling and folktales, students have been able to share different-ending versions of stories." Another stated, "I would include as final project students' own folklore or storytelling books. Nothing complicated but definitely interesting and personal."

Dear teachers, parents, guardians, and students,

The linguistic knowledge in MultiSemiotic refers to focusing on teaching language through culture to embrace students' identity. I use the term *identity* to refer to how students construct their language identity through interaction with their first language and then making connections to their second language using text genres.

You are going to learn how you can use the linguistic mode such as idioms, folktales, and identity texts in teaching and learning. The examples are provided in the context of New Mexico. You can follow the same structure and apply it in your own context.

This chapter will guide you to learn about the linguistic approach through semiotics. Some of the guiding questions to consider: Why do we need a linguistic semiotic in the classroom? How does this raciosemiotic/MultiSemiotic language approach encourage bilingual and multilingual learners, support their language competency, and bring awareness to global diversity? What linguistic instructional strategies foster culture, identity, and a sense of belonging? How can this approach support students' language development and competence?

What Is It About?

"The linguistic mode uses text, vocabulary, and metaphor, as well as information structure, local and global coherence relations, delivery, transitivity, and modality (the New London Group 1996). The pedagogical holistic model of new literacies focused on using the four approaches (i.e. authentic, didactic, critical, and functional). Teachers are responsible for selecting practical teaching approaches to engage students in analyzing multiple texts, evaluating and synthesizing information, giving constructive feedback to develop student problem-solving skills, and demonstrating how to categorize information (Karkar-Esperat, 2019). The MultiSemiotic linguistic mode includes words or phrases that refer to culture and historical words (Lazutina et al., 2016), popular lyrics, code-switching, phrases, folklore texts, storytelling, "semantics of proxematic sign" (Hall, 1966), vernacular, and identity texts (Cummins, 2006; Muhammad, 2020 and

Zaidi & El Chaar, 2020; see also Baker-Bell, 2020; Karkar-Esperat & Loftis 2021), humor in learning (Hurren, 2005)."
(Karkar-Esperat, 2025, p. 11)

The *raciosemiotic linguistic mode (Karkar-Esperat, 2023)* includes words or phrases that refer to culture, historical words, idioms (Lazutina et al., 2016), code switching, phrases, folklore texts, storytelling, "semantics of proxematic sign" (Hall, 1966), and identity texts (Zaidi & El Chaar, 2020; see also Baker-Bell, 2020).

Linguistic Knowledge

Academic language, also called academic English, includes lexical, grammar, and interpersonal skills students should master (Gottlieb & Slavit-Ernst, 2014). García (2009) indicated that language is a bilingual, observable, and natural form of communication rooted in discourse practices. Linguistic knowledge in this book refers to students using multiliteracies, semiotics, and culture to process language in reading, writing, listening, and communicating. The motivation for this chapter is that my belief that "language is identity. Learners use it to express their voice and culture" (Karkar-Esperat, 2025, p. 12). Language is a social practice (Street, 1984). It involves all signs in all forms of communication, such as spoken words, written texts, hand gestures, grammar and structure, and meaning. It is a process used to connect students to discover their world (Karkar-Esperat, 2023). The language practices of bilingual and multilingual students are often racialized (García et al., 2021; Ibrahim, 1999; Rosa & Flores, 2017), leading them to encounter challenges with academic language acceptance (Souto-Manning, 2021). Linguistic knowledge ensures that teachers have cultural and linguistic awareness of their students and use them in their teaching various genres to engage them, support their language development, and celebrate their identities.

Why Do We Need To Use It?

The linguistic knowledge elements used from the raciosemiotic architecture framework and the MultiSemiotic architecture framework "ensure teachers use a variety of pedagogical practices that engage background knowledge of their students" (Karkar-Esperat, 2023, p. 47). The frameworks remind teachers to be purposeful by being transparent in their teaching approaches. Language acquisition and word choice are part of one's identity (Wiley & Lukes, 1996). Multilingual and bilingual learners feel pressured to speak standard English (Rosa & Flores, 2017), and we need to acknowledge students' first language and support students' identities in the classroom. Focusing on fostering positive classroom environment will be "centered on love, compassion, dignity, and joy" (Karkar-Esperat, 2023, p. 47). García et al. (2021) encouraged us to "reject abyssal thinking and focu[s] on the vast linguistic complexity and heterogeneity of people and language" (p. 205). One way of doing that is using this linguistic understanding to reflect students' cultures through folktales and identity texts. "Additionally, learning the cultures helps learners obtain a thorough understanding of the cultures rooted in the target language" (Ratri et al., 2024, p. 37).

The use of the linguistic approach centers on students' identities. In their study, when asked by a student why identity matters, Moje answered, "Identity matters, whatever it is, shapes or is an aspect of how humans make sense of the world and their experiences in it, including their experiences with texts" (McCarthey & Moje, 2002, p. 228). Through this chapter, you'll learn to help students interact with language through their culture using various literacy-learning experiences.

How the Linguistic Approach Can Be Used in the Classroom

The linguistic approaches that spark bilingual and multilingual students' interests and engagement in reading and learning vary according to the student age group.

Of the various approaches, I have selected a few for elementary students. The first is the English Literature Teaching and Learning approach, which encompasses instructional methods, content selection, assessment strategies, and classroom management techniques (Barus et al., 2021). Another approach is the readers' response approach, which focuses on students' interpretations of literary texts. Students are encouraged to use critical thinking skills and express their thoughts about the texts, connecting with their perspectives and experiences (Barus et al.,

2021). The literature circles approach (Heydon, 2003; Kabouha & Elyas, 2015) is used to discuss literature that promotes learning and encourage in-depth and active exploration of texts. The cultural approach supports students in exploring literature and analyzing how culture and various perspectives are portrayed in the texts (Vural, 2013) to develop empathy and understanding (Kabouha & Elyas, 2015). The multimodal approach supports students' engagement with text using various modalities to enhance students' appreciation of texts (Choi & Yi, 2016; Karkar-Esperat & Loftis, 2021). The scaffolded reading approach provides students with guidance to read and comprehend literature to increase their confidence in reading and analyzing texts.

Multimodal and Cultural Approaches to Language Knowledge in an Elementary Class

Connecting students to the curriculum using cultural and multimodal approaches is significant. Korean elementary EFL learners were encouraged to express their emotions using graffiti to question the representation in the multimodal text (Gray & Lee, 2019). Burke and Hardware (2015) conducted a digital storytelling assignment with eight 13-year-old immigrant children in a second-language classroom. They found that this multimodal project, in which students were able to use language and visuals, was beneficial to students as they drew connections from their personal lives and supported students with limited English vocabulary. Similarly, Ajayi (2012) worked with 18 third-grade students, using socio-historical activities to interpret a video on Cinderella. Students successfully demonstrated their understanding in pictures and sentences. Norton and Vanderheyden (2004) used Archie graphic novels in an ESL context. Results showed that using this approach was a powerful cultural bridge for Asian learners that enhanced their understanding of Western values and helped them build friendships with native English speakers. Incorporating folktales into EFL classroom instruction captures students' attention and promotes linguistic and cultural competence (Safitri, 2023). Wijanarko (2021) explored the implementation of storytelling using Indonesian folktales to improve students' reading, and the results showed that folktale stories and illustrations stimulated students' interest and motivated them to engage deeply in reading the text comprehensively. Upa and Mangalik (2018) performed pre-experimental research using a pretest and posttest to inquire whether using Sulawesi folktales improved students' reading comprehension, and the results showed that this approach positively impacted students' reading. Using these various language genres develops students' cultural appreciation.

Conclusion

The linguistic approach facilitates bilingual and multilingual students' learning experiences, especially when teaching and learning are connected to students' cultures. This allows students to use their critical thinking skills, creativity, and imagination (Safitri, 2023).

The multimodal approach and cultural awareness are significant linguistic knowledge approaches that promote focusing on students' identities. Folktales, identity texts, and idioms allow students to learn about their cultural heritage, language, traditions, and values. Teachers design activities to integrate language skills, allowing students to explore materials that foster multicultural education in the classroom. Teachers can create collaborative opportunities for students—to inquire, analyze, and present information—that embrace their students' identity.

How Can We Use It?

There are three simple steps that you need to follow:

1. Read the national standards that guided these two lessons.
2. Study the learning materials, which will give you background about the chapter examples.
3. Review the instructional materials, which could be used with students in language art and social studies.

Guiding Table for This Chapter. The Modeled Lesson Uses the Linguistic Approach

Transmultiliteracies Sustaining Pedagogy Approach (Karkar-Esperat & Stickley, 2024)	♦ The use of the language arts standards and social studies standards. ♦ Applications for language arts and social studies classrooms.
The Pedagogical Holistic Model of New Literacies (Karkar-Esperat, 2019)	♦ Reading about biographies, identity texts, and folklore using different forms of texts. ♦ Creating a visual using a storyline or graphic organizer. ♦ Writing autobiographies and sharing them with their peers. ♦ Presenting autobiographies using digital media. ♦ Reading "I Am Poems" and then writing and sharing their poems. ♦ Developing a written autobiography with facts and concrete details. ♦ Creating a visual that portrays the story of the UFO crash. ♦ Sharing the information learned with peers using visuals (a storyline or graphic organizers).
The Raciosemiotic Architecture Framework (Karkar-Esperat, 2023)	♦ Connecting idioms, storytelling, and folktales to student cultures. ♦ Reflecting how folklore, folktale, and storytelling connect to culture and traditions. ♦ Synthesizing the use of folklore and storytelling supporting students' language learning. ♦ Identifying a critical figure that made a difference in social justice and cultural awareness. ♦ Writing about first language and culture, how that impacted learning, and how learners think about themselves. ♦ Describing the use of folklore and storytelling to engage students in thinking about power and equity. ♦ Demonstrating knowledge of family history and culture. ♦ Engaging in meaning-making using multiliteracies.

(Continued)

The MultiSemiotic Architecture Framework (Karkar-Esperat, 2025)	A MultiSemiotic Linguistic Approach: Idioms, Identity Text, and Storytelling
	"The MultiSemiotic linguistic mode includes words or phrases that refer to culture and historical words (Lazutina et al. 2016), popular lyrics, code-switching, phrases, folklore texts, storytelling, 'semantics of proxematic sign' (Hall 1966), vernacular, and identity texts (Cummins 2006; Muhammad 2020 and Zaidi & El Chaar 2020; see also Baker-Bell 2020; Karkar-Esperat & Loftis 2021), humor in learning (Hurren 2005)." (Karkar-Esperat, 2025, p. 11)

References

Ajayi, L. (2012). Video "reading" and multimodality: A study of ESL/literacy pupils' interpretation of Cinderella from their socio-historical perspective. *The Urban Review, 44*(1), 60–89. https://doi.org/10.1007/s11256-011-0175-0

Baker-Bell, A. (2020). Dismantling anti-black linguistic racism in english language arts classrooms: Toward an anti-racist black language pedagogy. *Theory Into Practice 59*(1), 8–21. https://doi.org/10.1080/00405841.2019.1665415

Barus, I. R. G., Simanjuntak, M. B., & Resmayasari, I. (2021). Reading literacies through Evieta- Based learning material: Students' perceptions (study case taken from Vocational School–IPB University). *Journal of Advanced English Studies, 4*(1), 15–20.

Burke, A., & Hardware, S. (2015). Honouring ESL students' lived experiences in school learning with multiliteracies pedagogy. *Language, Culture and Curriculum, 28*(2), 143–157. https://doi.org/10.1080/07908318.2015.1027214

Choi, J., & Yi, Y. (2016). Teachers' integration of multimodality into classroom practices for English language learners. *TESOL Journal, 7*(2), 304–327. https://doi.org/10.1002/tesj.204

Cummins, J. (2006). Identity texts: The imaginative construction of self through multiliteracies pedagogy. In *Imagining multilingual schools: Languages in education and glocalization*, 51–68. Wiley. https://doi.org/10.21832/9781853598968-003

García, O. (2009). *Bilingual education in the 21st century: A global perspective*. John Wiley & Sons.

García, O., Flores, N., Seltzer, K., Wei, L., Otheguy, R., & Rosa, J. (2021). Rejecting abyssal thinking in the language and education of racialized bilinguals: A manifesto. *Critical Inquiry in Language Studies*, *18*(3), 203–228. https://doi.org/10.1080/15427587.2021.1935957

Gottlieb, M., & Slavit-Ernst, G. (2014). *Academic language in diverse classrooms: Definitions and contexts*. Corwin.

Gray, S., & Lee, R. (2019). Textbook graffiti as a critical, multimodal classroom activity for Korean elementary EFL students. *Journal of English Teaching through Movies and Media*, *20*(2), 43–66. https://doi.org/10.16875/stem.2019.20.2.43

Hall, E. T. (1966). *The Hidden Dimension* (Vol. 609). Doubleday.

Heydon, R. (2003). Literature circles as a differentiated instructional strategy for including ESL students in mainstream classrooms. *Canadian Modern Language Review*, *59*(3), 463–475. https://doi.org/10.3138/cmlr.59.3.463

Hurren, B. L. (2005). Humor in school is serious business. *International Journal of Learning*, *12*(6), 79–83.

Ibrahim, A. E. K. M. (1999). Becoming Black: Rap and hip-hop, race, gender, identity, and the politics of ESL learning. *TESOL Quarterly*, *33*(3), 349–369. https://www.academia.edu/31136901/Becoming_Black_Rap_and_Hip_Hop_Race_Gender_Identity_and_the_Politics_of_ESL_Learning

Kabouha, R., & Elyas, T. (2015). Aligning teaching and assessment to course objectives: The case of preparatory year English program at King Abdulaziz University. *International Journal of Applied Linguistics and English Literature*, *4*(5), 82–91.

Karkar-Esperat, T. (2019). *Assessing preservice teachers' knowledge of new literacies* [Doctoral dissertation, Texas Tech University]. Texas Tech University Archive.

Karkar-Esperat, T., & Stickley, Z. (2024). Revisioning curriculum through the transmulitliteracies sustaining pedagogy approach. *Social Sciences & Humanities Open*, *9*, 100826.

Karkar-Esperat, T. M. (2023). Transparency in the classroom: The raciosemiotic architecture framework for multilingual learners. *Semiotics*, 39–53. https://doi.org/10.5840/cpsem20234

Karkar-Esperat, T. M. (2025). Multiliteracies for multilingual learners: The MultiSemiotic Architecture Framework. *International Journal of Bilingual Education and Bilingualism*, *28*(2), 117–134. https://doi.org/10.1080/13670050.2024.2409120

Karkar-Esperat, T. M., & Loftis, T. M. (2021). Using new literacies to foster student motivation. *Literacy Practice and Research*, *46*(1), Article 5. https://doi.org/10.25148/lpr.009339

Lazutina, T. V., I. N. Pupysheva, M. N. Shcherbinin, V. N. Baksheev, & G. V. Patrakova. (2016). Semiotics of art: Language of architecture as a complex system of signs. *International Journal of Environmental and Science Education*, *11*(17), 9991–9998.

McCarthey, S. J., & Moje, E. B. (2002). Identity matters. *Reading Research Quarterly*, *37*(2), 228–238. https://doi.org/10.1598/RRQ.37.2.6

Muhammad, G. E. (2020). *Cultivating genius: An equity framework for culturally and historically responsive literacy*. Scholastic Edge at the Cultural Interface.

New London Group (1996). A pedagogy of multiliteracies: Designing social futures. *Harvard Educational Review*, *66*(1), 60–92. https://doi.org/10.17763/haer.66.1.17370n67v22j160u

Norton, B., & Vanderheyden, K. (2004). Comic book culture and second language learners. In B. Norton & K. Toohey (Eds.), *Critical pedagogies and language learning* (pp. 201–221). Cambridge University Press. https://doi.org/10.1017/CBO9781139524834.011

Ratri, D. P., Widiati, U., Astutik, I., & Jonathans, P. M. (2024). A systematic review on the integration of local culture into English language teaching in Southeast Asia: Current practices and impacts on learners' attitude and engagement. *Pegem Journal of Education and Instruction*, *14*(2), 37–44. https://doi.org/10.47750/pegegog.14.02.05

Rosa, J., & Flores, N. (2017). Unsettling race and language: Toward a raciolinguistic perspective. *Language in Society*, *46*(5), 621–647. https://doi.org/10.1017/S0047404517000562

Safitri, I. (2023). Exploring the utilization of folktales as reading materials for EFL students. *Journal of English as a Foreign Language Education*, *4*(2), 115–125.

Souto-Manning, M. (2021). Righting the literacy teacher education debt: A matter of justice. *Journal of Literacy Research*, *53*(4), 588–600. https://doi.org/10.1177/1086296X211052240

Street, B. V. (1984). *Literacy in theory and practice* (Vol. 9). Cambridge University Press.

Upa, R., & Mangalik, H. (2018). Utilizing Sulawesi folktales into the teaching of reading comprehension. *Jurnal Studi Guru Dan Pembelajaran*, *1*(1), 37–41. https://doi.org/10.30605/jsgp.1.1.2018.19

Vural, H. (2013). Use of literature to enhance motivation in ELT classes. *Mevlana International Journal of Education*, *3*(4), 15–23. https://doi.org/10.13054/mije.13.44.3.4

Wijanarko, I. (2021). Storytelling using reconstructed Indonesian folktales in English translation to improve the reading skill of primary 2 students in school X. *Jurnal Teropong Pendidikan*, *1*(1), 14. https://doi.org/10.19166/jtp.v1i1.3131

Wiley, T. G., & Lukes, M. (1996). English-only and standard English ideologies in the US. *TESOL Quarterly*, *30*(3), 511–535. https://doi.org/10.2307/3587696

Zaidi, R., & D. El Chaar (2020). Identity texts: An intervention to internationalise the classroom. *Pedagogies: An International Journal*, *17*. https://doi.org/10.1080/1554480X.2020.1860060

Lesson Title: A Racio/MultiSemiotic Linguistic Approach (Council of Chief State School Officers, 2013; International Literacy Association, 2017; National Council of Teachers of English & International Reading Association, 2012)

NCTE/IRA Standards for the English Language Arts	International Literacy Association Standards	INTASC Standards
Standard #1: Students read a wide range of print and non-print texts to build an understanding of texts, of themselves, and of the cultures of the United States and the world; to acquire new information; to respond to the needs and demands of society and the workplace; and for personal fulfillment. Among these texts are fiction and nonfiction, classic and contemporary works. Standard #3: Students apply a wide range of strategies to comprehend, interpret, evaluate, and appreciate texts. They draw on their prior experience, their interactions with other readers and writers, their knowledge of word meaning and of other texts, their word identification strategies, and their understanding of textual features (e.g., sound-letter correspondence, sentence structure, context, graphics).	Standard #1: Foundational Knowledge Candidates demonstrate knowledge of the theoretical, historical, and evidence-based foundations of literacy and language and the ways in which they interrelate and the role of literacy professionals in schools. Standard #2: Curriculum and Instruction Candidates use foundational knowledge to critique and implement literacy curricula to meet the needs of all learners and to design, implement, and evaluate evidence-based literacy instruction for all learners. Standard #3: Assessment and Evaluation Candidates understand, select, and use valid, reliable, fair, and appropriate assessment tools to screen, diagnose, and measure student literacy achievement; inform instruction and evaluate interventions; participate in professional learning experiences; explain assessment results and advocate for appropriate literacy practices to relevant stakeholders.	Standard #1: Learner Development. The teacher understands how learners grow and develop, recognizing that patterns of learning and development vary individually within and across the cognitive, linguistic, social, emotional, and physical areas and designs and implements developmentally appropriate and challenging learning experiences. Standard #2: Learning Differences. The teacher uses understanding of individual differences and diverse cultures and communities to ensure inclusive learning environments that enable each learner to meet high standards.

Self-Discovery Through the Linguistic Mode ♦ 35

		Standard #3: Learning Environments. The teacher works with others to create environments that support individual and collaborative learning, and that encourage positive social interaction, active engagement in learning, and self-motivation.
	Standard #4: Diversity and Equity Candidates demonstrate knowledge of research, relevant theories, pedagogies, essential concepts of diversity and equity; demonstrate and provide opportunities for understanding all forms of diversity as central to students' identities; create classrooms and schools that are inclusive and affirming; advocate for equity at school, district, and community levels.	Standard #4: Content Knowledge. The teacher understands the central concepts, tools of inquiry, and structures of the discipline(s) he or she teaches and creates learning experiences that make the discipline accessible and meaningful for learners to assure mastery of the content.
	Standard #5: Learners and the Literacy Environment Candidates meet the developmental needs of all learners and collaborate with school personnel to use a variety of print and digital materials to engage and motivate all learners; integrate digital technologies in appropriate, safe, and effective ways; foster a positive climate that supports a literacy-rich learning environment.	Standard #5: Application of Content. The teacher understands how to connect concepts and use differing perspectives to engage learners in critical thinking, creativity, and collaborative problem solving related to authentic local and global issues.
	Standard #6: Professional Learning and Leadership. Candidates recognize the importance of, participate in, and facilitate ongoing professional learning as part of career-long leadership roles and responsibilities.	Standard #6: Assessment. The teacher understands and uses multiple methods of assessment to engage learners in their own growth, to monitor learner progress, and to guide the teacher's and learner's decision making.
Standard #8: Students use a variety of technological and information resources (e.g., libraries, databases, computer networks, video) to gather and synthesize information and to create and communicate knowledge.		
Standard #9: Students develop an understanding of and respect for diversity in language use, patterns, and dialects across cultures, ethnic groups, geographic regions, and social roles.		
Standard #10: Students whose first language is not English make use of their first language to develop competency in the English language arts and to develop understanding of content across the curriculum.		
Standard #11: Students participate as knowledgeable, reflective, creative, and critical members of a variety of literacy communities.		

(Continued)

NCTE/IRA Standards for the English Language Arts	International Literacy Association Standards	INTASC Standards
Standard #12: Students use spoken, written, and visual language to accomplish their own purposes (e.g., for learning, enjoyment, persuasion, and the exchange of information).		Standard #7: Planning for Instruction. The teacher plans instruction that supports every student in meeting rigorous learning goals by drawing upon knowledge of content areas, curriculum, cross-disciplinary skills, and pedagogy, as well as knowledge of learners and the community context. Standard #8: Instructional Strategies. The teacher understands and uses a variety of instructional strategies to encourage learners to develop deep understanding of content areas and their connections, and to build skills to apply knowledge in meaningful ways.

References

Council of Chief State School Officers. (2013). *InTASC model core teaching standards and learning progressions for teachers 1.0: A resource for ongoing teacher development*. https://learning.ccsso.org/intasc-model-core-teaching-standards-and-learning-progressions-for-teachers

International Literacy Association. (2017). *Standards for the preparation of literacy professionals 2017*. https://www.literacyworldwide.org/get-resources/standards/standards-2017

National Council of Teachers of English & International Reading Association (1996/2012). *Standards for the English language arts (Reaffirmed 2012)*. National Council of Teachers of English. https://ncte.org/resources/standards/ncte-ira-standards-for-the-english-language-arts/

Modeled Lesson 1: Linguistic Knowledge—Idioms
Linguistic Knowledge: Learning Module

Multilingual learners: "All children and youth who are, or have been, consistently exposed to multiple languages in addition to English" (WIDA, 2020, p. 11).

Translanguaging: "How multilingual learners access and use their full linguistic repertoires in communication and learning, including by using more than one language" (WIDA, 2020, p. 258.)

Multimodality: Engaging through varied modes of communication, including images, symbols, graphs, videos, maps, gestures, written and spoken language, facial expressions, and computer facilitated communications (Jewitt, 2009, Kress, 2010, Kress & van Leeuwen, 2001, WIDA, 2020). Multimodal texts are used to support students in text interpretation and composition (Reid, 2020; Reid & Serafini, 2018; Reid et al., 2025; Serafini & Gee, 2017).

Linguistic repertoire: "Languages, language varieties, and registers that combine into a set of dynamic resources from which language users can draw when they communicate.

A linguistic repertoire is not fixed from birth. Rather, people develop their language resources as they go through life by engaging in a variety of contexts in local and global communities" (WIDA, 2020, p. 255).

Lesson Overview

This lesson introduces an element of the Raciosemiotic Linguistic Framework: Idioms. It focuses on how we integrate students' vernacular into our teaching and learning experiences for our students. Using idioms is a way to consider students' linguistic repertoire. The Common Core State Standards that are used in this module focus on explaining the meaning of words and phrases as they are used in different text and media, including figurative, idioms, connotative, and technical meanings. Idioms are part of students' identities.

Keep in mind this is a lesson in which you can integrate the four language skills. However, I only chose reading and speaking standards for this module. There are some TESOL strategies used in the module. The readings give you a good background on the teaching skills that you need to introduce idioms to multilingual students. You have different text choices that you can use. Compassionate teaching stems from learning about student vernaculars and multilingualism. You are taught to use your students' background knowledge in planning instruction. The focus is connecting idioms to student cultures and language.

The example lesson that follows is guided by the International Literacy Standards for teacher preparation in literacy, the NCTE/IRA standards for English language arts, and the Common Core Standards for English language arts and social standards. Following this, activities for before, during, and after the lesson are presented to teachers so that they can use them to teach critical literacy, translanguaging, and multiliteracies. Opportunities are also presented in the lesson to guide third- to fifth grade students to use this approach.

Journaling: This is a diary that will document your learning journey and will be used to evaluate the effectiveness of this process.

Think of the tools (i.e., linguistic strategies) to teach a lesson on linguistic knowledge. What topics will you cover in your teaching? What activities can you use to teach students about language? How can you connect linguistic knowledge to teaching about culture?

Please discuss them in your journal.

A) Use the guiding questions in writing your response.
B) Start writing about the resources provided in the module.
C) Record your thought processes as you read the modules.
D) Consider how the presented information makes you think about your teaching of multilingual students in terms of content and teaching strategies.

Learning Outcomes (for Teachers)
After studying this chapter, you should be able to:

Content Objectives
1. Create an instructional lesson focusing on language connecting to culture.
2. Revisit the standards that focus on language in relation to culture based on the grade level being taught.
3. Engage in meaning-making using multiliteracies, such as audio and visual modes.
4. Reflect on the module.
5. Scaffold your lessons for third- to fifth grade learners to complete learning about idioms.
6. Use the raciosemiotic linguistic approach to create a product for your students.

TESOL Standards (for Teachers, TESOL International Association, 2018)
- ♦ **2a.** Candidates demonstrate knowledge of how dynamic academic, personal, familial, cultural, and social contexts, including sociopolitical factors, impact the education of ELLs.
- ♦ **2d.** Candidates devise and implement methods to learn about personal characteristics of the individual ELL

(e.g., interests, motivations, strengths, needs) and their family (e.g., language use, literacy practices, circumstances) to develop effective instructional practices.
- ♦ 3a. Candidates plan for culturally and linguistically relevant, supportive environments that promote ELLs' learning. Candidates design scaffolded instruction of language and literacies to support standards and curricular objectives for ELLs in the content areas.
- ♦ 3e. Candidates use and adapt relevant materials and resources, including digital resources, to plan lessons for ELLs, to support communication with other educators, school personnel, and ELLs, and to foster student learning of language and literacies in the content areas.

Language Objectives for Students
1. Use idioms to increase student vocabulary knowledge focusing on multiple meanings for words.
2. Use idioms to make inferences to improve reading comprehension.
3. Use idioms to improve inferential comprehension using different text.

Guiding Questions
1. What does it mean to have idiomatic competence?
2. How does the language approach (idioms) you present in relation to this topic bring awareness to global diversity?
3. How are you guiding students to analyze idioms?
4. What instructional strategies are you using, or could you use that scaffold for continuous exposure and planned practice for students?

Pre-Class Preparation Activities for Teachers
Idioms have a close relationship with historical background, economy, geographical environment, custom, and so on with a country. They more typically represent the cultural characteristics of a language than individual words. As you can see, the use of idioms brings cultural aspects to the language. Idioms offer cultural understandings into societal standards, principles, and

beliefs. Idioms allow us to gain insight into the thoughts, emotions, and views of the speaker's background. Think how vocabulary is used to convey meaning in comprehension.

- Think about three idioms you use. Include them in your journal.
- Think about how idioms reflect something about your worldview, culture, and traditions. Include them in your journal.

Preview the Reading

In the following readings, you will learn about idioms and reasons for including idioms in the curriculum, especially for language learners. Teaching idioms encourages learners to learn about the culture. Teaching of idioms should be purposeful and authentic. It encourages students to use language in socially responsible ways. You have examples of books that you can use in the classroom.

Read

- Why Teach Idioms? A Challenge to the Profession
- (Liontas, 2017). The article provides information on the definition of idioms, offers a rationale for teaching idioms to students, especially English language learners, and gives examples of how to teach idioms to your students https://files.eric.ed.gov/fulltext/EJ1156198.pdf.
- Multicultural Idioms Are a Golden Opportunity for Language Learners (Fin, 2021). Idioms are connected to students' cultures and languages. Learning about them is a way to celebrate student diversity. The link provides you with ideas on teaching idioms and lets you explore idioms in a multicultural setting https://www.diversebooks.org/blogposts/blog-post-title-one-a7bbn-z9gff-4r3zm-xgkxb-8clhm-7h74g-sb58b-2ctm9-8l9j4-8zx2h-djtnf-mgsbd.
- Hit Two Birds with One Stone: Idioms and Culture in FL Translation Class (Alharbi, 2013) https://awej.

org/images/AllIssues/Volume4/Volume4Number4Dec2013/16.pdf

This article examines the multilayered methods of teaching idioms and culture in a foreign language class and explores the significance of teaching idioms. You can teach culture through idioms. You will learn how idioms are connected to culture and cultural contexts. This source will help you connect with language arts and social studies through pedagogical applications that you can use.

Listen (these are audiovisual resources for you to explore idioms)

- What are idioms (My English Pages, 2018): https://www.youtube.com/watch?v=fgyoByXEKUU
- Getting to know your students (Colorin Colorado, 2020): https://youtu.be/wr9e8R4EYRY?si=JskV4RuVzodmLTdF
- 3 Points of Teaching Slang and Idioms in English (ITTT International TEFL & TESOL Training, 2021): https://youtu.be/zAtnR_9iqbY?si=frA93uWaAG8iMAO7

Thought Questions

1. Have you used any module material in your planning and instruction?
2. How were you able to connect idioms to your student culture?
3. What aspects of this unit supported your learning and teaching about idioms?
4. What adjustments to the unit would support your learning better?
5. Have you previously taught idioms? How did this unit enhance your teaching of idioms?

References

Alharbi, A. M. (2013). Hit two birds with one stone: Idioms and culture in FL Translation Class. *Arab World English Journal*, 4(4). https://awej.org/images/AllIssues/Volume4/Volume4Number4Dec2013/16.pdf

Colorin Colorado (2020, January 24). *Getting to know your ELLs and why it matters* [Video]. YouTube. https://www.youtube.com/watch?v=wr9e8R4EYRY

Fin, L. (2021, February 22). *Multicultural idioms are a golden opportunity for language learners.* WNDB DiverseBooks. https://www.diversebooks.org/blogposts/blog-post-title-one-a7bbn-z9gff-4r3zm-xgkxb-8clhm-7h74g-sb58b-2ctm9-8l9j4-8zx2h-djtnf-mgsbd

ITTT International TEFL & TESOL Training (2021, March 18). *3 points of teaching slang and idioms in English | ITTT | TEFL Blog* [Video]. Youtube. https://www.youtube.com/watch?v=zAtnR_9iqbY

Jewitt, C. (2009). *The Routledge handbook of multimodal analysis*. Routledge.

Kress, G., & van Leeuwen, T. (2001). *Multimodal discourse: The modes and media of contemporary communication*. Arnold.

Kress, G. (2010). *Multimodality: A social semiotic approach to contemporary communication*. Routledge.

Liontas, J. I. (2017). Why teach idioms? A challenge to the profession. *Iranian Journal of Language Teaching Research, 5*(3), 5–25. https://files.eric.ed.gov/fulltext/EJ1156198.pdf

My English Pages (2018, October 19). *What are idioms?* [Video]. YouTube. https://www.youtube.com/watch?v=fgyoByXEKUU

Reid, S. F., & Serafini, F. (2018). More than words: An investigation of the middle-grade multimodal novel. *Journal of Children's Literature, 44*(2), 32–44.

Reid, S. F., Moses, L., & Rylak, D. (2025). "That storrey reminse you to be cefl": A multimodal analysis of a first-grader's blended genre composition. *Journal of Early Childhood Literacy*, 14687984251337368.

Reid, S. F. (2020). *Multimodality matters: Exploring words, images, and design features in a seventh-grade English language arts classroom* (Doctoral dissertation, Arizona State University).

Serafini, F., & Gee, E. (Eds.). (2017). *Remixing multiliteracies: Theory and practice from New London to new times*. Teachers College Press.

TESOL International Association (2018). *Standards for initial TESOL Pre-K–12 teacher preparation programs*. Author. https://www.tesol.org/docs/default-source/advocacy/2018_tesol-teacher-prep-standards_final.pdf

WIDA. (2020). *WIDA English language development standards framework*, 2020 edition. Board of Regents of the University of Wisconsin System. https://wida.wisc.edu/sites/default/files/resource/WIDA-ELD-Standards-Framework-2020.Pdf

Lesson Title: A Linguistic Approach: Idioms (Karkar-Esperat, 2019, National Governors Association Center for Best Practices, & Council of Chief State School Officers, 2010; New Mexico Public Education Department, 2021)

Common Core State Language Arts Standards for 3rd–5th Grades	Social Studies Standards for 3rd–5th Grade	Pedagogical Holistic Model of New Literacies
Third Grade CCSS.ELA-LITERACY.RL.3.4 Determine the meaning of words and phrases as they are used in a text, distinguishing literal from nonliteral language. CCSS.ELA-LITERACY.L.3.5.A Distinguish the literal and nonliteral meanings of words and phrases in context (e.g., take steps). **Fourth Grade** CCSS.ELA-LITERACY.RL.4.1 Determine the meaning of words and phrases as they are used in a text, including those that allude to significant characters found in mythology. CCSS.ELA-LITERACY.L.4.5B Recognize and explain the meaning of common idioms, adages, and proverbs.	**Third Grade** 3.2. Use supporting questions to help answer the compelling question in an inquiry. 3.26. Express a positive view of themselves while demonstrating respect and empathy for others. 3.27. Compare and contrast their cultural identity with other people and groups. **Fourth Grade** 4.1 Generate compelling questions in an inquiry.	"The linguistic mode uses text, vocabulary, and metaphor, as well as information structure, local and global coherence relations, delivery, transitivity, and modality (the New London Group 1996). The pedagogical holistic model of new literacies focused on using the four approaches (i.e. authentic, didactic, critical, and functional). Teachers are responsible for selecting practical teaching approaches to engage students in analyzing multiple texts, evaluating and synthesizing information, giving constructive feedback to develop student problem-solving skills, and demonstrating how to categorize information (Karkar-Esperat 2019)." (Karkar-Esperat, 2025, p. 12)

CCSS.ELA-LITERACY.SL.4.6
Differentiate between contexts that call for formal English (e.g., presenting ideas) and situations where informal discourse is appropriate (e.g., small-group discussion); use formal English when appropriate to task and situation.

CCSS.ELA-LITERACY.SL.4.2
Paraphrase portions of a text read aloud or information presented in diverse media and formats, including visually, quantitatively, and orally.

Fifth Grade

CCSS.ELA-LITERACY.RL.5.4
Determine the meaning of words and phrases as they are used in a text, including figurative language such as metaphors and similes.

CCSS.ELA-LITERACY.RL.5.7
Analyze how visual and multimedia elements contribute to the meaning, tone, or beauty of a text (e.g., graphic novel myth, poem).

CCSS.ELA-LITERACY.SL.5.1C
Pose and respond to specific questions by making comments that contribute to the discussion and elaborate on the remarks of others.

CCSS.ELA-LITERACY.L.4.5B
Recognize and explain the meaning of common idioms, adages, and proverbs.

Fifth Grade

5.1. Generate compelling and related supporting questions in an inquiry.

5.30. Demonstrate knowledge of family history, culture, and past contributions of people in their main identity groups.

The *raciosemiotic linguistic mode* (Karkar-Esperat 2023) could include words or phrases that refer to culture, historical words, idioms (Lazutina et al., 2016), code-switching, phrases, folklore texts, storytelling, "semantics of proxematic sign" (Hall, 1966), and identity texts (Muhammad, 2020; Zaidi & El Chaar, 2020)

References

Hall, E. T. (1966). *The Hidden Dimension* (Vol. 609). Doubleday.

Karkar-Esperat, T. (2019). Assessing preservice teachers' knowledge of new literacies [Doctoral dissertation, Texas Tech University]. Texas Tech University Archive.

Karkar-Esperat, T. M. (2025). Multiliteracies for multilingual learners: The MultiSemiotic Architecture Framework. *International Journal of Bilingual Education and Bilingualism*, *28*(2), 117–134. https://doi.org/10.1080/13670050.2024.2409120

Karkar-Esperat, T. (2023). *Transparency in the classroom: The raciosemiotic architecture framework for multilingual learners*. Semiotics Society of America 2023 Yearbook.

Lazutina, T. V., I. N. Pupysheva, M. N. Shcherbinin, V. N. Baksheev, & G. V. Patrakova. (2016). Semiotics of art: Language of architecture as a complex system of signs. *International Journal of Environmental and Science Education*, *11*(17), 9991–9998.

Muhammad, G. E. (2020). Cultivating Genius: An Equity Framework for Culturally and Historically Responsive Literacy. Scholastic edge at the cultural interface.

National Governors Association Center for Best Practices, & Council of Chief State School Officers. (2010). *Common Core State Standards for English language arts & literacy in history/social studies, science, and technical subjects*. Washington, DC: Authors. https://www.corestandards.org/ELA-Literacy/

New Mexico Public Education Department. (2021). *New Mexico social studies standards*. https://webnew.ped.state.nm.us/bureaus/literacy-humanities/social-studies/

New London Group (1996). A Pedagogy of Multiliteracies: Designing Social Futures. *Harvard Educational Review*, *66*(1), 60–92. https://doi.org/10.17763/haer.66.1.17370n67v22j160u

Zaidi, R., & D. El Chaar (2020). Identity texts: An intervention to internationalise the classroom. *Pedagogies: An International Journal*, 17. https://doi.org/10.1080/1554480X.2020.1860060

Instructional Materials Used with Students
Lesson Title: A Raciosemiotic Linguistic Approach: Idioms

Language Objectives (for Students)
1. Use idioms to increase student vocabulary knowledge, focusing on multiple meanings for words.
2. Use idioms to make inferences to improve reading comprehension.
3. Use idioms to improve inferential comprehension using different texts.

During instruction activities that you can use for teaching your students
- Idiom Connection—100 Most Frequent Idioms (Audio; Idiom Connection, n.d.) https://www.idiomconnection.com/mostfrequent.html#AA
- Idiom Cartoon 1 (**Audio Visual**; (English In General, 2021a) https://youtu.be/KJS77wXttpI?si=cpF0MNXvXslaa7u6
- Idiom Cartoon 2 **(Audio Visual**; (English In General, 2021b) https://youtu.be/4cQqiMv4dc8?si=C3LvQFwKSg5rGM0h
- Velcro folder to pair idioms in both English and Spanish **(linguistic and visual)**
- Draw what you envision when you hear the idiom, draw an illustration of the correct meaning, and then compare both drawings **(audio visual)**
- Read mentor texts with idioms (Linguistic, visual, spatial; the Best Children's Books, n.d.) https://www.the-best-childrens-books.org/
  - Reach out to the school librarian to help you identify at least one book from the list provided

- **The social studies standard for this theme focuses on inquiry. To connect with social studies**, have students inquire about one or two idioms they use in their home. After students have identified at least one idiom, have them research the following: (a) How does the idiom reflect their culture or (b) is the idiom related to national customs? Have them write the idiom about using a visual (Pinterest, n.d.). https://www.pinterest.com/ideas/teaching-idioms/931498924473/
- **Differentiation includes** the use of audiovisual cartoons, class discussion, drawings and visuals, idioms in two languages, restatement, movement to make concepts clear, and online resources.

References

English In General. (2021a, January 30). *Learn English idioms with TV series & movies|10 Most common English idioms | Part 1* [Video]. YouTube. https://www.youtube.com/watch?v=KJS77wXttpI

English In General. (2021b, February 14). *Learn English idioms with TV series & movies|Part 3 most common English idioms - Vocabulary* [Video]. YouTube. https://www.youtube.com/watch?v=4cQqiMv4dc8

Idiom Connection (n.d.). *Top 100 English idioms*. Retrieved April 18, 2025, from https://www.idiomconnection.com/mostfrequent.html

Pinterest. (n.d.). *Teaching idioms*. Retrieved April 18, 2025, from https://www.pinterest.com/ideas/teaching-idioms/931498924473/

The Best Childrens Books (n.d.). *Find the best children's books matched to your child's reading ability*. https://www.the-best-childrens-books.org/

Modeled Lesson 2: Linguistic Knowledge

Linguistic Knowledge: Folklore Storytelling Learning Module

Lesson Overview

This lesson introduces an element of the MultiSemiotic Linguistic Approach: Folklore Storytelling. You will use your students' background knowledge in planning instruction. The Common

Core Standards used in this module focus on determining the meaning of words and phrases by drawing inferences from text (historic and cultural concepts) and examining literature from different cultures. In addition to using evidence to support particular points, students will add audio and visuals to presentations to enhance the development of ideas.

Folklore and storytelling are integral to student culture and history and support multilingual learners. Remember that this is a lesson in which you can integrate the four language skills. However, I only chose reading, speaking, and listening standards for this module, along with some TESOL strategies. The readings give you a good background on incorporating storytelling and folklore into multilingual classrooms. You have different text choices that you can use. Most importantly, you want your students to process the information by discussing concepts multiple times and helping them make clear connections with their own culture. Compassionate teaching stems from learning about student cultures and nurturing their cultures in your teaching practices. The focus is connecting folklore and storytelling to student cultures and language. In this module you will learn strategies that you can embed in your classroom.

The following example lesson is framed and guided by the International Literacy Standards for Teacher Preparation in Literacy, the NCTE/IRA standards for English language arts, the Common Core standards for English language arts, and social studies standards. Following this, activities for before, during, and after the lesson are presented, which you can use to teach critical literacy, translanguaging, and multiliteracies. The lesson also offers opportunities to guide your third–fifth graders in using this MultiSemiotic approach.

Journaling: This is a documentation of your learning journey and will be used to evaluate the effectiveness of this process.

Start writing about ways you have already worked with folklore and storytelling and your thought process as you read the modules. What ideas do you get from the information presented for teaching multilingual students in terms of content and teaching strategies?

Learning Outcomes (for Teachers)

After studying this chapter, teachers should be able to:

1) Create lessons focusing on language, connecting to folklore and storytelling.
2) Revisit the standards that focus on language in relation to culture based on the grade level being taught.
3) Recognize folktales as valuable cultural and linguistic resources to teach multilingual students.
4) Provide students with opportunities to learn independently.
5) Provide students with rich reading language experiences.
6) Engage in meaning-making using multiliteracies.
7) Use the MultiSemiotic linguistic approach to create a product for your students.
8) Complete a reflection on the module in your journal.
9) Scaffold learning for third–fifth grade learners to complete the process.

TESOL Standards (for Teachers, TESOL International Association, 2018)

- **2a**. Candidates demonstrate knowledge of how dynamic academic, personal, familial, cultural, and social contexts, including sociopolitical factors, impact the education of ELLs.
- **2d**. Candidates devise and implement methods to learn about personal characteristics of the individual ELL (e.g., interests, motivations, strengths, needs) and their family (e.g., language use, literacy practices, circumstances) to develop effective instructional practices.
- **3a**. Candidates plan for culturally and linguistically relevant, supportive environments that promote ELLs' learning. Candidates design scaffolded instruction of language and literacies to support standards and curricular objectives for ELLs in the content areas.
- **3b**. Candidates instruct ELLs using evidence-based, student-centered, developmentally appropriate interactive approaches.

- **3e.** Candidates use and adapt relevant materials and resources, including digital resources, to plan lessons for ELLs, support communication with other educators, school personnel, and ELLs and to foster student learning of language and literacies in the content areas.
- **5a.** Candidates demonstrate knowledge of effective collaboration strategies in order to plan ways to serve as a resource for ELL instruction, support educators and school staff, and advocate for ELLs.
- **5d.** Candidates engage in supervised teaching to apply and develop their professional practice using self-reflection and feedback from their cooperating teachers and supervising faculty.

Language Objectives (for Students)
1. Use context clues to discern the meaning of unfamiliar words.
2. Make inferences about the meaning of new words.
3. Connect storytelling and folklore to their own and others' cultures.
4. Choose words that are important for text comprehension.
5. Determine the meanings of words that have multiple meanings.

Guiding Questions
1) How are you using your knowledge of your student communities (culture and traditions) to plan your content lessons?
2) How is the use of folklore and storytelling supporting your students' language learning?
3) How does the use of folklore and storytelling engage students in thinking about power and equity?

Pre-Class Preparation Activities for Teachers
Folklore and storytelling preserve culture, heritage, and language. They give historical background about a region or a country. Integrating students' cultures through folklore and storytelling improves students' language skills. Using their knowledge assets

and embracing students' cultures increases student engagement as they access their funds of knowledge.

- ♦ Think how folklore, folktales, and storytelling reflect culture and traditions. Then, write about those reflections in your journal.
- ♦ Think about creating a thematic unit on culture, focusing on folklore and storytelling. What topic would you introduce? Please include them in your journal.

Preview the Reading

Language is rooted in the reality of a culture, its community life, and the people's customs. Folklore is made up of the customs, lifestyles, habits, and traditions of a community or a group of people, which are manifested through myths, legends, proverbs, riddles, tales, poetry, and other forms of artistic expression (Definitions of Folklore, 1996) and passed down through oral tradition. We preserve folklore through storytelling. You will learn how to integrate folklore and storytelling in your curriculum, especially for language learners. Teaching folklore and storytelling encourages learners to learn about culture through language. Teaching folklore and storytelling should be purposeful. It encourages students to use language. I have provided examples of books that you can use in the classroom, but there are many other good resources available to you.

Language and Folklore
Read

- ♦ Folklore has helped in documenting history, life experiences, and heritage. Elders used to teach about the cultural past. You will learn about the purpose of folktales, connect with stories, and listen to a folktale. Remember, folktales are part of folklore and are connected to culture and identity. "How African American folklore Saved the Cultural Memory and History of Slaves" (Ivanchina, n.d.)

- **Role of Traditional Stories for English Language Education** (Mahanand, 2021) https://www.fortell.org/wp-content/uploads/2021/10/issue42-74-83.pdf

  You will learn about how the use of folktales is critical for multilingual learners, as they can enrich their language by focusing on vocabulary, syntax, and discussion. Learners are able to make connections with their own cultures, and traditional stories can help create intercultural awareness.

- **Storytelling in a Transcultural, Translanguaging Dialogic Exchange** (Flynn, 2021) https://pdxscholar.library.pdx.edu/cgi/viewcontent.cgi?article=1501&context=socwork_fac.

  You will read the write-up of a study on storytelling that was conducted in a preschool with a culturally and linguistically diverse classroom. I want you to pay attention to the teaching strategies in connection to students' culture and language. From the first part of the report until the methodology section, you will learn some background about the topic. In the methodology section, you will learn what happened during the study and what the authors did that led to the results. In the discussion, you will learn how the findings of the study connect to the theories and literature introduced in the first parts of the report and why these results are important.

Listen

- Importance of Folklore (Yiddish Book Center, 2012) https://youtu.be/e7alWoiPOsM?si=I7CXj3WJryNNifVS
- Teaching Language with Stories (Ashley, 2015) https://youtu.be/RZOJv-1pcT0?si=0ScTJKPL1Xz97q8L
- Multicultural Folktales (Start with a Book, 2023) https://www.startwithabook.org/we-are-storytellers-exploring-multicultural-folktales-fairy-tales-and-myths#multicultural

Thought Questions
1. How have you used the module material in your planning and instruction?
2. How were you able to connect folktales and storytelling with your students?
3. What supported your learning?
4. What could be changed to support your learning?
5. Would you consider integrating storytelling and folklore in your class? If so, why do you think so? In what ways will you do that? Please explain and be specific.
6. What other standards would you consider using to teach a lesson on storytelling and folklore?

References

Ashley, M.. (2015, November 14). *Teaching language with stories* [Video]. YouTube. https://www.youtube.com/watch?v=RZOJv-1pcT0

Definitions of Folklore. (1996). *Journal of Folklore Research, 33*(3), 255–264. https://www.jstor.org/stable/3814683

Flynn, E. E. (2021). "Rapunzel, Rapunzel, lanza tu pelo": Storytelling in a transcultural, translanguaging dialogic exchange. *Reading Research Quarterly, 56*(4), 643–658.

Ivanchina, A. (n.d.). *How African American folklore saved the cultural memory and history of slaves*. Shutterstock. https://www.shutterstock.com/

Mahanand, A. (2021). Role of traditional stories for English language education. *FORTELL, 42*, 74–83.

Start with a Book (2023, September 26). *We are storytellers: Exploring multicultural folktales, fairy tales, and myths*. WETA. https://www.startwithabook.org/we-are-storytellers-exploring-multicultural-folktales-fairy-tales-and-myths#multicultural

TESOL International Association. (2018). *Standards for initial TESOL Pre-K–12 teacher preparation programs*. https://www.tesol.org/media/v33fewo0/2018-tesol-teacher-prep-standards-final.pdf

Yiddish Book Center. (2012, July 25). *Importance of folklore* [Video]. YouTube. https://www.youtube.com/watch?v=e7alWoiPOsM

Lesson Title: A Linguistic Approach: Folklore and Storytelling (Karkar-Esperat, 2019, National Governors Association Center for Best Practices, & Council of Chief State School Officers, 2010; New Mexico Public Education Department, 2021)

Common Core Standards for 3rd–5th Grades	Social Studies Standards for 4th–5th Grade	Pedagogical Holistic Model of New Literacies
Third Grade	**Third Grade**	"The linguistic mode uses text, vocabulary, and metaphor, as well as information structure, local and global coherence relations, delivery, transitivity, and modality (the New London Group 1996). The pedagogical holistic model of new literacies focused on using the four approaches (i.e. authentic, didactic, critical, and functional).
CCSS.ELA-LITERACY.RL.3.2 Recount stories, including fables, folktales, and myths from diverse cultures; determine the central message, lesson, or moral and explain how it is conveyed through key details in the text.	3.2. Use supporting questions to help answer the compelling question in an inquiry	
CCSS.ELA-LITERACY.RI.3.4 Determine the meaning of words and phrases as they are used in a text, distinguishing literal from nonliteral language.	3.5. Construct responses to compelling questions using reasoning, examples, and relevant details.	
CCSS.ELA-LITERACY.SL.3.4 Report on a topic or text, tell a story, or recount an experience with appropriate facts and relevant, descriptive details, speaking clearly at an understandable pace.	3.26. Express a positive view of themselves while demonstrating respect and empathy for others.	
Fourth Grade	3.27. Compare and contrast their cultural identity with other people and groups.	
CCSS.ELA-LITERACY.RL.4.1 Refer to details and examples in a text when explaining what the text says explicitly and when drawing inferences from the text.		

(Continued)

Common Core Standards for 3rd–5th Grades	Social Studies Standards for 4th–5th Grade	Pedagogical Holistic Model of New Literacies
Fourth Grade	**Fourth Grade**	Teachers are responsible for selecting practical teaching approaches to engage students in analyzing multiple texts, evaluating and synthesizing information, giving constructive feedback to develop student problem-solving skills, and demonstrating how to categorize information (Karkar-Esperat 2019). The *multisemiotic linguistic* mode includes words or phrases that refer to culture and historical words (Lazutina et al. 2016), popular lyrics, code-switching, phrases, folklore texts, storytelling, 'semantics of proxematic sign' (Hall 1966), vernacular, and identity texts (Cummins 2006; Muhammad 2020 and Zaidi and El Chaar 2020; see also Baker-Bell 2020; Karkar-Esperat & Loftis 2021), Humor in learning (Hurren 2005)." (Karkar-Esperat, 2025, p. 11)
CCSS.ELA-LITERACY.RL.4.4 Determine the meaning of words and phrases as they are used in a text, including those that allude to significant characters found in mythology (e.g., Herculean).	4.4 Construct responses to compelling questions using reasoning, examples, and relevant details.	
CCSS.ELA-LITERACY.RI.4.8 Explain how author uses reason and evidence to support particular points in a text.	4.25. Participate in inquiry of other people's lives and experiences while demonstrating respect and empathy for others.	
CCSS.ELA-LITERACY.RI.4.9 Compare and contrast the treatment of similar themes and topics (e.g., opposition of good and evil) and patterns of events (e.g., the quest) in stories, myths, and traditional literature from different cultures.	**Fifth Grade**	
CCSS.ELA-LITERACY.SL.4.2 Paraphrase portions of a text read aloud or information presented in diverse media and formats, including visually, quantitatively, and orally.	5.5. Construct responses to compelling questions supported by reasoning and evidence.	
Fifth Grade	5.13. Examine history from the perspectives of the participants using a variety of narratives.	
CCSS.ELA-LITERACY.SL.5.3 Summarize the points a speaker makes and explain how each claim is supported by reasons and evidence.		
CCSS.ELA-LITERACY.RI.5.3 Explain the relationships or interactions between two or more individuals, events, ideas, or concepts in a historical, scientific, or technical text based on specific information in the text.		

References

Baker-Bell, A. (2020). Dismantling Anti-Black Linguistic Racism in English Language Arts Classrooms: Toward an Anti-Racist Black Language Pedagogy. *Theory Into Practice*, *59*(1), 8–21. https://doi.org/10.1080/00405841.2019.1665415

Cummins, J. (2006). Identity texts: The imaginative construction of self through multiliteracies pedagogy. In *Imagining multilingual schools: Languages in education and glocalization*, 51–68. New York, NY: Wiley. https://doi.org/10.21832/9781853598968-003

Hall, E. T. (1966). *The hidden dimension*. Volume 609 Doubleday. Garden City, NY, USA.

Hurren, B. L. (2005). Humor in School is Serious Business. *International Journal of Learning*, *12*(6), 79–83.

Karkar-Esperat, T. (2019). Assessing preservice teachers' knowledge of new literacies [Doctoral dissertation, Texas Tech University]. Texas Tech University Archive.

Karkar-Esperat, T. (2023). *Transparency in the classroom: The raciosemiotic architecture framework for multilingual learners*. Semiotics Society of America 2023 Yearbook.

Karkar-Esperat, T. M. (2025). Multiliteracies for Multilingual Learners: The MultiSemiotic Architecture Framework. *International Journal of Bilingual Education and Bilingualism*, *28*(2), 117–134. https://doi.org/10.1080/13670050.2024.2409120

Karkar-Esperat, T. M., & Loftis, T. M.. (2021). Using new literacies to foster student motivation. *Literacy Practice and Research*, *46*(1), 5.

Lazutina, T. V., Pupysheva, I. N., Shcherbinin, M. N., Baksheev, V. N., & Patrakova, G. V. (2016). Semiotics of art: Language of architecture as a complex system of signs. *International Journal of Environmental and Science Education*, *11*(17), 9991–9998.

Muhammad, G. E. (2020). Cultivating Genius: An Equity Framework for Culturally and Historically Responsive Literacy. Scholastic edge at the cultural interface.

National Governors Association Center for Best Practices, & Council of Chief State School Officers. (2010). *Common core state standards for English language arts & literacy in history/social studies, science, and technical subjects*. Washington, DC: Authors. https://www.corestandards.org/ELA-Literacy/

New London Group (1996). A pedagogy of multiliteracies: Designing social futures. *Harvard Educational Review, 66*(1), 60–92. https://doi.org/10.17763/haer.66.1.17370n67v22j160u

New Mexico Public Education Department. (2021). *New Mexico social studies standards.* https://webnew.ped.state.nm.us/bureaus/literacy-humanities/social-studies/

Zaidi, R., & El Chaar, D. (2020). Identity texts: An intervention to internationalise the classroom. *Pedagogies: An International Journal, 17.* https://doi.org/10.1080/1554480X.2020.1860060

Instructional Materials Used with Students

Lesson Title: A MultiSemiotic Linguistic Approach: Folklore and Storytelling

Language Objectives (for Students)

1. Use context clues to discern the meanings of unfamiliar words.
2. Make inferences about the meanings of new words.
3. Connect storytelling and folklore to students' culture.
4. Choose words that are important for text comprehension.
5. Determine the meanings of words that have multiple meanings.

During-Instruction Activities

- Create a foldable about Mexican heritage
- Use storyboard to create a short play
- Direct a play about culture
- Read works and books that are written in both English and Spanish

Connecting to Social Studies

- To connect with social studies, have students inquire about the UFO crash outside Roswell, New Mexico using different resources. It could be visiting the museum, watching a movie, reading articles, or listening to a storyteller. Students will participate in a discussion and create a visual that portrays what happened. Some students can tell the story using PowerPoint presentations.

♦ **Differentiations include** the use of audio, class discussions, drawings and visuals, movement to make concepts clear, online resources, and varying text levels.

Modeled Lesson 3: Linguistic Knowledge
Lesson Title: A Linguistic Approach: Identity

Lesson Overview
This lesson introduces an element of the Raciosemiotic/Multi-Semiotic Linguistic Approach: Identity. We must teach our students about their identity in connection to multilingualism and culture. We do that by introducing them to texts to which they can make connections. The Common Core state standards that are used in this module focus on using narrative, comparing and contrasting biographies, drawing information from multiple print text sources, and producing clear and coherent writing. This module asks you to use culture as a lens to explore topics.

Keep in mind this is a lesson in which you can integrate the four language skills. However, I only chose reading and speaking/listening standards for this module. There are also some TESOL strategies used in the module. The readings give you a good background on the teaching skills that you need to introduce identity texts to multilingual students. You have different text choices that you can use. You are being taught to use your students' background knowledge in planning instruction. The focus is connecting identity to student cultures and language.

The example lesson that follows is guided by the International Literacy Standards for teacher preparation in literacy, the NCTE/IRA standards for English language arts, the Common Core Standards for English language arts and social studies standards. Following this, activities for before, during, and after are presented for teachers to use to teach critical literacy, translanguaging, and multiliteracies. Opportunities are also presented in the lesson to guide third–fifth grade students to use this approach.

Journaling: This is a documentation of your learning journey and will be used to evaluate the effectiveness of this process.

Start writing about what materials you've previously used to introduce identity, as well as your thought process as you read the modules. What new ideas does the information presented give you for teaching multilingual students in terms of content and teaching strategies?

Learning Outcomes (for Teachers)

After studying this chapter, teachers should be able to:

- Create a lesson focusing on language and culture, connecting to identity.
- Revisit the standards that focus on language in relation to culture based on the grade level being taught.
- Provide students with texts that help them learn how people are similar and different.
- Support students to create a positive perception about their identity.
- Provide students with rich reading language experiences.
- Engage in meaning-making using multiliteracies.
- Use the raciosemiotic/MultiSemiotic linguistic approach to create a product for your students.
- Complete a reflection on the module.
- Scaffold learning for their third–fifth graders to complete the process.

TESOL Standards (for Teachers, TESOL International Association, 2018)

- **2a**. Candidates demonstrate knowledge of how dynamic academic, personal, familial, cultural, and social contexts, including sociopolitical factors, impact the education of ELLs.
- **2d**. Candidates devise and implement methods to learn about personal characteristics of the individual ELL (e.g., interests, motivations, strengths, needs) and their family (e.g., language use, literacy practices, circumstances) to develop effective instructional practices.
- **3a**. Candidates plan for culturally and linguistically relevant, supportive environments that promote ELLs'

learning. Candidates design scaffolded instruction of language and literacies to support standards and curricular objectives for ELLs in the content areas.
- ♦ **3b.** Candidates instruct ELLs using evidence-based, student-centered, developmentally appropriate interactive approaches.
- ♦ **3e.** Candidates use and adapt relevant materials and resources, including digital resources, to plan lessons for ELLs, support communication with other educators, school personnel, and ELLs and to foster student learning of language and literacies in the content areas.
- ♦ **5a.** Candidates demonstrate knowledge of effective collaboration strategies in order to plan ways to serve as a resource for ELL instruction, support educators and school staff, and advocate for ELLs.
- ♦ **5d.** Candidates engage in supervised teaching to apply and develop their professional practice using self-reflection and feedback from their cooperating teachers and supervising faculty.

Language Objectives (for Students)
1. Develop a written autobiography with facts and concrete details.
2. Produce clear and coherent writing.
3. Compare different biographies orally.
4. Read autobiographies clearly and with adequate fluency and pace.

Guiding Questions
1. How does culture impact student identity and learning?
2. How can the teacher create lessons using the students' cultural identities?
3. How can the teacher learn about the students' cultures, create a safe environment for the students, and support relationships with the students and families?
4. How can you use language to empower students to frame their identities?

5. How can focusing on identity bring equity into the classroom?
6. How can autobiography help in understanding someone's personal history?

Pre-Class Preparation Activities for Teachers
Think of a text set you can create to teach a unit on identity. What theme on identity would you teach? What visual aids would you use? Please discuss them in your journal.

Preview the Reading
Culture can mean different things, but we want to think about students' assets and how we can use students' language, multilingualism, background, family, and interests to create content and also help students identify their own identity. We want our students to celebrate their unique cultures in our classroom. We also want our students to learn about other cultures in the classroom and identify their biases and assist them in reflection on their own biases. Through recognizing our student cultures in the classroom, we empower them and affirm their cultural identity.

Read

- The Relationship Between Cultural Identity and Learning (Sosyal Altugan, 2015) https://www.sciencedirect.com/science/article/pii/S1877042815024210?ref=pdf_download&fr=RR-2&rr=950c60181c1bd68b

  The purpose of this reading is to understand that there is a relationship between learning and cultural identity. You will learn about cultural identity and how it increases student motivation toward learning. Think of cultural strategies that you have used or can use to increase student motivation.

- Why Cultural Diversity and Awareness in the Classroom Is Important (Walden University, n.d.) https://www.waldenu.edu/online-bachelors-programs/

bs-in-elementary-education/resource/why-cultural-diversity-and-awareness-in-the-classroom-is-important

This article focuses on why fostering cultural diversity in the classroom is imperative for your students' success.

- I am poems (ReadWriteThink, n.d.) https://www.readwritethink.org/sites/default/files/resources/lesson_images/lesson391/I-am-poem.pdf

  Students create short poems describing themselves. In addition to being a simple writing activity to introduce students to poetry, this is a great way to help students express themselves.

- How to Write an Autobiography https://literacyideas.com/how-to-write-an-autobiography/ (Donnchaidh, 2023)

  This source will show you how to teach students to write an autobiography.

- These are resources that you could use to teach your fourth–sixth graders about biographies:
  - Best Biographies for Kids (The best Childrens Books, n.d.) https://www.the-best-childrens-books.org/
  - Biographies for Middle School (Conie, 2021) https://www.toledolibrary.org/blog/biographies-for-middle-school-grades-6-8/

Listen

- Writing an Autobiography: Format, Steps & Tips (Woerner, 2023) https://study.com/academy/lesson/writing-an-autobiography-format-steps-tips.html

Thought Questions

1. How have you used the module material in your planning and instruction?
2. How were you able to connect to your students?
3. What supported your learning?
4. What could be changed to support your learning?

5. Would you consider teaching about identity? In what ways will you do that? Please explain and be specific.
6. What other standards would you consider using to teach a lesson on identity?

References

Conie, C. (2021, March 22). *Biographies for middle school (Grades 6-8)*. Toledo Library. https://www.toledolibrary.org/blog/biographies-for-middle-school-grades-6-8

Donnchaidh, S. M. (2023, June 9). *How to write an autobiography*. Literacy Ideas. https://literacyideas.com/how-to-write-an-autobiography/

ReadWriteThink (n.d.). *Writing an "I am" poem*. Retrieved April 18, 2025, from https://www.readwritethink.org/sites/default/files/resources/lesson_images/lesson391/I-am-poem.pdf

Sosyal Altugan, A. (2015). The relationship between cultural identity and learning. *Procedia, 186*, 1159–1162. https://doi.org/10.1016/j.sbspro.2015.04.161

TESOL International Association. (2018). *Standards for initial TESOL Pre-K–12 teacher preparation programs*. Alexandria. https://www.tesol.org/docs/default-source/advocacy/2018_tesol-teacher-prep-standards_final.pdf

The Best Childrens Books (n.d.). *Find the Best Children's Books Matched to Your Child's Reading Ability*. https://www.the-best-childrens-books.org/

Walden University. (n.d.). *Why cultural diversity and awareness in the classroom is important*. Retrieved April 18, 2025, from https://www.waldenu.edu/online-bachelors-programs/bs-in-elementary-education/resource/why-cultural-diversity-and-awareness-in-the-classroom-is-important

Woerner, J. (2023, November 21). *Writing an autobiography | Format, example & template*. Study.com. https://study.com/academy/lesson/writing-an-autobiography-format-steps-tips.html?src=ppc_adwords_nonbrand&rcntxt=aws&crt=631249708240&kwd=&kwid=aud-681311930872:dsa-1253079156202&agid=125582019081&mt=&device=c&network=s&_campaign=SeoPPC&gclid=Cj0KCQiAiJSeBhCCARIsAHnAzT_hArc-pfNsOenP7Tnx9539Zlt18tQg8r4qzLxIshwTyqkubPXIEDMaApnBEALw_wcB

Lesson Title: A Racio/MultiSemiotic Linguistic Approach: Identity (Karkar-Esperat, 2019, National Governors Association Center for Best Practices, & Council of Chief State School Officers, 2010; New Mexico Public Education Department, 2021)

Common Core Standards for 3r.d–5th Grades	*Social Studies Standards for 3rd–5th Grade*	*Pedagogical Holistic Model of New Literacies*
Third Grade	**Third Grade**	"The linguistic mode uses text, vocabulary, and metaphor, as well as information structure, local and global coherence relations, delivery, transitivity, and modality (the New London Group 1996). The pedagogical holistic model of new literacies focused on using the four approaches (i.e. authentic, didactic, critical, and functional). Teachers are responsible for selecting practical teaching approaches to engage students in analyzing multiple texts, evaluating and synthesizing information, giving constructive feedback to develop student problem-solving skills, and demonstrating how to categorize information (Karkar-Esperat 2019).
CCSS.ELA-LITERACY.RL.3.9 Compare and contrast the themes, settings, and plots of stories written by the same author about the same or similar characters (e.g., in books from a series).	3.2. Use supporting questions to help answer the compelling question in an inquiry.	
CCSS.ELA-LITERACY.W.3.2B Develop the topic with facts, definitions, and details.	3.26. Express a positive view of themselves while demonstrating respect and empathy for others.	
CCSS.ELA-LITERACY.W.3.4 With guidance and support from adults, produce writing in which the development and organization are appropriate to task and purpose.	3.27. Compare and contrast their cultural identity with other people and groups.	
CCSS.ELA-LITERACY.SL.3.5 Create engaging audio recordings of stories or poems that demonstrate fluid reading at an understandable pace; add visual displays when appropriate to emphasize or enhance certain facts or details.		

(Continued)

Common Core Standards for 3r.d–5th Grades	Social Studies Standards for 3rd–5th Grade	Pedagogical Holistic Model of New Literacies
Fourth Grade	**Fourth Grade**	The *MultiSemiotic linguistic* mode includes words or phrases that refer to culture and historical words (Lazutina et al. 2016), popular lyrics, code-switching, phrases, folklore texts, storytelling, 'semantics of proxematic sign" (Hall 1966), vernacular, and identity texts (Cummins 2006; Muhammad 2020 and Zaidi and El Chaar 2020; see also Baker-Bell 2020; Karkar-Esperat and Loftis 2021), Humor in learning (Hurren 2005)." (Karkar-Esperat, 2025, p. 12)
CCSS.ELA-LITERACY.RL.4.9 Compare and contrast the treatment of similar themes and topics (e.g., opposition of good and evil) in stories, myths, and traditional literature from different cultures.	4.3. Cite evidence that supports a response to supporting or compelling questions.	
CCSS.ELA-LITERACY.W.4.2B Develop the topic with facts, definitions, concrete details, quotations, or other information and examples related to the topic.	4.25. Participate in inquiry of other people's lives and experiences while demonstrating respect and empathy for others.	
CCSS.ELA-LITERACY.W.4.4 Produce clear and coherent writing in which the development and organization are appropriate to task, purpose, and audience.	4.26. Explain connections among historical contexts and people's perspectives at the time.	
CCSS.ELA-LITERACY.SL.4.5 Add audio recordings and visual displays to presentations when appropriate to enhance the development of main ideas or themes.		The *raciosemiotic linguistic* mode could include words or phrases that refer to culture, historical words, idioms (Lazutina et al., 2016), code-switching, phrases, folklore texts, storytelling, "semantics of proxematic sign" (Hall, 1966), and identity texts (Zaidi & El Chaar, 2020; see also Baker-Bell, 2020).
Fifth Grade		
CCSS.ELA-LITERACY.RL.5.9 Compare and contrast stories in the same genre (e.g., mysteries and adventure stories) on their approaches to similar themes and topics.		
CCSS.ELA-LITERACY.RI.5.2 Determine two or more main ideas of a text and explain how they are supported by key details; summarize the text.		

	Fifth Grade
CCSS.ELA-LITERACY.RI.5.7 Draw on information from multiple print or digital sources, demonstrating the ability to locate an answer to a question quickly or to solve a problem efficiently.	5.30. Demonstrate knowledge of family history, culture, and past contributions of people in their main identity groups.
CCSS.ELA-LITERACY.W.5.2B Develop the topic with facts, definitions, concrete details, quotations, or other information and examples related to the topic.	5.13. Examine history from the perspectives of the participants using a variety of narratives.
CCSS.ELA-LITERACY.W.5.4 Produce clear and coherent writing in which the development and organization are appropriate to task, purpose, and audience.	

References

Baker-Bell, A. (2020). Dismantling anti-black linguistic racism in English language arts classrooms: Toward an anti-racist black language pedagogy. *Theory into Practice*, *59*(1), 8–21. https://doi.org/10.1080/00405841.2019.1665415

Cummins, J. (2006). Identity texts: The imaginative construction of self through multiliteracies pedagogy. In *Imagining multilingual schools: Languages in education and glocalization*, 51–68. New York, NY: Wiley. https://doi.org/10.21832/9781853598968-003

Hall, E. T. (1966). *The hidden dimension. Volume 609*. Garden City, NY, USA: Doubleday.

Hurren, B. L. (2005). Humor in school is serious business. *International Journal of Learning*, *12*(6), 79–83.

Karkar-Esperat, T. (2019). Assessing preservice teachers' knowledge of new literacies [Doctoral dissertation, Texas Tech University]. Texas Tech University Archive.

Karkar-Esperat, T. M., & T. M. Loftis. (2021). Using new literacies to foster student motivation. *Literacy Practice and Research*, *46*(1), 5.

Karkar-Esperat, T. (2023). Transparency in the Classroom: The Raciosemiotic Architecture Framework for Multilingual Learners. Semiotics Society of America 2023 Yearbook.

Karkar-Esperat, T. M. (2025). Multiliteracies for multilingual learners: The multisemiotic architecture framework. *International Journal of Bilingual Education and Bilingualism*, *28*(2), 117–134 https://doi.org/10.1080/13670050.2024.2409120

Lazutina, T. V., I. N. Pupysheva, M. N. Shcherbinin, V. N. Baksheev, & G. V. Patrakova. (2016). Semiotics of art: Language of architecture as a complex system of signs. *International Journal of Environmental and Science Education*, *11*(17), 9991–9998.

Muhammad, G. E. (2020). Cultivating Genius: An Equity Framework for Culturally and Historically Responsive Literacy. Scholastic edge at the cultural interface.

National Governors Association Center for Best Practices, & Council of Chief State School Officers. (2010). *Common core state standards for English language arts & literacy in history/social studies, science, and technical subjects*. Washington, DC: Authors. https://www.corestandards.org/ELA-Literacy/

New Mexico Public Education Department. (2021). *New Mexico social studies standards*. https://webnew.ped.state.nm.us/bureaus/literacy-humanities/social-studies/

New London Group (1996). A pedagogy of multiliteracies: Designing social futures." *Harvard Educational Review, 66*(1), 60–92. https://doi.org/10.17763/haer.66.1.17370n67v22j160u

Zaidi, R., & D. El Chaar (2020). Identity texts: An intervention to internationalise the classroom. *Pedagogies: An International Journal*, 17. https://doi.org/10.1080/1554480X.2020.1860060

Instructional Materials Used with Students
Lesson Title: A Racio/MultiSemiotic Linguistic Approach: Identity

Language Objectives (for Students)
1. To develop a written autobiography with facts and concrete details.
2. To produce clear and coherent writing.
3. To orally compare different biographies.
4. To read autobiography clearly and with adequate pace.

- During-Instruction Activities
  - Reading about biographies.
  - Creating a visual using a storyline or graphic organizer.
  - Writing their autobiographies and sharing them with their peers.
  - Presenting their autobiographies using digital media.
  - Reading example "I Am Poems" and then writing and sharing their poems.

The social studies standards for this theme focus on students identifying primary and secondary sources, examining history from different perspectives, and citing evidence.

- To connect with social studies, have students identify a critical figure that made a difference in social justice and cultural awareness. After they read the biography, they

will share the information they learned with their peers using visuals (a storyline or graphic organizer).
- ◆ Then, ask students to write about their first language and culture and how that impacts their learning and how they think about themselves.

Differentiation includes the use of paraphrasing, supplementary materials, audio supports, class discussion, drawings and visuals, online resources, and text levels, as well as varying the length of the "I am" poems from three to five stanzas.

3

Self-Discovery Through the Visual Mode

Examining Customs and Traditions and Visual Knowledge

> **VIGNETTE**
>
> Teaching ESL at an elementary school for 4th grade abroad, I found that the students had diverse abilities and interests, and the use of visuals helped them be included immediately. It became a tool for them to explore texts and find their individual voices. The department chair asked me to have students read stories and rotate students among the groups. Looking at students' diverse needs and motivation to read, I divided them into groups, and each group decided on a *Magic Tree House* story. Students read chapters from the book at home and came prepared to share their thoughts in class. I asked them to take notes by drawing pictures of their understanding, writing short sentences, and developing paragraphs. My goal was to cultivate their interest in reading. Students' relationships grew stronger, and they were able to

include other viewpoints in their thinking. I saw how invested the students were in reading their stories, so I asked them to write their own scripts for the stories. At that point, I knew I needed to include visuals to dramatize their scenes. I invited a storyteller who taught them how to make their hand puppets. Each student chose a character to portray. Student engagement reached a different level by adding an audience, which included their parents. Using puppets helped my students discover their talents and abilities to write, present, and portray characters using their voices and hands during readers' theater. I remember that this experience was life-changing for my students as they started enjoying a new talent through reading and communication. One student stuttered, and with this creative experience and constant practice, he was able to communicate clearly during this experience. As a teacher educator now, I advocate for the use of visuals to connect to students' identities and enhance their reading skills. This chapter celebrates using visuals to embrace the richness of cultures that could and should be part of their reading experiences.

One of the in-service teachers who implemented these modules shared, "I was able to connect to my students by realizing that they need to learn about the cultural heritage New Mexico has to offer." Another teacher conveyed, "Teaching and utilizing visuals develop vocabulary, word recognition, reading for comprehension, writing, and critical thinking skills across all subject areas. An endless number of topics could be covered when teaching visual knowledge." One teacher added, "I find that I am myself am a visual learner and it helps me better understand the expectations, and I see this in my students as well." Another teacher expressed, "Visual learning is key on learning new concepts." A different teacher specified, "My students and I are able to connect through our culture and traditions. We share many things in common and so they are able to be comfortable and share things about their life." A teacher concluded, "Learning about visual knowledge helps students learn about their culture by researching and being able to see where their families came from as well as their ancestors."

> *A final teacher added, "It [Visual knowledge] aids by providing a more explicit explanation of new concepts, and this creates an easier way for understanding and applying knowledge."*

Dear teachers, parents, guardians, and students,

You are going to learn how you can use visuals in teaching and learning. The examples are provided in the context of New Mexico. You can follow the same structure and apply it in your own context.

This chapter will guide you to learn about what is a visual semiotic. Why do we need a visual semiotic in the classroom? How can you adapt this approach in the classroom?

What Is It About?

"The visual mode, according to the New London Group (1996), focuses on concepts such as "colors," "vectors," "perspective," and "background," as well as "foregrounding and backgrounding." The holistic pedagogical model of new literacies used various words to describe this visual mode, such as graphs, interactive texts, visual resources (e.g., texts, message boards, blogs), visual aids (e.g., graphs, maps, charts, tables), and technologies (Karkar-Esperat, 2019). The MultiSemiotic visual mode could refer to signs (i.e., Black Lives Matter signs, signs to promote social equity at work, visuals of people from different backgrounds coming together), timelines (referring to history), and customs and traditions with cultural connections (dress, colors, symbols, gender roles; see Mills and Godley, 2017; see also Watson et al., 2021)." (Karkar-Esperat, 2025, p. 11)

Visual Literacy

Visual literacy "is the communicative mode" (Duncum, 2004, p. 252). Teachers use visuals to scaffold or shelter instruction

(Echevarría et al., 2017) and provide clear and understandable information using visuals, simulations, and graphic organizers (Krashen, 1985).

Visual literacies are essential in learning experiences because individuals learn about topics through exposure to advertisements, art, social media, and so on. Teachers use visuals to communicate new information to students. Students are encouraged to analyze the messages and emotions conveyed in the visuals (Loerts & Belcher, 2019). Schools that adopt the visual literacy mode tend to increase bilingual and multilingual students' grades and skills learning and comprehension (Hailey et al., 2015). According to Deetsch et al. (2018), visual literacy can help students connect what they see to the object's meaning. For instance, a kindergarten teacher uses visuals when teaching colors, connecting red to apple and green to tree. The use of visuals encourages language skills. Dialogue is essential in understanding pictures (Duncum, 2004), and through visuals, learners incorporate self-reflection (Serafini, 2014). Visual literacy encourages creativity and helps students internalize a topic (Kędra and Žakevičiūtė, 2019). Students engage in the visual thinking process when they use visual aids such as diagrams, charts, and images that organize information to solve issues and communicate ideas.

Why Do We Need to Use It?

Teaching and learning should be more than reading a text and answering questions using didactic literacy. Students should be involved in recognizing the value of working with each other by exploring visuals. The use of visuals inspires students to identify details and encourages self-discovery. It also reminds teachers to be empathetic and compassionate toward personalizing instruction, helping students connect with the learned material, and applying what they learned into a meaningful process using functional and authentic literacy approaches.

Examples of How Visuals Have Been Used In the Classroom

Visual literacy is a powerful tool for students speaking more than one language in the classroom. It not only bridges language barriers but also empowers them to grasp content more effectively (Catalano & Hamann, 2016). Images and visual cues serve as a universal language that transcends linguistic differences, making it easier for bilingual students to comprehend concepts and ideas. By integrating visual literacy strategies in the classroom, teachers can foster a more inclusive learning environment that respects the diverse linguistic backgrounds of students. This approach not only supports language development but also fosters a sense of empowerment among bilingual learners. As De Jong and Gao (2023) assert, "a multilingual stance includes teacher beliefs, attitudes, and knowledge about the significant role of bilingual students' home languages in education, and it requires teachers to develop critical multilingual language awareness" (p. 473).

There are several factors that should be addressed in the classroom, and teachers should be open to trying as many teaching methods as possible to ensure a positive learning outcome for their students. Culture is one of the most common factors that needs to be addressed in the classroom. Each student is unique, coming from a different background and practicing different cultures. It is crucial for students to receive an education where they feel comfortable. Culture, particularly for bilingual learners, can influence the interpretation and comprehension of visual media (De Oliveira, 2016). As Catalano and Hamann (2016) point out, effectively using visual literacies involves understanding how bilingual students can perceive visual information in a different way based on their cultural experience. The incorporation of cultural elements in visual materials is not just beneficial but essential, significantly impacting the learning of students and underscoring the crucial role of educators.

Visual strategies and culture are crucial in the classroom, especially when working with bilingual students. By mixing culturally appropriate visual materials and resources, teachers can generate a more engaging and comprehensive learning environment that resonates with students' backgrounds (Maijala, 2020). Visual strategies support bridging cultural gaps, encouraging understanding, and increasing the general learning experience for bilingual learners. Additionally, incorporating elements of students' cultures in visual materials can validate their identities and develop a sense of belonging in the classroom, developing a positive and supportive learning atmosphere. By incorporating cultural events, teachers can create engaging and inclusive learning environments that help multilingual academic development (Aisami, 2015).

Visual Literacies Strategies In An Elementary Class

Visual literacy strategies in elementary classes can be advantageous for bilingual students. Visual aids such as pictures, illustrations, and videos can help enhance understanding of the content and engagement with others, especially for students learning a different language (Huilcapi-Collantes et al., 2020). Visuals can also offer context, support vocabulary progress, and help understand multifaceted concepts. Integrating diverse cultures can also help bilingual students relate to the content and make a more comprehensive learning environment (Berg & Huang, 2015). In addition, according to Radke et al. (2022), interactive visual activities such as drawing, labeling, and creating visual presentations can further strengthen learning and language acquisition for bilingual students in elementary classrooms.

There are many ways to support bilingual and multilingual students with visual aids. For instance, some teachers help their ELLs "associate reading and writing with meaning and literacy knowledge derived from their home experiences" (Sunseri & Sunseri, 2019, p. 119). Providing students with pictures from their country or anything that connects with their culture will help them feel comfortable in the classroom, and they will be willing to learn as much as possible. According to Quecan (2021), "the benefits of using visual aids in the classroom are robust as they can improve motivation, comprehension, and vocabulary acquisition among English learners" (p.7). Nuñez (2019) showed that students from Central and South America more easily learned English as a second language when they were supported with visual aids such as videos or images, especially on social media. Implementing interactive activities such as drawing and labeling images and creating DIY visual presentations can reinforce learning and language skills for bilingual and multilingual students. Interactive activities not only help students learn a new language but can also increase the students' knowledge and skills in the classroom (Anderson et al., 2018). Even better, the joy and fun in these activities can make educators feel more enthusiastic and engaged.

Utilizing culturally relevant visual aids is essential for creating a connecting and inclusive learning environment. Not only will students learn from one another, but the teacher can also share their experiences with other teachers who have bilingual students in their classrooms. A learning activity where students share their traditional stories and folktales through pictures can help them connect with their heritage and understand cultural values (Agbenyega et al., 2017). This sense of connection can make educators feel more empathetic and connected to their students. Rewarding students with a celebration or festival can also boost their learning and engagement skills. Festivals are part of the visual mode because students can provide numerous cultural practices that students might be interested in sharing with their classmates and others in their community. Visualizing what other cultures look like can make students feel more comfortable in their learning environment. Having students paint, create, or color artifacts or cultural symbols can provide insight into promoting cultural awareness.

Many studies have been conducted about the use of visual aids for bilingual students and their connection to culture. According to Laird-Arnold (2022), landscapes and cuisine are some of the more important aspects that can be used as visual aids in learning strategies. Displaying visuals of well-known landscapes and historic sites from around the world can spark curiosity in learning new cultures. By welcoming new visual material in the classroom, such as by showcasing of traditional foods and cuisines from all around the world, educators can promote cultural awareness and make students more appreciative of diversity. This emphasis on cultural awareness can make educators themselves more fully appreciate of diversity, fostering a sense of inclusivity and respect in their teaching.

Conclusion

Visual aids can help bilingual students in elementary school understand concepts better. The visuals provide a way to grasp ideas beyond words, making learning more accessible for students in a second language. Teachers who use visuals tend to connect more with their students by providing them with different cultures and backgrounds (Loerts & Belcher, 2019). Interactive activities involving visuals, such as drawings or image representations, can strengthen learning and language skills for bilingual students in elementary schools. Sharing cultural cuisine, costumes, and symbols can increase students' interest in learning new material or learning about traditions they have never seen before.

How Can We Use It?

There are three simple steps that you need to follow:

1. Read the national standards that guided these two lessons.
2. Study the learning materials, which will give you background about the chapter examples.
3. Review the instructional materials, which could be used with students in language art and social studies.

The modeled lessons are on Customs and Traditions and then Visual Knowledge.

Guiding Table for This Chapter

Transmultiliteracies Sustaining Pedagogy Approach (Karkar-Esperat & Stickley, 2024)	♦ The use of the Language Arts Standards and Social Studies Standards. ♦ Applications for language arts and social studies classrooms.
The Pedagogical Holistic Model of New Literacies (Karkar-Esperat, 2019)	♦ Reading about the topic using different forms of texts. ♦ Creating a text set on a particular culture. ♦ Using Glogster or Piktochart to create a visual. ♦ Presenting about a particular cultural heritage electronically or using a paper poster. ♦ Filming a subject that presents cultures, traditions, and customs.
The Raciosemiotic Architecture Framework (Karkar-Esperat, 2023)	♦ Synthesize on art forms signifying meanings and discuss interpretations. ♦ Recognize how art represents the characterization of human beings and supports social advocacy and/or social justice. ♦ Discuss a piece of art considering time, culture, place, story, and colors. ♦ Engage in meaning-making using multiliteracies.
The MultiSemiotic Architecture Framework (Karkar-Esperat, 2025)	**A MultiSemiotic Visual Approach: Visual Knowledge & Customs and Traditions** ♦ The MultiSemiotic visual mode could refer to signs, customs, and traditions with cultural connections that the lessons were developed around.

References

Agbenyega, J. S., Tamakloe, D. E., & Klibthong, S. (2017). Folklore epistemology: How does traditional folklore contribute to children's thinking and concept development?. *International Journal of Early Years Education*, *25*(2), 112–126.

Aisami, R. S. (2015). Learning styles and visual literacy for learning and performance. *Procedia-Social and Behavioral Sciences*, *176*, 538–545.

Anderson, J. A., Chung-Fat-Yim, A., Bellana, B., Luk, G., & Bialystok, E. (2018). Language and cognitive control networks in bilinguals and monolinguals. *Neuropsychologia, 117*, 352–363.

Berg, M. A., & Huang, J. (2015). Improving in-service teachers' effectiveness: K-12 academic literacy for the linguistically diverse. *Functional Linguistics, 2*, 1–21. https://doi.org/10.1186/s40554-015-0017-6

Castro-Garcés, A. Y. (2021). Awakening sociocultural realities in pre-service teachers through a pedagogy of multiliteracies. *GIST Education and Learning Research Journal, 22*, 173–197. https://doi.org/10.26817/16925777.844

Catalano, T., & Hamann, E. T. (2016). Multilingual pedagogies and pre-service teachers: Implementing "language as a resource" orientations in teacher education programs. *Bilingual Research Journal, 39*(3–4), 263–278. https://doi.org/10.1080/15235882.2016.1229701

De Jong, E., & Gao, J. (2023). Preparing teacher candidates for bilingual practices: Toward a multilingual stance in mainstream teacher education. *International Journal of Bilingual Education and Bilingualism, 26*(4), 472–482. https://doi.org/10.1080/13670050.2022.2119072

De Oliveira, L. C. (2016). A language-based approach to content instruction (LACI) for English language learners: Examples from two elementary teachers. *International Multilingual Research Journal, 10*(3), 217–231. https://doi.org/10.1080/19313152.2016.1185911

Deetsch, M., Glass, R., Jankowski, R., Mylander, E., Roth, P., & Wharton, E. (2018). Visual literacy and its impact on pre-literacy development. *Journal of Museum Education, 43*(2), 148–158. https://doi.org/10.1080/10598650.2018.1426332

Deng, Q., & Hayden, H. E. (2021). How preservice teachers begin to develop equitable visions for teaching multilingual learners. *Peabody Journal of Education, 96*(4), 406–422. https://doi.org/10.1080/0161956X.2021.1965413

Duncum, P. (2004). Visual culture isn't just visual: Multiliteracy, multimodality and meaning. *Studies in Art Education, 45*(3), 252–264. https://doi.org/10.1080/00393541.2004.11651771

Echevarría, J., Vogt, M. E., & Short, D. (2017). *Making content comprehensible for English learners: The SIOP model* (4th ed.). Pearson Education.

Hailey, D., Miller, A., & Yenawine, P. (2015). Understanding visual literacy: The visual thinking strategies approach. In *Essentials of teaching and integrating visual and media literacy: Visualizing learning* (pp. 49–73). Springer International Publishing.

Huilcapi-Collantes, C., Hernández, A., & Hernández-Ramos, J. P. (2020). The effect of a blended learning course of visual literacy for in-service teachers. *Journal of Information Technology Education: Research, 19.* https://doi.org/10.28945/4533

Humphrey, S. (2020). The role of teachers' disciplinary semiotic knowledge in supporting young bi/multilingual learners' academic and reflexive multiliteracies. *Language and Education, 35*(2), 140–159. https://doi.org/10.1080/09500782.2020.1772282

Karkar-Esperat, T. (2019). Assessing preservice teachers' knowledge of new literacies [Doctoral dissertation, Texas Tech University]. Texas Tech University Archive.

Karkar-Esperat, T. & Stickley, Z. (2024). Revisioning curriculum through the transmulitliteracies sustaining pedagogy approach. *Social Sciences & Humanities Open, 9,* 100826.

Karkar-Esperat, T. M. (2023). Transparency in the classroom: The Raciosemiotic Architecture Framework for multilingual learners. *Semiotics,* 39–53. https://doi.org/10.5840/cpsem20234

Karkar-Esperat, T. M. (2025). Multiliteracies for multilingual learners: The MultiSemiotic Architecture Framework. *International Journal of Bilingual Education and Bilingualism, 28*(2), 117–134. https://doi.org/10.1080/13670050.2024.2409120

Kędra, J. (2018). What does it mean to be visually literate? Examination of visual literacy definitions in a con- text of higher education. *Journal of Visual Literacy, 37,* 67–84. https://doi.org/10.1080/1051144X.2018.1492234

Kędra, J., & Žakevičiūtė, R. (2019). Visual literacy practices in higher education: What, why and how? *Journal of Visual Literacy, 38*(1–2), 1–7. https://doi.org/10.1080/1051144X.2019.1580438

Krashen, S. D. (1985). *The input hypothesis: Issues and implications.* Longman.

Kukner, J. M., & Orr, A. M. (2015). Inquiring into pre-service content area teachers development of literacy practices and pedagogical content knowledge. *Australian Journal of Teacher Education, 40*(5), 41–60. https://doi.org/10.14221/ajte.2015v40n5.3

Laird-Arnold, K. N. (2022). A Case Study of Cultural Awareness Integration Throughout the Elementary Education Curriculum. (Doctoral dissertation)

Loerts, T., & Belcher, C. (2019). Developing visual literacy competencies while learning course content through visual journaling: Teacher candidate perspectives. *Journal of Visual Literacy*, *38*(1–2), 46–65. https://doi.org/10.1080/1051144X.2018.1564603

Maijala, M. (2020). Culture teaching methods in foreign language education: pre-service teachers' reported beliefs and practices. *Innovation in Language Learning and Teaching*, *14*(2), 133–149. https://doi.org/10.1080/17501229.2018.1509981

McKoy, C. L., MacLeod, R. B., Walter, J. S., & Nolker, D. B. (2017). The impact of an in-service workshop on cooperating teachers' perceptions of culturally responsive teaching. *Journal of Music Teacher Education*, *26*(2), 50–63. https://doi.org/10.1177/1057083716629392

Mills, K. A., & Godley, A. (2017). Race and racism in digital media: What can critical race theory contribute to research on techno-cultures?. In *Handbook of writing, literacies, and education in digital cultures*. Taylor & Francis Group.

Mitton-Kükner, J., & Murray Orr, A. (2018). A multi-year study of pre-service teachers' literacy practices in the content areas: Time epistemologies and indicators of stasis and growth. *Pedagogies*, *13*(1), 19–35. https://doi.org/10.1080/1554480X.2017.1376670

Nuñez, I. (2019). "Le hacemos la lucha": Learning from madres mexicanas' multimodal approaches to raising bilingual, biliterate children. *Language Arts*, *97*(1), 7–16. https://doi.org/10.58680/la201930233

Pitkänen-Huhta, A., & Mäntylä, K. (2021). Teachers negotiating multilingualism in the EFL classroom. *European Journal of Applied Linguistics*, *9*(2), 283–306. https://doi.org/10.1515/eujal-2018-0020

Quecan, L. (2021). *Visual aids make a big impact on ESL students: A guidebook for ESL teachers* (No. 1157) [Master's thesis, University of San Francisco]. Scholarship Repository. https://repository.usfca.edu/capstone/1157/

Radke, S. C., Vogel, S. E., Ma, J. Y., Hoadley, C., & Ascenzi-Moreno, L. (2022). Emergent bilingual middle schoolers' syncretic reasoning in statistical modeling. *Teachers College Record*, *124*(5), 206–228. https://doi.org/10.1177/01614681221104141

Serafini, F. (2014). *Reading the visual: An introduction to teaching multimodal literacy*. Teachers College Press.

Song, S. (2022). Digital service-learning: Creating translanguaging spaces for emergent bilinguals' literacy learning and culturally responsive family engagement in mainstream preservice teacher education. *TESL-EJ*, *26*(3), Article 3. https://doi.org/10.55593/ej.26103a5

Sunseri, A. B., & Sunseri, M. A. (2019). The write aid for ELLs: The strategies bilingual student teachers use to help their ELL students write effectively. *CATESOL Journal*, *31*(1), 117–131.

Tan, L., Chai, C. S., Deng, F., Zheng, C. P., & Drajati, N. A. (2019). Examining pre-service teachers' knowledge of teaching multimodal literacies: A validation of a TPACK survey. *Educational Media International*, *56*(4), 285–299. https://doi.org/10.1080/09523987.2019.1681110

Vogt, K., Tsagari, D., & Spanoudis, G. (2020). What do teachers think they want? A comparative study of in-service language teachers' beliefs on LAL training needs. *Language Assessment Quarterly*, *17*(4), 386–409. https://doi.org/10.1080/15434303.2020.1781128

Watson, V. W., L. E. Reine Johnson, R. S. Peña-Pincheira, J. E. Berends, & S. Chen. 2021. Locating a pedagogy of love: (Re)framing pedagogies of loss in popular-media narratives of African immigrant communities. *International Journal of Qualitative Studies in Education* 35: 1–21. https://doi.org/10.1080/09518398.2021.1982057.

Wernicke, M., Hammer, S., Hansen, A., & Schroedler, T. (Eds.). (2021). *Preparing teachers to work with multilingual learners* (Vol. 130). Multilingual Matters. https://doi.org/10.21832/WERNIC6102

Lesson Title: A MultiSemiotic Visual Approach: Customs and Traditions (Council of Chief State School Officers, 2017; International Literacy Association, 2017; National Council of Teachers of English & International Reading Association, 2012)

NCTE/IRA Standards for the English Language Arts	International Literacy Association Standards	INTASC standards
Standard #1: Students read a wide range of print and non-print texts to build an understanding of texts, of themselves, and of the cultures of the United States and the world; to acquire new information; to respond to the needs and demands of society and the workplace; and for personal fulfillment. Among these texts are fiction and nonfiction, classic and contemporary works.	**Standard#1: Foundational Knowledge** Candidates demonstrate knowledge of the theoretical, historical, and evidence-based foundations of literacy and language and the ways in which they interrelate, as well as the role of literacy professionals in schools.	**Standard #1: Learner Development.** The teacher understands how learners grow and develop, recognizing that patterns of learning and development vary individually within and across the cognitive, linguistic, social, emotional, and physical areas and designs and implements developmentally appropriate and challenging learning experiences.
Standard # 3: Students apply a wide range of strategies to comprehend, interpret, evaluate, and appreciate texts. They draw on their prior experience, their interactions with other readers and writers, their knowledge of word meaning and of other texts, their word identification strategies, and their understanding of textual features (e.g., sound-letter correspondence, sentence structure, context, graphics).	**Standard#2: Curriculum and Instruction** Candidates use foundational knowledge to critique and implement literacy curricula to meet the needs of all learners and to design, implement, and evaluate evidence-based literacy instruction for all learners. **Standard #3: Assessment and Evaluation** Candidates understand, select, and use valid, reliable, fair, and appropriate assessment tools to screen, diagnose, and measure student literacy achievement; inform instruction and evaluate interventions; participate in professional learning experiences; explain assessment results and advocate for appropriate literacy practices to relevant stakeholders.	**Standard #2: Learning Differences.** The teacher uses understanding of individual differences and diverse cultures and communities to ensure inclusive learning environments that enable each learner to meet high standards.

Standard #3: Learning Environments. The teacher works with others to create environments that support individual and collaborative learning, and that encourage positive social interaction, active engagement in learning, and self motivation.

Standard #4: Content Knowledge. The teacher understands the central concepts, tools of inquiry, and structures of the discipline(s) he or she teaches and creates learning experiences that make the discipline accessible and meaningful for learners to assure mastery of the content.

Standard #5: Application of Content. The teacher understands how to connect concepts and use differing perspectives to engage learners in critical thinking, creativity, and collaborative problem solving related to authentic local and global issues.

Standard #4: Diversity and Equity
Candidates demonstrate knowledge of research, relevant theories, pedagogies, essential concepts of diversity and equity; demonstrate and provide opportunities for understanding all forms of diversity as central to students' identities; create classrooms and schools that are inclusive and affirming; and advocate for equity at school, district, and community levels.

Standard #5: Learners and the Literacy Environment
Candidates meet the developmental needs of all learners and collaborate with school personnel to use a variety of print and digital materials to engage and motivate all learners; integrate digital technologies in appropriate, safe, and effective ways; and foster a positive climate that supports a literacy-rich learning environment.

Standard #6: Professional Learning and Leadership. Candidates recognize the importance of, participate in, and facilitate ongoing professional learning as part of career-long leadership roles and responsibilities.

Standard #7: Practicum/Clinical Experiences
Candidates apply theory and best practice in multiple supervised practicum/clinical experiences.

Standard #8: Students use a variety of technological and information resources (e.g., libraries, databases, computer networks, video) to gather and synthesize information and to create and communicate knowledge.

Standard #9: Students develop an understanding of and respect for diversity in language use, patterns, and dialects across cultures, ethnic groups, geographic regions, and social roles.

Standard #10: Students whose first language is not English make use of their first language to develop competency in the English language arts and to develop understanding of content across the curriculum.

Standard #11: Students participate as knowledgeable, reflective, creative, and critical members of a variety of literacy communities.

Standard #12: Students use spoken, written, and visual language to accomplish their own purposes (e.g., for learning, enjoyment, persuasion, and the exchange of information).

References

Council of Chief State School Officers. (2013). *InTASC model core teaching standards and learning progressions for teachers 1.0: A resource for ongoing teacher development.* https://learning.ccsso.org/intasc-model-core-teaching-standards-and-learning-progressions-for-teachers

International Literacy Association. (2017). *Standards for the preparation of literacy professionals 2017.* https://www.literacyworldwide.org/get-resources/standards/standards-2017

National Council of Teachers of English & International Reading Association. (1996/2012). *Standards for the English language arts (Reaffirmed 2012).* National Council of Teachers of English.

Modeled Lesson 1: Customs and Traditions

Customs and Traditions: Learning Module

Lesson Overview

This lesson introduces an element of the MultiSemiotic Visual Approach: Customs and Traditions. We must teach our students about their own culture. Students are going to read about diversity in New Mexico, the history of Roswell, and ways to promote cultural awareness through informational texts.

In the last module, you learned about identity and how culture and language are an integral part of identity. You are encouraged to think about creating a text set to teach this unit. Students are going to create a visual and present the information they learned about New Mexico. The Common Core state standards are used to interrogate information, explain resources, summarize text, and conduct short research and compare and contrast information and concepts. We use culture as a lens to explore topics.

Keep in mind this is a lesson in which you could integrate the four language skills (reading, writing, speaking, and listening). There are some TESOL strategies used in the module. The readings give you a good background on the teaching skills that you need to introduce the culture celebrated in New Mexico, specifically Roswell, and it explores how culture is connected to history and heritage. You are being taught to use your students' background knowledge in planning instruction. The focus is connecting customs and traditions to student language.

The example lesson that follows is guided by the International Literacy Standards for teacher preparation in literacy, the NCTE/IRA standards for English language arts, the Common Core Standards for English language arts, and social studies standards. Following this, before, during, and after activities are presented that you can use to teach critical literacy, translanguaging, and multiliteracies. Opportunities are also presented in the lesson to guide your fourth- through sixth-grade students to use this approach.

Journaling: This is a documentation of your learning journey and will be used to evaluate the effectiveness of this process.

Start writing about your resources, including any material that can introduce customs and traditions, and your thought process as you read the modules. Consider how the information presented makes you think about your teaching of multilingual students in terms of content and teaching strategies.

Learning Outcomes for Teachers

After studying this chapter, you should be able to:

- ♦ Create instructional text focusing on the culture and traditions in New Mexico.
- ♦ Revisit the standards that focus on language in relation to culture based on the grade level being taught.
- ♦ Provide students with texts that help them learn about New Mexico, especially Roswell.
- ♦ Support students to create an understanding of how they can preserve their culture.
- ♦ Provide students with rich reading experiences.
- ♦ Engage in meaning-making using multiliteracies.
- ♦ Use the MultiSemiotic visual approach to create a learning product for your students.
- ♦ Complete a reflection on the module.
- ♦ Scaffold your fourth- through sixth-grade learners to complete the process.

TESOL Standards (for teachers, TESOL International Association, 2018)

- **2a**: Candidates demonstrate knowledge of how dynamic academic, personal, familial, cultural, and social contexts, including sociopolitical factors, impact the education of ELLs.
- **2d**: Candidates devise and implement methods to learn about personal characteristics of the individual ELL (e.g., interests, motivations, strengths, needs) and their family (e.g., language use, literacy practices, circumstances) to develop effective instructional practices.
- **3a**: Candidates plan for culturally and linguistically relevant, supportive environments that promote ELLs' learning. Candidates design scaffolded instruction of language and literacies to support standards and curricular objectives for ELLs in the content areas.
- **3b**: Candidates instruct ELLs using evidence-based, student-centered, developmentally appropriate interactive approaches.
- **3e**: Candidates use and adapt relevant materials and resources, including digital resources, to plan lessons for ELLs, support communication with other educators, school personnel, and ELLs and to foster student learning of language and literacies in the content areas.
- **5a**: Candidates demonstrate knowledge of effective collaboration strategies in order to plan ways to serve as a resource for ELL instruction, support educators and school staff, and advocate for ELLs.
- **5d**: Candidates engage in supervised teaching to apply and develop their professional practices using self-reflection and feedback from their cooperating teachers and supervising faculty.

Language Objectives (for Students)

1. To comprehend varied genres of text on the culture of New Mexico.
2. To write a summary about New Mexico culture.
3. To present information using a visual about New Mexico culture.

Guiding Questions
1. What are the cultural attributes in the state of New Mexico?
2. What are the cultural groups that make up New Mexico?
3. How can we instill in students their cultural values and how they can protect their cultural heritage?
4. How can you help students connect with their cultural heritage?
5. How is the student's culture similar and different from other cultures?
6. How can students develop appreciation of other cultures?
7. How can you be culturally responsive to your students' needs?
8. How does this culture fit in with other cultures in the United States?

Preview the Reading
We celebrate student identities through culture. Culture and traditions shape our students' values. As educators, we need to learn about our students' cultures and include them in our curriculum. There are vast topics on culture that include history, religion, food, music, and so on. For the purpose of this unit, we will focus on history, since we will focus on music in the next unit. Teaching students about the history of New Mexico, Roswell specifically, helps them make more connections with their state and city.

Pre-Class Preparation Activities for Teachers
Read

Think of a text set you can create to teach a unit on customs and traditions. What theme would you teach? What visual aids would you use? Please discuss them in your journal.

Preview the Reading
Culture is an integral part of our students' language and heritage. Therefore, it is essential to start thinking of how we can use our students' backgrounds (customs and traditions) in creating lessons. We want our students to be engaged in learning, and

using their culture will help them have a meaningful experience. The goal is also to use the student context, encourage them to be proud of their culture, and instill how to protect their heritage. We also want our students to learn about each other' cultures and have rich conversations.

Read

You will read about a brief history of Roswell that covers important events that you can choose to focus on with your students

- "New Mexico is home to 19 distinct Pueblos, populations of Apache, Navajo, and various other Native groups. Indigenous people in the state fought hard to preserve their cultures.... The strength, tenacity, spirituality, and tradition of each individual tribe is as solid as the bedrock beneath the soil of the Earth they honor and protect." After you read the article, you can explore the links provided on the website.
  Roswell History (Roswell New Mexico, n.d.) https://roswell-nm.gov/654/Our-History
- You will read a short article that focuses on teachers creating and using culturally sustaining informational texts using various genres to promote literacy learning using the students' assets. There is a survey of children's literacy practices that you could use. (Preservation, n.d.).
  Historic Preservation division https://www.newmexicoculture.org/preservation/

Creating and Using Culturally Sustaining Informational Texts: (Watangabe Kganetso, 2016)

- These are resources that you could use to teach your 4th–6th grade students about history and culture in New Mexico
  - *How the Stars Fell Into the Sky: A Navajo Legend* by Jerrie Oughton
  - *The Goat in the Rug* by Charles L. Blood

- *Navajo Life: A Bilingual Children's Picture Book* by Hildegard Thompson
- *The Navajo (A True Book: American Indians)* by Kevin Cunningham
- *That Roswell: An Alien Looks Back* by John Camp
- *Malgro Beanfield War*—book and a movie by John Nichols

Listen

- The Navajo Nation (The Planet Project, 2018) https://youtu.be/DCZkJ9XcP8Y?si=BrXTwS8n_0smP4EI
- Virtual Field Trip: Acoma Pueblo (Steve, 2020) https://youtu.be/M6tScqcTcEg?si=zA7P-osbAi6XDGl
- Virtual Tours in New Mexico (New Mexico True, n.d.) https://www.newmexico.org/virtualtours/

These are activities that you can use during instruction for teaching your students:

- Reading about New Mexico.
- Creating a text set on New Mexico culture.
- Using Glogster or Piktochart to create a visual.
- Students present about New Mexico cultural heritage electronically or using a paper poster.
- Students film something that shows culture, traditions, and customs.

The social studies standards for this theme focus on students explaining connections among historical contents and demonstrating knowledge of family history, culture, and past contributions of people in their main identity groups.

- To connect with social studies, have students read about New Mexico and Roswell, and create a poster that portrays their customs and traditions or customs and traditions in New Mexico. Keep in mind students' backgrounds, especially that students may come from a wide variety of ethnicities (African American, Indigenous,

Mexican, Native American). If students are new to the area, this unit is a great opportunity for them to present about their traditions.
- Field trip in Roswell: Art and Culture in New Mexico (See Roswell, n.d.) https://seeroswell.com/project/arts-and-culture/

Differentiation includes paraphrasing, visuals and supplementary materials, audio and visual, class discussion, drawing/visuals, online resources, and text levels.

Thought Questions
1. How have you used any module material in your planning and instruction?
2. How were you able to connect to your students?
3. What supported your learning?
4. What could be changed to support your learning?
5. Would you consider teaching about culture? In what ways will you do that? Please explain and be specific.
6. What other standards would you consider using to teach a lesson on culture?

References

New Mexico True (n.d.). *Virtual Tours: Interactive 360 Views of New Mexico Attractions*. New Mexico Tourism Department. https://www.newmexico.org/virtualtours/

Preservation (n.d.). *Historic Preservation*. New Mexico Department of Cultural Affairs. https://www.newmexicoculture.org/preservation/

Roswell New Mexico. (n.d.). *Our History*. Roswell New Mexico. https://roswell-nm.gov/654/Our-History

See Roswell. (n.d.). *Arts and Culture|Roswell, NM*. See Roswell.com. from https://seeroswell.com/project/arts-and-culture/

Steve, S. [KOB4Kids]. (2020, October 9). *Virtual Field Trip: Acoma Pueblo* [Video]. YouTube. https://www.youtube.com/watch?v=M6tScqcTcEg

[The Planet Project]. (2018, December 9). *The Navajo Nation|The Story of America's Largest Tribe* [Video]. YouTube. https://www.youtube.com/watch?v=DCZkJ9XcP8Y

TESOL International Association. (2018). *Standards for initial TESOL Pre-K–12 teacher preparation programs*. Alexandria. https://www.tesol.org/docs/default-source/advocacy/2018_tesol-teacher-prep-standards_final.pdf

Watanabe Kganetso, L. M. (2016, November 8). *Creating and Using Culturally Sustaining Informational Texts*. International Literacy Association. https://ila.onlinelibrary.wiley.com/doi/abs/10.1002/trtr.1546?casa_token=eWl_RQJPieIAAAAA%3AWslCPhWHkMT1rUZ_7YAuYiNKOrYiS8ssMF2tOnMPx_zEM3T9eRf1pFhn8E1VlucKUETEh_ptV5DM61sE

Lesson Title: A MultiSemiotic Visual Approach: Customs and Traditions (Karkar-Esperat, 2019, National Governors Association Center for Best Practices, & Council of Chief State School Officers, 2010; New Mexico Public Education Department, 2021)

Common Core Standards for 4th–6th Grades	*Social Studies Standards for 4th–5th Grade*	*Pedagogical Holistic Model of New Literacies*
Fourth Grade	**Fourth Grade**	"The visual mode, according to the New London Group (1996), focuses on concepts such as "colors," "vectors," "perspective," and "background," "foregrounding," and "backgrounding." The pedagogical holistic model of new literacies used various words to describe this visual mode, such as graphs, interactive texts, visual resources (e.g., texts, message board, blogs), visual aids (e.g., graphs, maps, charts, tables), and technologies (Karkar-Esperat, 2019).
CCSS.ELA-LITERACY.RI.4.1 Refer to details and examples in a text when explaining what the text says explicitly and when drawing inferences from the text.	4.3. Cite evidence that supports a response to supporting or compelling questions.	
CCSS.ELA-LITERACY.RI.4.3 Explain events, procedures, or concepts in historical, scientific, or technical text, including what happened and why, based on specific information in the text.	4.26. Explain connections among historical contexts and people's perspectives at the time.	
CCSS.ELA-LITERACY.RI.4.9 Integrate information from two texts on the same topic in order to write or speak about the subject knowledgeably.	4.11. Describe the different groups of people that have settled in New Mexico throughout history and describe their contributions to New Mexico cultures.	
CCSS.ELA-LITERACY.W.4.7 Conduct short research projects that build knowledge through investigation of different aspects of a topic.		

Self-Discovery Through the Visual Mode ◆ 95

CCSS.ELA-LITERACY.SL.4.2 Paraphrase portions of a text read aloud or information presented in diverse media and formats, including visually, quantitatively, and orally. **Fifth Grade** CCSS.ELA-LITERACY.RI.5.1 Quote accurately from a text when explaining what the text says explicitly and when drawing inferences from the text. CCSS.ELA-LITERACY.RI.5.5 Compare and contrast the overall structure (e.g., chronology, comparison, cause/effect, problem/solution) of events, ideas, concepts, or information in two or more texts. CCSS.ELA-LITERACY.RI.5.9 Integrate information from several texts on the same topic in order to write or speak about the subject knowledgeably. CCSS.ELA-LITERACY.W.5.7 Conduct short research projects that use several sources to build knowledge through investigation of different aspects of a topic. CCSS.ELA-LITERACY.SL.5.2 Summarize a written text read aloud or information presented in diverse media and formats, including visually, quantitatively, and orally.	**Fifth Grade** 5.5. Construct responses to compelling questions supported by reasoning and evidence. 5.30. Demonstrate knowledge of family history, culture, and past contributions of people in their main identity groups.	The MultiSemiotic visual mode could refer to signs (i.e., Black Lives Matter signs, signs to promote social equity at work, visuals of people from different backgrounds coming together), timelines (referring to history), and customs and traditions with cultural connections (dress, color, symbols, gender role; see Mills and Godley, 2017; see also Watson et al., 2021)" (Karkar-Esperat, 2025, p. 12).

(Continued)

Common Core Standards for 4th–6th Grades	Social Studies Standards for 4th–5th Grade	Pedagogical Holistic Model of New Literacies
Sixth Grade		
CCSS.ELA-LITERACY.RI.6.1 Cite textual evidence to support analysis of what the text says explicitly as well as inferences drawn from the text.		
CCSS.ELA-LITERACY.RI.6.4 Integrate information presented in different media or formats (e.g., visually, quantitatively) as well as in words to develop a coherent understanding of a topic or issue.		
CCSS.ELA-LITERACY.W. 6.7 Conduct short research projects to answer a question, drawing on several sources and refocusing the inquiry when appropriate.		
CCSS.ELA-LITERACY.SL. 6.4 Present claims and findings; sequencing ideas logically and using pertinent descriptions, facts, and details to accentuate main ideas or themes; use appropriate eye contact, adequate volume, and clear pronunciation.		

References

Council of Chief State School Officers. (2013). *InTASC model core teaching standards and learning progressions for teachers 1.0: A resource for ongoing teacher development.* https://learning.ccsso.org/intasc-model-core-teaching-standards-and-learning-progressions-for-teachers

International Literacy Association. (2017). *Standards for the preparation of literacy professionals 2017.* https://www.literacyworldwide.org/get-resources/standards/standards-2017

Karkar-Esperat, T. (2019). Assessing preservice teachers' knowledge of new literacies [Doctoral dissertation, Texas Tech University]. Texas Tech University Archive.

Karkar-Esperat, T. M. (2025). Multiliteracies for Multilingual Learners: The MultiSemiotic Architecture Framework. *International Journal of Bilingual Education and Bilingualism. 28*(2), 117–134 doi.org/10.1080/13670050.2024.2409120

Mills, K. A., & Godley, A. (2017). Race and racism in digital media: What can critical race theory contribute to research on techno-cultures?. In *Handbook of writing, literacies, and education in digital cultures.* Taylor & Francis Group.

National Council of Teachers of English & International Reading Association. (1996/2012). *Standards for the English language arts* (Reaffirmed 2012). National Council of Teachers of English.

National Governors Association Center for Best Practices, & Council of Chief State School Officers. (2010). *Common Core State Standards for English language arts & literacy in history/social studies, science, and technical subjects.* Washington, DC. https://www.corestandards.org/ELA-Literacy/

New London Group (1996). "A Pedagogy of Multiliteracies: Designing Social Futures." *Harvard Educational Review 66*(1), 60–92. https://doi.org/10.17763/haer.66.1.17370n67v22j160u

New Mexico Public Education Department. (2021). *New Mexico social studies standards.* https://webnew.ped.state.nm.us/bureaus/literacy-humanities/social-studies/

Watson, V. W., L. E. Reine Johnson, R. S. Peña-Pincheira, J. E. Berends, & S. Chen. 2021. "Locating a Pedagogy of Love: (Re)framing Pedagogies of Loss in Popular-Media Narratives of African Immigrant Communities." *International Journal of Qualitative Studies in Education* 35: 1–21. https://doi.org/10.1080/09518398.2021.1982057.

Instructional Materials Used with Students

Lesson Title: A MultiSemiotic Visual Approach: Customs and Traditions

Language Objectives (for students)
1. To comprehend varied genre text on the culture of New Mexico.
2. To write a summary about New Mexico culture.
3. To present information using a visual about New Mexico culture.

These are Activities that You can use During Instruction for Teaching Your Students
- Reading about New Mexico.
- Creating a text set on New Mexico culture.
- Using Glogster or Piktochart to create a visual.
- Presenting about New Mexico cultural heritage electronically or using a paper poster.
- Filming something that shows culture, traditions, and customs.

The social studies standards for this theme focus on students explaining connections among historical contents and demonstrating knowledge of family history, culture, and past contributions of people in their main identity groups.

- To connect with social studies, have students read about New Mexico and Roswell and create a poster that portrays their customs and traditions or customs and traditions in New Mexico. Keep in mind students' backgrounds, especially that students come from diverse ethnicities (African American, Indigenous, Mexican, Native American). If students are new to the area it is a great opportunity for them to present about their traditions.
  - Field trip in Roswell: Art and Culture in New Mexico (See Roswell, n.d.) https://seeroswell.com/project/arts-and-culture/

Differentiation includes paraphrasing, visuals and supplementary materials, audio and visual, class discussion, drawing/visuals, online resources, text levels.

Reference

See Roswell. (n.d.). *Arts and Culture|Roswell, NM.* . from https://seeroswell.com/project/arts-and-culture/

Modeled Lesson 2: Visual Knowledge
Lesson Title: A MultiSemiotic Synesthesia Approach: Visual Knowledge

Lesson Overview
This lesson introduces an element of the MultiSemiotic visual approach.

Visual knowledge in this module refers to using an art object, which could include a mural, paintings, landscape, portraits, movements, stories, calligraphy, and music, in addition to text, as a tool to develop an understanding about a topic considering culture and language. Adopting art in the classroom supports all learners and also encourages students to form an appreciation for art. Art is a form of storytelling that has a story and background. Teaching students about art helps them learn to express ideas and emotions and develop essential skills that foster critical thinking and expression. For students to develop a deeper understanding of art, they need to make a connection to the space and culture using language. Incorporating art in teaching helps the students to pay attention to details such color, texture, values, forms, space, and shapes. This attention to detail will encourage the students to analyze the arts.

In this module, teachers are encouraged to start teaching students about local artworks, murals, paintings, and posters. Students learn about artwork across the state including artists, symbols, and artistic movements. From learning about works of art at local and state level, the students could branch out to the broader use of art. Art can be seen as a form of storytelling that draws on the background of the art and artist. Students engage in self-discovery throughout different forms of art. Art reflects the artistic movement and period in which it was created. Art could also be used to express movements. Art is used to connect to the students' cultures and identities and embrace their sense of belonging to their community. The goal of this module is to connect language to visuals and cultures. Students learn about visuals using a multicultural and multiliteracies lens. Teachers must make curricular decisions that shape the students' identities positively.

Each student learns differently; they have their unique abilities and strengths. They could prefer to learn through images, graphs, posters, or PowerPoint presentations. As teachers, we need to address our students' needs. MultiSemiotic visuals could be used as an approach to support student learning and to differentiate instruction. Additionally, you could use visual literacy to focus on teaching the four language skills. In the module, we focus on all language skills, specifically teaching writing by concentrating on voice (one of the traits of writing).

Students will use their own voices when exposed to different works of arts. Students will write down a description of the pictures on the back of the cards or present them orally. Students will first connect with local art, then art throughout the states, and then with signs used for movements around the world. The teacher will provide some resources and model and guide students on writing, drawing (if needed), and then writing with guidance and independently following the gradual release of responsibility.

Teachers are encouraged to follow the step-by-step process provided in the instructional materials. They should encourage students to gather materials that reflect their community's visual knowledge before learning about art from other states or the world.

The Common Core state standards are used to build visual knowledge using multimedia and other resources. In this professional learning experience, we use culture as a lens to explore topics.

Keep in mind that this is a lesson in which you could integrate reading, listening, writing, and speaking language skills. There are some TESOL strategies used in the module. The readings give you the explanation on how you can teach visual knowledge.

The example lesson that follows is guided by the International Literacy Standards for teacher preparation in literacy, the NCTE/ILA standards for English language arts, the Common Core Standards for English language arts, and social studies standards. Following this, pre-, during-, and post-activities are presented that you can use to teach critical literacy, translanguaging, and multiliteracies. Opportunities are also presented in the lesson to guide your fourth–sixth grade students to use this approach.

Journaling: This is a diary that will document your learning journey, and it will be used to evaluate the effectiveness of this process.

Think of the tools (i.e., visuals and audiovisuals) to teach a lesson on visual knowledge. What topics would you cover in your teaching? What activities could you use? How can you connect visual knowledge to teaching language (listening, speaking, reading, and writing)?

Please discuss them in your journal.

A) Use the guiding questions in writing your response.
B) Start writing about the resources provided in the module.
C) Record your thought processes as you read the modules.
D) Consider how the presented information makes you think about your teaching of multilingual students, in terms of content, and teaching strategies.

Learning Outcomes for Teachers

After studying this module, you should be able to:

- Build a lesson or a unit on visual knowledge.
- Guide students in making connections with art and culture.
- Develop the students' writing skills using voice, a writing trait.

- Guide students in using their critical thinking skills to analyze a piece of art.
- Connect art with the students' identities considering the work of art's message, time, and background.
- Provide students with opportunities to learn about local artists!
- Support students to create a photo story to assist them in connecting art to language, culture, and identity.
- Provide students with rich reading language experiences.
- Guide students to use resources to create a photo story/photovoice to represent their language and culture.
- Engage in meaning-making using multiliteracies.
- Use the MultiSemiotic visual approach to create a learning product for your students.
- Complete a reflection on the module.

TESOL Standards (for Teachers, TESOL International Association, 2018)

- **2a**: Candidates demonstrate knowledge of how dynamic academic, personal, familial, cultural, and social contexts, including sociopolitical factors, impact the education of ELLs.
- **2d**: Candidates devise and implement methods to learn about personal characteristics of the individual ELL (e.g., interests, motivations, strengths, needs) and their family (e.g., language use, literacy practices, circumstances) to develop effective instructional practices.
- **3a**: Candidates plan for culturally and linguistically relevant, supportive environments that promote ELLs' learning. Candidates design scaffolded instruction of language and literacies to support standards and curricular objectives for ELLs in the content areas.
- **3b**: Candidates instruct ELLs using evidence-based, student-centered, developmentally appropriate interactive approaches.
- **3e**: Candidates use and adapt relevant materials and resources, including digital resources, to plan lessons for ELLs, support communication with other educators,

school personnel, and ELLs and to foster student learning of language and literacies in the content areas.
- **5a**: Candidates demonstrate knowledge of effective collaboration strategies in order to plan ways to serve as a resource for ELL instruction, support educators and school staff, and advocate for ELLs.
- **5d**: Candidates engage in supervised teaching to apply and develop their professional practices using self-reflection and feedback from their cooperating teachers and supervising faculty.

Language Objectives (for students)
1. To read about local artists and the local art community.
2. To reflect on art (murals, paintings, and posters), analyze meaning, and discuss interpretations.
3. To recognize local, national, or international art by naming, drawing, and writing about them.
4. To write how art represents the characterization of human beings and supports social advocacy and/or social justice.
5. To gather information using various sources, such as readings and visiting local museums.
6. To discuss a piece of art considering time, culture, place, and colors.
7. To produce a photo story using pictures and technology.
8. To present the project to student peers in various spaces.

Guiding Questions
1. How can we teach students about how culture is represented in art? What representations (public art, mural, paintings, landscape, portraits, movements, stories, calligraphy, and music) materials would you use?
2. How can we preserve historical arts and cultural heritage, centering visual knowledge?
3. How can we teach students language skills (speaking, reading, listening, and writing) through connecting with visuals or using visuals to teach language?

4. What resources (anything that includes visuals) are provided in the classroom that support the students learning about art?
5. How do these connections support multilingual and bilingual student learning?
6. How can students in New Mexico connect to people around the country or outside the United States through art?
7. How is art connected to culture and traditions?
8. What activities could be used to connect with art with social justice and or identity?
9. How can you be culturally responsive to your students' needs, focusing on visual knowledge in the classroom?

Preview the Reading

The readings cover different aspects of visual knowledge that will support you in understanding how visual knowledge could be used in the classroom, the state requirement in teaching about art. Also, you will learn how to connect culture to art and language. There are different readings that will support your understanding and building visual knowledge in the classroom.

Pre-Class Preparation Activities for Teachers
Read

Background
- ♦ The New Mexico Advisory Council on Arts Education (NMACAE) advocates for the needs of New Mexico students and educators in music, dance, theatre, visual arts https://artsednm.org/resources/

Art and Curriculum
- ♦ A lesson plan on connecting art to curriculum https://humanities.nmartmuseum.org/curriculum/connecting-cultures-in-architecture-lesson-plan/
- ♦ How to use art to teaching writing https://twowritingteachers.org/2021/12/13/getting-craft-y-using-art-to-teach-writing/

Art and Culture
- ♦ Identity and Art (Močnik, 2011) https://www.moma.org/interactives/exhibitions/2011/sanjaivekovic/essays/RM%20Identity%20and%20the%20Arts.pdf
- ♦ Smokey Bear, Iconic Symbol of Wildfire Prevention, Still Going Strong at 70 (Sosbe, 2014) https://www.usda.gov/about-usda/news/blog/smokey-bear-iconic-symbol-wildfire-prevention-still-going-strong-70
- ♦ Exploring Identity Through African Art: Perspectives and Techniques (Ross, 2023) https://momaa.org/exploring-identity-through-african-art-perspectives-and-techniques/
- ♦ Fostering a Culture of Connection through the Arts (The Kennedy Center, n.d.) https://www.kennedy-center.org/education/resources-for-educators/classroom-resources/articles-and-how-tos/articles/educators/professional-development/fostering-a-culture-of-connection-through-the-arts2/

Art and storytelling
- ♦ LaToya M. Hobbs: It's Time (Harvard, n.d.) https://harvardartmuseums.org/exhibitions/6322/latoya-m-hobbs-its-time
- ♦ Teach Your Students to Use Art as a Tool for Social Advocacy (Hoeve, 2023) https://theartofeducation.edu/2016/06/june-art-tool-social-advocacy/

Art and storytelling
- ♦ Exploring how graffiti and street art calls attention to movement (Ross, 2023) https://jeffreyianross.medium.com/exploring-how-graffiti-and-street-art-calls-attention-to-social-justice-issues-6c967fe9ddd0

Boston Mural Map (Boston mural map, 2021) https://www.boston.gov/departments/arts-and-culture/boston-mural-map

Listen
- Art and Social Justice (The institute for arts integration and STEAM, 2021) https://www.youtube.com/watch?v=MP0UHiP-Y3k
- Children's picture books: (Diverse BookFinder, n.d.) https://diversebookfinder.org/setting/new-mexico/

Photovoice
- Photovoice tutorial (YES Forum, 2023): https://www.youtube.com/watch?v=aZM8fb32rN8
- Students can create a photovoice, or a videonote by taking a video on a cellphone.
- Photovoice application (Google, n.d.): https://play.google.com/store/apps/details?id=com.edukunapps.picvoice&hl=en_US&gl=US
- How to Create a Children's Book Storyboard (Becky's Graphic Design, 2021) https://www.youtube.com/watch?v=uKuDYEceGa4

Thought Questions

1. Why do you think visual knowledge should be included in the curriculum?
2. How does learning about visual knowledge foster cultural identity?
3. In what ways do you think researching visual knowledge would support student learning?
4. After reading about visual knowledge and reviewing the module materials, what resonated most with you? In what way will you incorporate it in your class?
5. The module covered the Common Core Standards focusing on all the language skills. How are you planning to incorporate them in your classroom?
6. How are you planning to teach about visual knowledge in social studies using the standards provided?
7. What kinds of creativity (think about the modes of meanings that could be used) do you hope to discover through your students' responses and reactions?

8. Do you see any challenges in implementing this approach into your classrooms? Explain.
9. What did not work? Why?
10. Any additional thoughts? Please share!

References

Visual Knowledge-Learning Materials

[Becky's Graphic Design®, LLC]. (2021, November 24). *How to Create a Children's Book Storyboard • CANVA • Free!!* [Video]. YouTube. https://www.youtube.com/watch?v=uKuDYEceGa4

Boston mural map. Boston.gov. (2021, February 24). https://www.boston.gov/departments/arts-and-culture/boston-mural-map

Diverse BookFinder (n.d.). *Children's picture books: Stories set in New Mexico*. Diverse BookFinder. https://diversebookfinder.org/setting/new-mexico/

Fostering a culture of connection through the arts. (n.d.). The Kennedy Center. https://www.kennedy-center.org/education/resources-for-educators/classroom-resources/articles-and-how-tos/articles/educators/professional-development/fostering-a-culture-of-connection-through-the-arts2/

Google. (n.d.). *PicVoice: Add voice to photos - apps on Google Play*. Google. https://play.google.com/store/apps/details?id=com.edukunapps.picvoice&hl=en_US&gl=US&pli=1

Harvard. (n.d.). *Exhibitions, Latoya M. Hobbs: It's time*. Harvard Art Museums. https://harvardartmuseums.org/exhibitions/6322/latoya-m-hobbs-its-time

Hoeve, L. T. (2023, March 27). *Teach your students to use art as a tool for social advocacy*. The Art of Education University. https://theartofeducation.edu/2016/06/june-art-tool-social-advocacy/

Ross, J.D. (2023, May 20). *Exploring how graffiti and street art calls attention to social justice issues*. Medium. https://jeffreyianross.medium.com/exploring-how-graffiti-and-street-art-calls-attention-to-social-justice-issues-6c967fe9ddd0

Levin, L. (2021, December 13). *Getting craft-y: Using art to teach writing*. Two Writing Teachers. https://twowritingteachers.org/2021/12/13/getting-craft-y-using-art-to-teach-writing/

Močnik, R. (2011). Identity and the arts. *Contemporary Art and Nationalism*, 40–55.

MoMAA, E. (2023, April 30). *Exploring identity through African art: Perspectives and techniques*. https://momaa.org/exploring-identity-through-african-art-perspectives-and-techniques/

New Mexico Museum of Art (n.d.). *Connecting cultures in architecture*. New Mexico Museum of Art. https://humanities.nmartmuseum.org/curriculum/connecting-cultures-in-architecture-lesson-plan/

New Mexico Advisory Council on Arts Education. (2021, December 10). *New Mexico Advisory Council on Arts Education*. New Mexico Advisory Council on Arts Education | Advocating for students in music, dance, theater, media and visual art. https://artsednm.org/resources/

Sosbe, K. (2014, August 7). *Smokey Bear, iconic symbol of wildfire prevention, still going strong at 70*. USDA. https://www.usda.gov/about-usda/news/blog/smokey-bear-iconic-symbol-wildfire-prevention-still-going-strong-70

The Institute for Arts Integration and STEAM. (2021, June 15). *Art and Social Justice [Video]*. YouTube. https://www.youtube.com/watch?v=MP0UHiP-Y3k

YES Forum. (2023, January 24). *VOICE - Photovoice tutorial* [Video]. YouTube. https://www.youtube.com/watch?v=aZM8fb32rN8

MultiSemiotic Visual Approach: Visual Knowledge (Karkar-Esperat, 2019, National Governors Association Center for Best Practices, & Council of Chief State School Officers, 2010; New Mexico Public Education Department, 2021)

Common Core Standards for 4th–6th Grades	Social Studies Standards for 4th–5th Grade	Pedagogical Holistic Model of New Literacies
Fourth Grade	**Fourth Grade**	"The visual mode, according to the New London Group (1996), focuses on concepts such as "colors," "vectors," "perspective," and "background," "foregrounding" and "backgrounding." The pedagogical holistic model of new literacies used various words to describe this visual mode, such as graphs, interactive texts, visual resources (e.g., texts, message board, blogs), visual aids (e.g., graphs, maps, charts, tables), and technologies (Karkar-Esperat, 2019).
CCSS.ELA-LITERACY.RI.4.7 Interpret information presented visually, orally, or quantitatively (e.g., in charts, graphs, diagrams, timelines, animations, or interactive elements on Web pages) and explain how the information contributes to an understanding of the text in which it appears.	4.4. Construct responses to compelling questions using reasoning, examples, and relevant details.	
CCSS.ELA-LITERACY.RI.4.7 Integrate information from two texts on the same topic in order to write or speak about the subject knowledgeably.	4.9. Demonstrate understanding that state symbols, holidays, traditions, and songs represent various cultural heritages, natural treasures, and the democratic values of New Mexico.	
CCSS.ELA-LITERACY.SL.4.5 Add audio recordings and visual displays to presentations when appropriate to enhance the development of main ideas or themes.	4.25. Participate in inquiry of other people's lives and experiences while demonstrating respect and empathy for others.	

(Continued)

Common Core Standards for 4th–6th Grades	Social Studies Standards for 4th–5th Grade	Pedagogical Holistic Model of New Literacies
CCSS.ELA-LITERACY.SL.4.4 Report on a topic or text, tell a story, or recount an experience in an organized manner, using appropriate facts and relevant, descriptive details to support main ideas or themes; speak clearly at an understandable pace. CCSS.ELA-LITERACY.W.4.1A Introduce a topic or text clearly, state an opinion, and create an organizational structure in which related ideas are grouped to support the writer's purpose. CCSS.ELA-LITERACY.W.4.2A Introduce a topic clearly and group related information in paragraphs and sections; include formatting (e.g., headings), illustrations, and multimedia when useful to aid comprehension. CCSS.ELA-LITERACY.W.3D Use concrete words and phrases and sensory details to convey experiences and events precisely. CCSS.ELA-LITERACY.W.4.7 Conduct short research projects that build knowledge through investigation of different aspects of a topic.	**Fifth Grade** 5.2. Use supporting questions to help answer the compelling question in an inquiry. 5.5. Construct responses to compelling questions supported by reasoning and evidence.5.30. Demonstrate knowledge of family history, culture, and past contributions of people in their main identity groups.	The *multisemiotic visual* mode refers to signs (i.e., Black Lives Matter signs, signs to promote social equity at work, visuals of people from different backgrounds coming together), timelines (referring to history), philosophy of colors and materials used in context, and customs and traditions with cultural connections (dress, color, symbols, gender role; see Mills and Godley, 2017; see also Watson et al., 2021)" (Karkar-Esperat, 2025, p. 12).

Fifth Grade

CCSS.ELA-LITERACY.RI.5.7
Draw on information from multiple print or digital sources, demonstrating the ability to locate an answer to a question quickly or to solve a problem efficiently.

CCSS.ELA-LITERACY.RI.5.9
Integrate information from several texts on the same topic in order to write or speak about the subject knowledgeably.

CCSS.ELA-LITERACY.SL.5.1A
Come to discussions prepared, having read or studied required material; explicitly draw on that preparation and other information known about the topic to explore ideas under discussion.

CCSS.ELA-LITERACY.SL.5.4
Report on a topic or text or present an opinion, sequencing ideas logically and using appropriate facts and relevant, descriptive details to support main ideas or themes; speak clearly at an understandable pace.

CCSS.ELA-LITERACY.SL.5.5
Include multimedia components (e.g., graphics, sound) and visual displays in presentations when appropriate to enhance the development of main ideas or themes.

CCSS.ELA-LITERACY.W.5.1A
Introduce a topic or text clearly, state an opinion, and create an organizational structure in which ideas are logically grouped to support the writer's purpose.

(*Continued*)

Common Core Standards for 4th–6th Grades	Social Studies Standards for 4th–5th Grade	Pedagogical Holistic Model of New Literacies
CCSS.ELA-LITERACY.W.5.3D Use concrete words and phrases and sensory details to convey experiences and events precisely.		
CCSS.ELA-LITERACY.W.5.7 Conduct short research projects that use several sources to build knowledge through investigation of different aspects of a topic.		
Sixth Grade		
CCSS.ELA-LITERACY.RI.6.3 Determine a central idea of a text and how it is conveyed through particular details; provide a summary of the text distinct from personal opinions or judgments.		
CCSS.ELA-LITERACY.RI.6.7 Integrate information presented in different media or formats (e.g., visually, quantitatively) as well as in words to develop a coherent understanding of a topic or issue.		
CCSS.ELA-LITERACY.SL.6.1A Include multimedia components (e.g., graphics, images, music, sound) and visual displays in presentations to clarify information.		
CCSS.ELA-LITERACY.SL.6.2 Interpret information presented in diverse media and formats (e.g., visually, quantitatively, orally) and explain how it contributes to a topic, text, or issue under study.		

CCSS.ELA-LITERACY.W.6.8
Gather relevant information from multiple print and digital sources; assess the credibility of each source; and quote or paraphrase the data and conclusions of others while avoiding plagiarism and providing basic bibliographic information for sources.

CCSS.ELA-LITERACY.W.6.7
Conduct short research projects to answer a question, drawing on several sources and refocusing the inquiry when appropriate.

CCSS.ELA-LITERACY.W.6.6
Use technology, including the Internet, to produce and publish writing as well as to interact and collaborate with others; demonstrate sufficient command of keyboarding skills to type a minimum of three pages in a single sitting.

References

Council of Chief State School Officers. (2013). *InTASC model core teaching standards and learning progressions for teachers 1.0: A resource for ongoing teacher development.* https://learning.ccsso.org/intasc-model-core-teaching-standards-and-learning-progressions-for-teachers

International Literacy Association. (2017). *Standards for the preparation of literacy Professionals 2017.* https://www.literacyworldwide.org/get-resources/standards/standards-2017

Karkar-Esperat, T. (2019). Assessing preservice teachers' knowledge of new literacies [Doctoral dissertation, Texas Tech University]. Texas Tech University Archive.

Karkar-Esperat, T. M. (2025). Multiliteracies for Multilingual Learners: The MultiSemiotic Architecture Framework. *International Journal of Bilingual Education and Bilingualism. 28*(2), 117–134 doi.org/10.1080/13670050.2024.2409120

National Council of Teachers of English & International Reading Association. (1996/2012). *Standards for the English language arts (Reaffirmed 2012).* National Council of Teachers of English.

New London Group (1996). "A Pedagogy of Multiliteracies: Designing Social Futures." *Harvard Educational Review 66*(1), 60–92. https://doi.org/10.17763/haer.66.1.17370n67v22j160u

Mills, K. A., & Godley, A. (2017). Race and racism in digital media: What can critical race theory contribute to research on techno-cultures?. In *Handbook of writing, literacies, and education in digital cultures.* Taylor & Francis Group.

Watson, V. W., L. E. Reine Johnson, R. S. Peña-Pincheira, J. E. Berends, & S. Chen. 2021. "Locating a Pedagogy of Love: (Re)framing Pedagogies of Loss in Popular-Media Narratives of African Immigrant Communities." *International Journal of Qualitative Studies in Education 35*, 1–21. https://doi.org/10.1080/09518398.2021.1982057

Instructional Material for the Classroom—A MultiSemiotic Visual Approach: Visual Knowledge

Language Objectives (for students)
- To read about local artists and the local art community.
- To reflect on art (murals, paintings, and posters), analyze meaning, and discuss interpretations.
- To recognize local, national, or international art by naming, drawing, and writing about it.
- To write how art represents the characterization of human beings and supports social advocacy and/or social justice.
- To gather information using various sources, such as readings and visiting local museums.
- To discuss a piece of art considering time, culture, place, and colors.
- To produce a photostory using pictures and technology.
- To present the project to student peers in various spaces.

During Instruction, These are Activities that You can use for Teaching Your Students
- **Home**: Students think of art around them and describe it. It could be a church, a museum, building, or a park (nature). Students can look for art in the form of a mural, painting, or symbols. Then they describe what they see as much as they can. Why does it appeal to them? What is the voice of the artist? What does this art resemble? What emotions does it evoke? (This question will promote self-discovery.) Then, the students research this art to gather more information about it in terms of time, artist, culture, and background (thinking about the movement associated with it such as social justice). They could ask these questions: How does the time and culture impact the choice of painting? Where would you see this in life? How was the painting received and/or critiqued? How would you describe this painting?
- **State**: Students visit a virtual state museum and describe it with details, following the same steps mentioned previously.

- **World**: Students search online for famous world art, or the teacher could show different areas of art.
- Students write about the art or draw based on the art, with the teacher's guidance if needed.
- Students will be asked to create a photovoice on one of the art genres they found. First, they will describe in detail what they see. Then, they will integrate what they found about the art (background, culture, movement, genre). Lastly, they will express why they chose this art and how they connect with this art.

Aligning with the social studies standards (for students) Students will inquire about the art object they chose by asking question and finding resources that will give them information about the background of that object.

Differentiation includes leveled text, visuals and supplementary materials, audio and visual, class discussion, drawing/visuals, online resources, and videos.

4

Self-Discovery Through the Audio Mode

Examining Language Using Music Genres - Mariachi, Hip-Hop, Folk Music

---

VIGNETTE

Teachers need to recognize students' interests and needs. As a teacher, I realized that students enjoy connecting words with music, as language is both rhythm and harmony. We want students to utilize music for that development. In my work with in-service teachers, I've noticed that the common challenge is engaging students. After listening to the teachers and their needs to engage students in a way that's guided by culture, I developed materials covering folk, hip-hop, and mariachi music genres.

Once teachers started implementing these materials, they unanimously shared that music had captured their students' attention, and the shy students had joined in and were now talking. Teachers discussed music as a great way to connect with students, and they were surprised to learn about the different cultures involved in the music in their area. One teacher expressed: "I would have never really thought about how important folk music is to the students' understanding of their own cultures." Music was important in connecting with students; a teacher talked about "getting students' emotions, their grief, or their happiness, or just how their thoughts and feelings out, and people use poetry and music, or sometimes they combine it." Some in-service teachers used hip-hop in their classroom, and one teacher communicated, "In my opinion, hip-hop helps students relate to life, hardship, and triumph, depending on the singer and the message." Another teacher voiced, "My Spanish students advised me that hip-hop sung in Spanish is the same and really speaks to the same events in people's lives and how it has affected them and those around them."

One of the teachers who implemented mariachi shared, "I feel that mariachi music helps communities feel validated by including their traditions and music." Music improved engagement in the classroom. As one teacher attested, "It was just a really engaging thing. And then the conversations they were holding with their partners were really good because then they started talking about songs that they know had the rhyming in them because we went into the rhyming and the hip-hop." Music brings balance and harmony to the classroom. It guides students to pay attention to words and expressions. It inspires self-awareness and discovery and guides students in academics. Teachers get to know their students through their music helping them become more compassionate educators.

Dear teachers, parents, guardians, and students,

You are going to learn how you can use the music genres such as folk music, hip-hop, and mariachi in teaching and learning. The examples are provided in the context of New Mexico. You can follow the same structure and apply it in your own context.

This chapter will guide you to learn about what is an audio semiotic. Why do we need an audio semiotic in the classroom? How can you be culturally responsive to your students' needs using music as one of the genres in the classroom? How can you help students connect with their cultures through music? How can you adapt this approach in your classroom?

What Is It About?

The audio mode, according to the New London Group (1996), focuses on music as well as "the employment of any sound effect to support student learning." The pedagogical holistic model of new literacies used words like "theater," "different types of audio," "singing," "dialogue," and "monologue" to reflect different classroom experiences (Karkar-Esperat, 2019). The MultiSemiotic audio mode could refer to using different genres of music (hip-hop that connects with history and culture, country music, mariachi), voice, and tone (see also Mills et al., 2016; Ramjattan, 2019), as well as folk music, which draws on lyrics and rhyme and rhythm (Karkar-Esperat, 2025).

Audio Literacy

Teachers use knowledge of audio, or audio literacy, to make learning experiences accessible and engaging. Some of the audio literacy formats teachers use are audiobooks, videos, sound recordings, podcasts, and other forms to scaffold student learning, especially for bilingual and multilingual students. Literacy encompasses communication, connection, and the expectation that interaction be accessible to everyone. Literacy can empower individuals (Keefe & Copeland, 2011). It is critical as teacher educators that despite the discipline they teach, literacy is embedded in their curricula, which is the ability to negotiate meaning through reading, listening, analyzing, and creating meaning by writing, producing songs, acting, and speaking (Draper et al., 2012). "Literacy is a collective responsibility of every individual in the community; that is, to develop meaning-making with all human modes of communication to transmit and receive information" (Keefe & Copeland, 2011, p. 95). The audio mode is one of the communication modes connected to music literacy (Abrahams, 2015; Broomhead, 2021), which is the focus of this chapter. This chapter will explore some popular music genres connected to students' cultures. Csíkos and Dohány (2016) suggest that music literacy refers to culturally shaped systems of knowledge in music and musical skills and abilities. Cultures shape the music within them. Students are going to use music as a way to learn about language and use music and language to express themselves.

Why Do We Need to Use It?

Learning is usually focused on using traditional texts, which focus on learning academic vocabulary and answering comprehension questions using didactic teaching. Many students feel disconnected from this material and enjoy creative learning methods, such as music. Creative teachers use students' talents, skills, and cultures. Instead of relying on reading to answer questions, with the audio mode students critically analyze the audio content and understand the underlying messages and tone. Using audio supports students' learning and paves the way for self-discovery. Music helps students discover themselves and their cultures. As students learn about their culture through music, they learn how to write and analyze songs using functional and authentic literacy approaches.

Examples of How Music Has Been Used in the Classroom

Music in literacy instruction supports students' learning through auditory modalities (Kimball & O'Connor, 2010) and helps develop their critical thinking skills (Graham & Ward, 2024). It is an interactive and positive educational tool. Integrating music in the literacy classroom supports students in inquiry and conceptual learning and adds to their interests (Kimball & O'Connor, 2010). It has been shown to increase students' reading scores as an instructional approach (Andrews, 1997). Music is "interdisciplinary, multimodal, and collaborative" (Beckendorf et al., 2024. p. 252), and incorporating it in the classroom includes exploration, music analysis, and research. The use of music involves movement, singing, listening, and language skills.

Music is incorporated in foreign language classrooms as a creative approach to deepen students' awareness of other cultures, history, and language (Failoni, 1993). Music includes various genres such as traditional folk, jazz, hip-hop, mariachi, and children's songs. Incorporating music (audio), visuals, technology, role-playing, videos, and musical activities supports foreign language classrooms (Failoni, 1993). Music impacts children's learning abilities, develops listening skills, vocabulary, and phonemic awareness (Stone, 2015) and enhances linguistic abilities such as phonological memory and metacognition (Bolduc, 2008). Music also supports students' language proficiency as it integrates speaking, reading, writing, and listening skills. For instance, students may practice reading the lyrics or song texts and, in doing so, learn vocabulary words in the songs and the cultural contexts of the songs. Teachers can include a writing activity such as writing summaries of the songs.

For example, mariachi music has evolved into a global genre of music, gaining popularity across the world (Salazar, 2015). Some authors have viewed mariachi as an educational genre (Smith, 2018). Using it in the classroom supports building relationships with students, parents, and peers. In one study parents found a way to support their children in the classroom through mariachi music, and as a result students' academic motivation grew, fostering their sense of belonging and strengthened their ability to connect to peers (Liu, 2017). Using hip-hop in the classroom supports students' critical literacy, where they learn about multiple perspectives and focus on sociopolitical contemporary issues: "Hip-hop pedagogies can be the catalyst for that transformation" (Hall & Devirgilio, p. 40). Hip-hop music provides students the means to explore their identity and find affirmation (Hall & Devirgilio). It enhances engagement and achievement in the classroom (Emdin, 2017; Ladson-Billings, 1994; Meacham et al., 2018).

Audio Literacy Strategies In An Elementary Class

One of the core definitional principles for literacy is that "literacy is not a trait that resides solely in the individual person. It requires and creates a connections (relationship) with others" (Keefe & Copeland, 2011, p. 97). Audio literacy, music or otherwise, creates those relationships with students and their peers with their teachers. Audio literacy strategies provide multilingual and bilingual students with ways to learn and scaffold the learned information. One form of audio literacy is audiobooks, which allow learners to focus on listening and which are considered useful reading tools

(McGill, 2016). Audiobooks demonstrate for learners fluent reading (accuracy, intonation, and pitch) and support comprehension (McGill, 2016). They are easily shared with the whole class since everyone can listen to the same story at the same time. That creates community within the classroom. Teachers and students can use them as resources for modeling, providing feedback, and pacing students' responses to questions (Freeman & McLaughlin, 1984).

Music reflects the country's culture, history, and literature and reinforces using the four language skills (Failoni, 1993). Students can practice comprehension questions about the lyrics, define vocabulary words, translate the lyrics, and identify grammar structures within the lyrics (Failoni, 1993). Music can support students' literacy growth by increasing their oral language development (Fisher & McDonald, 2001) and vocabulary knowledge and improving their listening and sound discrimination (Mascle, 2009). Students use their prior knowledge as they make predictions about the song; furthermore, music promotes reading fluency (Algozzine & Douville, 2001). Music can be integrated into the classroom as a powerful teaching tool where the teachers can present advanced texts through music. Engaging students with music through reading activities will keep students engaged (Hare and Smallwood, 2008). Using music in learning is an important key to building cognitive skills.

Picture books with audio are another form of audio literacy. Picture books can be used with music as a multisensory experience, using text, sounds, and illustrations to tell a story (Villarreal et al., 2015). Teachers can connect music to picture books (i.e. singing "The Wheels on the Bus" when reading the book version of the song) and reinforce music concepts like melody and rhythm (Hall, 2021). Using a multisensory approach enhances students' learning as it provides a differentiated learning environment (Kimball & O'Connor, 2010). Music motivates students to learn, enhances communication skills, and improves students' cultural awareness.

Conclusion

Music motivates students to learn, enhances communication skills, and improves students' cultural awareness. Music connects with identity (Campbell, 2018; Kelly-McHale, 2013) as it is present in all cultures (Huron, 2006). It aids teachers in creating inclusive classrooms (Hall, 2021). Teachers can use music as a multicultural pedagogical tool to reflect the cultural diversity of the world (Anderson & Campbell, 2011). Using music in teaching and learning provides opportunities for the teacher to use a variety of techniques (Hill-Clarke & Robinson, 2004) so that they can support students' language development and increase their engagement.

How Can We Use It?

There are three simple steps that you need to follow:

1. Read the national standards that guided these two lessons.
2. Study the learning materials, which will give you background about the chapter examples.
3. Review the instructional materials, which could be used with students in language art and social studies.

The modeled lessons cover folk music, hip-hop, and mariachi.

Guiding Table for this chapter

Transmultiliteracies Sustaining Pedagogy Approach (Karkar-Esperat & Stickley, 2024)	♦ The use of the Language Arts Standards and Social Studies Standards. ♦ Applications for language arts and social studies classrooms.
The Pedagogical Holistic Model of New Literacies(Karkar-Esperat, 2019)	♦ Reading about the topic using different forms of texts. ♦ Creating storyboards and cardboard displays that represent the different aspects and history of a music genre. ♦ Reading about the music genres and how they are connected to history, culture, and identity (visual map). ♦ Creating a graffiti. ♦ Gathering information about the music genre from their families. ♦ Presenting the folk music that students brought to class.

(Continued)

The Raciosemiotic Architecture Framework (Karkar-Esperat, 2023)	◆ Synthesizing information on the three music genres through different artists in a storyboard. Students add other elements not expressed in what they read. ◆ Describing the music genres and their connection to customs and traditions. ◆ Discussing how mariachi music is connected to migration and immigration. ◆ Demonstrating knowledge of family history, culture, and past contributions of people in their main identity groups to the music genre (i.e. hip-hop, mariachi). ◆ Engaging in meaning-making using multiliteracies.
The MultiSemiotic Architecture Framework	**A MultiSemiotic Audio Approach: Mariachi, Hip-Hop, and Folk Music** The MultiSemiotic audio mode refers to using different genres of music (hip-hop that connects with history and culture, country music, mariachi), voice, and tone (see also Mills et al., 2016; Ramjattan, 2019), as well as folk music (lyrics and rhyme and rhythm).

References

Abrahams, F. (2015). Another perspective: Teaching music to millennial students. *Music Educators Journal*, *102*(1), 97–100.

Algozzine, B., & Douville, P. (2001). Teaching tips. *Preventing School Failure*, *45*(4), 187–188.

Anderson, W. M., & Campbell, P. S. (Eds.). (2011). *Multicultural perspectives in music education* (Vol. 3). R&L Education.

Andrews, L. J. (1997). *Effects of an integrated reading and music instructional approach on fifth-grade students' reading achievement, reading attitude, music achievement, and music attitude* (Publication No. 9729987) [Doctoral dissertation, University of North Carolina]. Proquest.

Beckendorf, A. L., Bickley, T., Conor, E., Grau Schmidt, A., Pratesi, A. L., & Wells, V. A. (2024). Music Companion to the Framework for Information Literacy. *Notes*, *81*(2), 252.

Bolduc, J. (2008). The effects of music instruction on emergent literacy capacities among preschool children: A literature review. *Early Childhood Research and Practice*, *10* (1), 1–5. https://eric.ed.gov/?id=EJ848819

Broomhead, P. (2021). A new definition of music literacy: What, why, and how? *Music Educators Journal*, *107*(3), 15–21. https://doi.org/10.1177/0027432121991644

Campbell, P. S. (2018). *Music, education and diversity: Building cultures and communities*. Teachers College Press.

Csíkos, C., & Dohány, G. (2016). Connections between music literacy and music-related background variables: An empirical investigation. *Visions of Research in Music Education*, *28*(1), Article 2. https://digitalcommons.lib.uconn.edu/vrme/vol28/iss1/2

Draper, R. J., Broomhead, P., Jensen, A. P., & Nokes, J. D. (2012). (Re)imagining literacy and teacher preparation through collaboration. *Reading Psychology*, *33*(4), 367–398. https://doi.org/10.1080/02702711.2010.515858

Graham, P., & Ward, A. (2024). Music as symbolic action. *Discourse & Society*, *35*(1), 66–82. https://doi.org/10.1177/09579265231195713

Hall, S. (2021). Using picture books to create a culturally inclusive elementary music classroom. *General Music Today*, *34*(2), 19–25. https://doi.org/10.1177/1048371320961378

Hare, K., & Smallwood, J. (2008). *Music and learning*. https://www.training-games.com/free/TtT_Hare_Smallwood.pdf

Hill-Clarke, K., & Robinson, N. R. (2004). It's as easy as a-b-c and do-re-mi: Music, rhythm, and rhyme enhance children's literacy skills. *Young Children*, *59*(5), 91–95.

Huron, D. (2006). Is music an evolutionary adaptation? *Annals of the New York Academy of Sciences*, *930*(1), 43–61. https://doi.org/10.1111/j.1749-6632.2001.tb05724.x

Failoni, J. W. (1993). Music as means to enhance cultural awareness and literacy in the foreign language classroom. *Mid-Atlantic Journal of Foreign Language Pedagogy*, *1*, 97–108.

Fisher, D., & McDonald, N. (2001). The intersection between music and early literacy instruction: Listening to literacy! *Reading Improvement*, *38*, 106–115.

Freeman, T. J., & McLaughlin, T. F. (1984). Effects of a taped-words treatment procedure on learning disabled students' sight-word reading. *Learning Disability Quarterly, 7*(1), 49–54. https://doi.org/10.2307/1510261

Karkar-Esperat, T. (2019). *Assessing preservice teachers' knowledge of new literacies* [Doctoral dissertation, Texas Tech University]. Texas Tech University Archive.

Karkar-Esperat, T. (2023) Transparency in the Classroom: The Raciosemiotic Architecture Framework for Multilingual Learners. *Semiotics Society of America 2023 Yearbook*.

Karkar-Esperat, T. & Stickley, Z. (2024). Revisioning Curriculum Through the Transmulitliteracies Sustaining Pedagogy Approach. *Social Sciences & Humanities Open, 9*, 100826.

Karkar-Esperat, T. M. (2025). Multiliteracies for multilingual learners: The multisemiotic architecture framework. *International Journal of Bilingual Education and Bilingualism. 28*(2), 117–134. https://doi.org/10.1080/13670050.2024.2409120

Keefe, E. B., & Copeland, S. R. (2011). What is literacy? The power of a definition. *Research and practice for persons with severe disabilities, 36*(3–4), 92–99. https://doi.org/10.2511/027494811800824507

Kelly-McHale, J. (2013). The influence of music teacher beliefs and practices on the expression of musical identity in an elementary general music classroom. *Journal of Research in Music Education, 61*(2), 195–216. https://doi.org/10.1177/0022429413485439

Kimball, K., & O'Connor, L. (2010). Engaging auditory modalities through the use of music in information literacy instruction. *Reference & User Services Quarterly, 49*(4), 316–319. http://www.jstor.org/stable/20865289

Ladson-Billings, G. (1994). *The dreamkeepers: Successful teachers of African American children*. Jossey-Bass.

Liu, F. (2017). *The impact of mariachi education on academic achievement in Tucson High Magnet School and Pueblo Magnet High School* [Master's thesis, University of Arizona]. ProQuest Dissertations Publishing.

Mascle, D. (2009). *Why teach your preschooler using rhyme and song?* Retrieved January 11, 2025, from http://www.ezinearticles.com

Meacham, S., Muhammad, L., & Mennenga, K. (2018). The fifth element? Using the tradition of knowledge and education in Hip-hop to transform classroom outcomes. *Journal of Popular Music Education, 2*(1–2), 133–148. https://doi.org/10.1386/jpme.2.1-2.133_1

McGill, A. H. (2016). *Audiobooks with struggling readers at the elementary school level* (Publication No. 3181) [Doctoral dissertation, Walden University]. Walden Dissertations and Doctoral Studies. https://scholarworks.waldenu.edu/dissertations/3181/

Mills, K. A., Davis-Warra, J., Sewell, M., & Anderson, M. (2016). Indigenous ways with literacies: transgenerational, multimodal, placed and collective. *Language and Education, 30*(1), 1–21. https://doi.org/10.1080/09500782.2015.1069836

New London Group (1996). A pedagogy of multiliteracies: Designing social futures. *Harvard Educational Review, 66*(1), 60–92. https://doi.org/10.17763/haer.66.1.17370n67v22j160u

Ramadani, I. (2017). The Importance of Music in the Development of the Child. *International Advisory Board, 20,* 303.

Ramjattan, V. A. 2019. "Raciolinguistics and the Aesthetic Labourer." *Journal of Industrial Relations* 61(5), 726–738. https://doi.org/10.1177/0022185618792990

Salazar, L. (2015). Mariachi music as a pathway to higher education in the United States. *Journal of the Vernacular Music Center, 1*(1), 1–74.

Sheehy, D. E. (2006). *Mariachi music in America: Experiencing music, expressing culture (Global Music Series)*. Oxford University Press.

Smith, V. L. (2018). *The influences of a mariachi education on student perceptions of academic achievement, academic attainment, and student engagement* (Publication No. 3140) [Master's thesis, University of the Pacific]. University of the Pacific Theses and Dissertations. https://scholarlycommons.pacific.edu/uop_etds/3140/

Stone, T. (2015). *The impact of music on language & early literacy: A research summary of Kinder Musik's ABC Music & Me*. ABCMM. https://media2.kindermusik.com/website/2016/11/Research_Schools_Kindermusik_Impact-of-MM-on-Language-Early-Literacy_2016.pdf

Villarreal, A., Minton, S., & Martinex, M. (2015). Child illustrators. *The Reading Teacher, 69*(3), 265–275. https://doi.org/10.1002/trtr.1405

Lesson Title: A MultiSemiotic Music Approach (Council of Chief State School Officers, 2013; International Literacy Association, 2017; National Council of Teachers of English & International Reading Association, 2012)

NCTE/IRA Standards for the English Language Arts	International Literacy Association Standards	INTASC standards
Standard # 1: Students read a wide range of print and non-print texts to build an understanding of texts, of themselves, and of the cultures of the United States and the world; to acquire new information; to respond to the needs and demands of society and the workplace; and for personal fulfillment. Among these texts are fiction and nonfiction, classic and contemporary works.	Standard#1: Foundational Knowledge Candidates demonstrate knowledge of the theoretical, historical, and evidence-based foundations of literacy and language and the ways in which they interrelate and the role of literacy professionals in schools.	Standard #1: Learner Development. The teacher understands how learners grow and develop, recognizing that patterns of learning and development vary individually within and across the cognitive, linguistic, social, emotional, and physical areas and designs and implements developmentally appropriate and challenging learning experiences.
Standard #3: Students apply a wide range of strategies to comprehend, interpret, evaluate, and appreciate texts. They draw on their prior experience, their interactions with other readers and writers, their knowledge of word meaning and of other texts, their word identification strategies, and their understanding of textual features (e.g., sound-letter correspondence, sentence structure, context, graphics).	Standard#2: Curriculum and Instruction Candidates use foundational knowledge to critique and implement literacy curricula to meet the needs of all learners and to design, implement, and evaluate evidence-based literacy instruction for all learners. Standard #3: Assessment and Evaluation Candidates understand, select, and use valid, reliable, fair, and appropriate assessment tools to screen, diagnose, and measure student literacy achievement; inform instruction and evaluate interventions; participate in professional learning experiences; explain assessment results and advocate for appropriate literacy practices to relevant stakeholders.	Standard #2: Learning Differences. The teacher uses understanding of individual differences and diverse cultures and communities to ensure inclusive learning environments that enable each learner to meet high standards. Standard #3: Learning Environments. The teacher works with others to create environments that support individual and collaborative learning, and that encourage positive social interaction, active engagement in learning, and self motivation.

Standard #4: Diversity and Equity Candidates demonstrate knowledge of research, relevant theories, pedagogies, and essential concepts of diversity and equity; demonstrate and provide opportunities for understanding all forms of diversity as central to students' identities; create classrooms and schools that are inclusive and affirming; advocate for equity at school, district, and community levels.

Standard #5: Learners and the Literacy Environment
Candidates meet the developmental needs of all learners and collaborate with school personnel to use a variety of print and digital materials to engage and motivate all learners; integrate digital technologies in appropriate, safe, and effective ways; and foster a positive climate that supports a literacy-rich learning environment.

Standard #6: Professional Learning and Leadership. Candidates recognize the importance of, participate in, and facilitate ongoing professional learning as part of career-long leadership roles.

Standard #4: Content Knowledge. The teacher understands the central concepts, tools of inquiry, and structures of the discipline(s) he or she teaches and creates learning experiences that make the discipline accessible and meaningful for learners to assure mastery of the content.

Standard #5: Application of Content. The teacher understands how to connect concepts and use differing perspectives to engage learners in critical thinking, creativity, and collaborative problem solving related to authentic local and global issues.

Standard #6: Assessment. The teacher understands and uses multiple methods of assessment to engage learners in their own growth, to monitor learner progress, and to guide the teacher's and learner's decision making.

Standard #7: Planning for Instruction. The teacher plans instruction that supports every student in meeting rigorous learning goals by drawing upon knowledge of content areas, curriculum, cross-disciplinary skills, and pedagogy, as well as knowledge of learners and the community context.

Standard #8: Students use a variety of technological and information resources (e.g., libraries, databases, computer networks, video) to gather and synthesize information and to create and communicate knowledge.

Standard #9: Students develop an understanding of and respect for diversity in language use, patterns, and dialects across cultures, ethnic groups, geographic regions, and social roles.

Standard #10: Students whose first language is not English make use of their firstlanguage to develop competency in the English language arts and to develop understanding of content across the curriculum.

Standard #11: Students participate as knowledgeable, reflective, creative, and critical members of a variety of literacy communities.

(Continued)

NCTE/IRA Standards for the English Language Arts	International Literacy Association Standards	INTASC standards
Standard #12: Students use spoken, written, and visual language to accomplish their own purposes (e.g., for learning, enjoyment, persuasion, and the exchange of information).	Standard #7: Practicum/Clinical Experiences Candidates apply theory and best practice in multiple supervised practicum/clinical experiences.	Standard #8: Instructional Strategies. The teacher understands and uses a variety of instructional strategies to encourage learners to develop deep understanding of content areas and their connections and to build skills to apply knowledge in meaningful ways.

References

Council of Chief State School Officers. (2013). *InTASC model core teaching standards and learning progressions for teachers 1.0: A resource for ongoing teacher development.* https://learning.ccsso.org/intasc-model-core-teaching-standards-and-learning-progressions-for-teachers

International Literacy Association. (2017). *Standards for the preparation of literacy professionals 2017.* https://www.literacyworldwide.org/get-resources/standards/standards-2017

National Council of Teachers of English & International Reading Association. (1996/2012). *Standards for the English language arts (Reaffirmed 2012).* National Council of Teachers of English. https://ncte.org/resources/standards/ncte-ira-standards-for-the-english-language-arts/

Modeled Lesson 1: Audio Knowledge
Lesson Title: A MultiSemiotic Music Approach: Mariachi

Lesson Overview
This lesson introduces the first element of the MultiSemiotic Audio Approach: Mariachi Music. Mariachi is one form of Latin American music. Professional mariachi musicians sing and play trumpets, guitars, and violins at different events such as birthdays, civic celebrations, weddings, baptisms, and quinceañeras (Sheehy, 2006). Mariachi is a symbol of the Mexican culture and identity.

Music represents national identity, and it includes social and cultural aspects. You are going to learn how mariachi music could help you develop your students' identities by integrating it in writing, listening, speaking, and musical activities. Think of how mariachi music is connected to storytelling, tone, and affect, which are all ways you could encourage students to use language skills.

You are encouraged to ask students to gather the mariachi music that they are acquainted with, that they listen to, or that family members can identify with.

Students are encouraged to create storylines and cardboard displays to present the information that they have learned about mariachi. Some videos provided in the module will help you complete these activities. You are expected to help your students reflect critically in writing or speaking about how this genre connects to culture and identity. This genre builds all the language skills.

The Common Core state standards are used to build knowledge of mariachi using multimedia and different resources. Additionally, the standards guide you to use research to learn through mariachi about migration and about music traditions concerning mariachi, involving mariachi attire, instruments, and dancing. In this professional learning expereience, we use culture as a lens to explore these topics.

Keep in mind that this is a lesson in which you could integrate reading, listening, writing, and speaking language skills, and the module includes TESOL strategies. The readings give you an explanation of how you can teach mariachi music.

The following example lesson is guided by the International Literacy Standards for teacher preparation in literacy, the NCTE/IRA standards for English language arts, the Common Core Standards for English language arts, and social studies standards. Following this, pre-, during, and post-activities are presented that you can use to teach critical literacy, translanguaging, and multiliteracies. Opportunities are also presented in the lesson to guide your third–fifth-grade students to use this approach.

Journaling: This journal will document your learning journey and will be used to evaluate the effectiveness of this process.

Think of tools (i.e., audiovisuals) to teach a lesson on mariachi. What topics would you cover in your teaching? What activities could you use? Please discuss them in your journal.

A) Use the guiding questions in writing your response.
B) Start writing about your resources, considering any materials that can introduce mariachi.
C) Record your thought processes as you read the modules.
D) Consider how the presented information makes you think about your teaching of multilingual students in terms of content and teaching strategies.

Learning Outcomes for Teachers

After studying this module, you should be able to:

- Connect mariachi to culture and language use.
- Create a storyboards and cardboard displays that represent the different aspects and the history of mariachi.
- Gather and organize the mariachi music students have brought to classroom.
- Guide students to reflect on their learning processes and social interactions while learning about mariachi.
- Highlight the connection that mariachi music has with people's lives.
- Revisit the standards that focus on language in relation to mariachi music based on the grade level being taught.
- Provide students with texts that help them learn about mariachi music.
- Support students to create an understanding of how mariachi music represents identity in some cultures.
- Provide students with rich reading language experiences.
- Engage in meaning-making using multiliteracies.
- Use the MultiSemiotic audio approach to create a learning product for your students.
- Complete a reflection on the module.
- Guide learners in third through fifth grade to learn and apply their knowledge of mariachi.

TESOL Standards (for Teachers, TESOL International Association, 2018)

- **1c.** Candidates demonstrate knowledge of language processes (e.g., interlanguage and language progressions) to facilitate and monitor ELLs' language learning in English.
- **1d.** Candidates apply knowledge of English academic language functions, learning domains, content-specific language anddiscourse structures, and vocabulary to promote ELLs' academic achievement across content areas.

- **2a.** Candidates demonstrate knowledge of how dynamic academic, personal, familial, cultural, and social contexts, including sociopolitical factors, impact the education of ELLs.
- **2b.** Candidates demonstrate knowledge of research and theories of cultural and linguistic diversity and equity that promote academic and social language learning for ELLs.
- **2c.** Candidates devise and implement methods to understand each ELL's academic characteristics, including background knowledge, educational history, and current performance data, to develop effective, individualized instructional and assessment practices for their ELLs.
- **2d.** Candidates devise and implement methods to learn about personal characteristics of the individual ELL (e.g., interests, motivations, strengths, needs) and their family (e.g., language use, literacy practices, circumstances) to develop effective instructional practices.
- **2e.** Candidates identify and describe the impact of his/her identity, role, cultural understandings, and personal biases and conscious knowledge of US culture on his/her interpretation of the educational strengths and needs of individual ELLs and ELLs in general.
- **3a.** Candidates plan for culturally and linguistically relevant, supportive environments that promote ELLs' learning. Candidates design scaffolded instruction of language and literacies to support standards and curricular objectives for ELLs in the content areas.
- **3b.** Candidates instruct ELLs using evidence-based, student-centered, developmentally appropriate interactive approaches.
- **3c.** Candidates adjust instructional decisions after critical reflection on individual ELLs' learning outcomes in both language and content.
- **3d.** Candidates plan strategies to collaborate with other educators, school personnel, and families in order to support their ELLs' learning of language and literacies in the content areas.

- **3e.** Candidates use and adapt relevant materials and resources, including digital resources, to plan lessons for ELLs, support communication with other educators, school personnel, and ELLs and to foster student learning of language and literacies in the content areas.
- **4b.** Candidates demonstrate understanding of classroom-based formative, summative, and diagnostic assessments scaffolded for both English language and content assessment. Candidates determine language and content learning goals based on assessment data.
- **5.a.** Candidates demonstrate knowledge of effective collaboration strategies in order to plan ways to serve as a resource for ELL instruction, support educators and school staff, and advocate for ELLs.
- **5c.** Candidates practice self-assessment and reflection, make adjustments for self-improvement, and plan for continuous professional development in the field of English language learning and teaching.

Language Objectives (for Students)
- To explain how mariachi music is connected to history, culture, and identity.
- To describe mariachi and its connection to customs and traditions.
- To discuss how mariachi music is connected to migration and immigration.

Guiding Questions
1. What type of mariachi music do your students listen to?
2. How does mariachi music reflect the culture and human activity?
3. How can you connect writing and reading to mariachi?
4. How can we instill in students their cultural values, and how they can protect their cultural heritage through mariachi music, if applicable?
5. How can you help students connect with their culture through music?

6. How can you be culturally responsive to your students' needs using music as one of the genres in the classroom?
7. How does mariachi music represent other cultures in New Mexico and United States?
8. How has mariachi been adopted in New Mexico?

Preview on the Reading
Music is a way to connect to students' interests, form relationships, and increase their engagement in the classroom. It involves all the language skills and helps students in sharing their voice, culture, and language. Mariachi music supports students in integrating all the language skills and supports their social and emotional growth. Through mariachi music, students learn about others and self. Using mariachi is an engaging approach that empowers the students by learning about their cultures and backgrounds.

Pre-Class Preparation Activities for Teachers
Read

- Read about Mariachi music in the classroom.
  Celebrating & Honoring Hispanic Culture through Traditional Mariachi (Neel, 2020) https://www.musicconstructed.com/tool/celebrating-honoring-hispanic-culture-through-the-traditional-mariachi-genre/
- Understand how integrating Mariachi in the classroom empowers marginalized students.
  Making a Difference with Mariachi Music (Morales, 2024) https://ensemblenews.org/region/making-a-difference-with-mariachi-music/
- Examine cultural responsiveness as an effective teaching practice through a review of literature, focusing on instruction in the mariachi classroom.
  Cultural Responsiveness as Best Practice for Teaching Mariachi https://www.academia.edu/6270637/Cultural_Responsiveness_as_Best_Practice_for_Teaching_Mariachi

Listen

- A Mariachi Tradition: The Story of Mexico's Music (Footpints, n.d.) https://www.youtube.com/watch?v=CDsYsii0Mj8
- The Art of Learning through Mariachi (Crayola Education, 2003) https://www.youtube.com/watch?v=RuERAd3L6FQ
- The Best Mariachi in the World (McCormick, 2020) https://www.youtube.com/watch?v=7GMzHdEJLhs
- Mariachi Girl the bilingual play (KGET News, 2019) https://www.youtube.com/watch?v=0k7acpyyMc4&t=53s
- Top 10 Most Popular Mariachi Songs (Encore, 2021) https://www.youtube.com/watch?v=B5bASCKCZT0
- Torres-Ramos, J. R. Cultural Responsiveness as Best Practice: Implications for Teaching Mariachi José R. Torres-Ramos University of North Texas.

Plan

These are activities that you can use during instruction for teaching your students:
- Read about mariachi music and how it is connected to history, culture, and identity (visual map).
- Gather mariachi music from different areas through different artists in a storyboard using a United States map. Students add other elements not expressed that they want to include. Students will go deep on one period.
- Students describe mariachi and its connection to customs and traditions.
- Students use cardboard to make art projects for mariachi.

The social studies standards for this theme focus on migration, exploring history and describing their contributions to New Mexico cultures, and demonstrating knowledge of family history, culture, and past contributions of people in their main identity groups.

- To connect with social studies, have students inquire about and provide context for the mariachi music in context of migration and immigration. Students give the background of the mariachi music that they brought to class and research how different groups of people settled in New Mexico and influenced the culture and identity.

Thought Questions
1. Why do you think mariachi music should be included in the curriculum?
2. How does mariachi music represent a symbol of cultural identity?
3. After reading about mariachi music and reviewing the module materials, what resonated more with you? In what way will you incorporate it in your class?
4. The module covered the common core standards focusing on all the language skills. How are you planning to incorporate them in your classroom?
5. How are you planning to teach about mariachi in social studies using the standards provided?
6. What kinds of creativity (think about the modes of meanings that could be used) do you hope to discover through your students' responses and reactions?
7. Do you see any challenges in implementing this approach into your classrooms? Explain.
8. Any additional thoughts? Please share!

References

Crayola Education. (2003, April 26). *Create music with the world's youngest mariachi Mateo Lopez* [Video]. YouTube. https://www.youtube.com/watch?v=RuERAd3L6FQ

Encore. (2021, August 2). *Top 10 most popular mariachi songs* [Video]. YouTube. https://www.youtube.com/watch?v=B5bASCKCZT0

Footprints. (n.d.). *Mexican Mariachi music | Mariachi – A genre of Mexican regional music | History and journey*[Video]. YouTube. https://www.youtube.com/watch?v=CDsYsii0Mj8

KGET News. (2019, September 12). *"Mariachi girl" the bilingual play* [Video]. YouTube. https://www.youtube.com/watch?v=0k7acpyyMc4&t=53s

McCormick, A. (2020, September 28). *The best mariachi in the world* [Video]. YouTube. https://www.youtube.com/watch?v=7GMzHdEJLhs

Morales, J. (2024, May 1). *Making a difference with mariachi music*. The Ensemble. https://ensemblenews.org/region/making-a-difference-with-mariachi-music/

Neel, M. (2020, July 28). *Celebrating & honoring Hispanic culture through traditional mariachi*. Music ConstructED. https://www.musicconstructed.com/tool/celebrating-honoring-hispanic-culture-through-the-traditional-mariachi-genre/

Sheehy, D. E. (2006). *Mariachi music in America: Experiencing music, expressing culture* (Global Music Series). Oxford University Press.

TESOL International Association. (2018). *Standards for initial TESOL Pre-K–12 teacher preparation programs*. https://www.tesol.org/media/v33fewo0/2018-tesol-teacher-prep-standards-final.pdf

Lesson Title: A MultiSemiotic Audio Knowledge: Mariachi (Karkar-Esperat, 2019; National Governors Association Center for Best Practices, & Council of Chief State School Officers, 2010; New Mexico Public Education Department, 2021)

Common Core Standards for 3rd–5th Grades	Social Studies Standards for 3rd–5th Grade	Pedagogical Holistic Model of New Literacies
Third Grade CCSS.ELA-LITERACY. RI.3.10 By the end of the year, read and comprehend informational texts, including history/social studies, science, and technical texts, at the high end of the grades 2–3 text complexity band independently and proficiently. CCSS.ELA-LITERACY. SL.3.6 Speak in complete sentences when appropriate to task and situation in order to provide requested detail or clarification. CCSS.ELA-LITERACY. W.3.7 Conduct short research projects that build knowledge about a topic.	**Third Grade** 3.5. Construct responses to compelling questions using reasoning, examples, and relevant details. 3.10. Evaluate the reasons for migration and immigration and the effects on people, culture, and ideas in world communities. **Fourth Grade** 4.4. Construct responses to compelling questions using reasoning, examples, and relevant details. 4.11. Describe the different groups of people that have settled in New Mexico throughout history and describe their contributions to New Mexico cultures.	The audio mode, according to the New London Group (1996), focuses on concepts such as music as well as "the employment of any sound effect to support student learning." The pedagogical holistic model of new literacies uses words such as "theater," "different types of audio," "singing," "dialogue," and "monologue" to reflect different pedagogical approaches (Karkar-Esperat, 2019). The MultiSemiotic audio mode (Karkar-Esperat, 2025) refers to using different genres of music (hip-hop that connects with history and culture, country music, mariachi), voice, and tone (see also Mills et al., 2016; Ramjattan, 2019) and folk music (lyrics and rhyme and rhythm).

Fourth Grade

CCSS.ELA-LITERACY.RL.4.10
By the end of the year, read and comprehend literature, including stories, dramas, and poetry, in the grades 4–5 text complexity band proficiently, with scaffolding as needed at the high end of the range.

CCSS.ELA-LITERACY.SL.4.5
Add audio recordings and visual displays to presentations when appropriate to enhance the development of main ideas or themes.

CCSS.ELA-LITERACY.W.4.7
Conduct short research projects that build knowledge through investigation of different aspects of a topic.

Fifth Grade

CCSS.ELA-LITERACY.RL.5.10
By the end of the year, read and comprehend informational texts, including history/social studies, science, and technical texts, at the high end of the grades 4–5 text complexity band independently and proficiently.

Fifth Grade

5.5. Construct responses to compelling questions supported by reasoning and evidence.

5.30. Demonstrate knowledge of family history, culture, and past contributions of people in their main identity groups.

(Continued)

Common Core Standards for 3rd–5th Grades	Social Studies Standards for 3rd–5th Grade	Pedagogical Holistic Model of New Literacies
CCSS.ELA-LITERACY.SL.5.5 Include multimedia components (e.g., graphics, sound) and visual displays in presentations when appropriate to enhance the development of main ideas or themes. CCSS.ELA-LITERACY.W.5.7 Conduct short research projects that use several sources to build knowledge through investigation of different aspects of a topic.		

References

Karkar-Esperat, T. (2019). *Assessing preservice teachers' knowledge of new literacies [Doctoral dissertation, Texas Tech University]*. Texas Tech University Archive.

Karkar-Esperat, T. M. (2025). Multiliteracies for multilingual learners: The multisemiotic architecture framework. *International Journal of Bilingual Education and Bilingualism. 28*(2), 117–134. https://doi.org/10.1080/13670050.2024.2409120

Mills, K. A., Davis-Warra, J., Sewell, M., & Anderson, M. (2016). Indigenous ways with literacies: Transgenerational, multimodal, placed and collective. *Language and Education 30*(1), 1–21. https://doi.org/10.1080/09500782.2015.1069836

National Governors Association Center for Best Practices, & Council of Chief State School Officers. (2010). *Common Core State Standards for English language arts & literacy in history/social studies, science, and technical subjects*. Authors. https://www.corestandards.org/ELA-Literacy/

New Mexico Public Education Department. (2021). *New Mexico social studies standards*. https://webnew.ped.state.nm.us/bureaus/literacy-humanities/social-studies/

New London Group (1996). A Pedagogy of Multiliteracies: Designing Social Futures. *Harvard Educational Review, 66*(1), 60–92. https://doi.org/10.17763/haer.66.1.17370n67v22j160u

Ramjattan, V. A. 2019. Raciolinguistics and the Aesthetic Labourer. *Journal of Industrial Relations, 61*(5), 726–738. https://doi.org/10.1177/0022185618792990

Instructional Materials Used with Students
Lesson Title: A MultiSemiotic Music Approach: Mariachi

Language Objectives (for Students)
- ♦ To explain how mariachi music is connected to history, culture, and identity.
- ♦ To describe mariachi music and its connection to customs and traditions.
- ♦ To discuss how mariachi music is connected to migration and immigration.

During instruction, these are activities that you can use for teaching your students:

- Reading about mariachi music and how it is connected to history, culture, and identity (visual map).
- Gathering mariachi music from different areas through different artists in a storyboard using the United States map. Students add other elements not expressed that they want to include. Students will go deep on one period.
- Students describing mariachi and its connection to customs and traditions.
- Students using cardboard to make art projects for mariachi.

During instruction, these are activities that you can use aligning with the social studies standards (for students)

- Students provide context to the teacher-provided mariachi music in context of migration and immigration.
- Students give the background of the mariachi music that they brought to class and research how different groups of people settled in New Mexico and influenced the culture and identity.
- **Differentiation includes** maps, visuals and supplementary materials, audio and visual supports, class discussion, drawings, online resources, and videos.

Modeled Lesson 2: Audio Knowledge
Lesson Title: A MultiSemiotic Music Approach: Hip-Hop

Lesson Overview
This lesson introduces an element of the MultiSemiotic Audio Approach: Hip-Hop Music. Music represents national identity and social and cultural aspects. You are going to learn how hip-hop music can help you develop students' identities by integrating it in reading, listening, speaking, and musical activities. Hip-hop supports students' developing opinions by helping them think critically. Think about the ways hip-hop music is connected to rhyming words, allowing students to use all their language skills.

In the last module, you learned about mariachi music and how it is connected to culture and history. You are encouraged to ask students to gather the hip-hop music they are acquainted with, that they listen to, or that family members can identify with.

Students are encouraged to create graffiti and storyboards to present the information that they have learned about hip-hop. Some videos provided in the module will help you complete these activities. You are expected to help your students practice writing their own lyrics. This genre builds all the language skills.

The Common Core state standards are used to determine the meanings words and phrases as they are used in a text. This will help interpret information presented using multimedia. Additionally, the standards guide you to analyze language involving rapping, dancing, and rhythm. In this guide, we use culture as a lens to explore topics.

Keep in mind that because this is a lesson in which you could integrate reading, listening, writing, and speaking language skills, there are some TESOL strategies used in the module. The readings explain how you can teach hip-hop music and will give you good background on the teaching skills that will help you introduce hip-hop.

The following example lesson is guided by the International Literacy Standards for teacher preparation in literacy, the NCTE/IRA standards for English language arts, the Common Core Standards for English language arts, and social studies standards. Following this, activities for before, during, and after the lesson are presented that you can use to teach critical literacy, translanguaging, and multiliteracies. Opportunities are also presented in the lesson to guide your third- to fifth-grade students to use this approach.

Journaling: This is a diary that will document your learning journey

- A) Start writing about your resources and any material that can introduce hip-hop.
- B) Record your thought processes as you read the modules.
- C) Consider how the presented information makes you think about your teaching of multilingual students in terms of content and teaching strategies.

Learning Outcomes for Teachers

After studying this module, you should be able to:

- Connect hip-hip to language in New Mexico culture.
- Create a model using a storyboard that represents the different aspects and the history of hip-hop.
- Gather and organize the hip-hop music students have brought to classroom.
- Guide students to reflect on their learning processes and their social interactions while learning about hip-hop.
- Highlight the connection between hip-hop music and people's lives.
- Revisit the standards that focus on language in relation to hip-hop music based on the grade level being taught.
- Provide students with texts that help them learn about hip-hop music.
- Support students to create an understanding of how hip-hop music represents identity in some cultures.
- Provide students with rich reading language experiences.
- Engage in meaning-making using multiliteracies.
- Use the MultiSemiotic audio approach to create a learning product with your students.
- Complete a reflection on the module.
- Guide third- to fifth-grade learners to learn and apply their knowledge of hip-hop.

TESOL Standards (for Teachers, TESOL International Association, 2018)

- **1c.** Candidates demonstrate knowledge of language processes (e.g., interlanguage and language progressions) to facilitate and monitor ELLs' language learning in English.
- **1d.** Candidates apply knowledge of English academic language functions, learning domains, content-specific language and discourse structures, and vocabulary to promote ELLs' academic achievement across content areas.
- **2a.** Candidates demonstrate knowledge of how dynamic academic, personal, familial, cultural, and social contexts,

including sociopolitical factors, impact the education of ELLs.
- **2b.** Candidates demonstrate knowledge of research and theories of cultural and linguistic diversity and equity that promote academic and social language learning for ELLs.
- **2c.** Candidates devise and implement methods to understand each ELL's academic characteristics, including background knowledge, educational history, and current performance data, to develop effective, individualized instructional and assessment practices for their ELLs.
- **2d.** Candidates devise and implement methods to learn about personal characteristics of the individual ELL (e.g., interests, motivations, strengths, needs) and their family (e.g., language use, literacy practices, circumstances) to develop effective instructional practices.
- **2e.** Candidates identify and describe the impact of his/her identity, role, cultural understandings, and personal biases and conscious knowledge of US culture on his/her interpretation of the educational strengths and needs of individual ELLs and ELLs in general.
- **3a.** Candidates plan for culturally and linguistically relevant, supportive environments that promote ELLs' learning. Candidates design scaffolded instruction of language and literacies to support standards and curricular objectives for ELLs in the content areas.
- **3b.** Candidates instruct ELLs using evidence-based, student-centered, developmentally appropriate interactive approaches.
- **3c.** Candidates adjust instructional decisions after critical reflection on individual ELLs' learning outcomes in both language and content.
- **3d.** Candidates plan strategies to collaborate with other educators, school personnel, and families in order to support their ELLs' learning of language and literacies in the content areas.
- **3e.** Candidates use and adapt relevant materials and resources, including digital resources, to plan lessons for ELLs, support communication with other educators,

school personnel, and ELLs and to foster student learning of language and literacies in the content areas.
- **5b.** Candidates demonstrate knowledge of effective collaboration strategies in order to plan ways to serve as a resource for ELL instruction, support educators and school staff, and advocate for ELLs.
- **4b.** Candidates demonstrate understanding of classroom-based formative, summative, and diagnostic assessments scaffolded for both English language and content assessment. Candidates determine language and content learning goals based on assessment data.
- **5C.** Candidates practice self-assessment and reflection, make adjustments for self-improvement, and plan for continuous professional development in the field of English language learning and teaching.

Language Objectives (for Students)
- To determine the meaning of words and phrases in relation to hip-hop.
- To write hip-hop lyrics and produce their song using technology (i.e., sound, typed lyrics, poster to present the lyrics, a cover using graffiti for their presentation).
- To explain connections among historical and cultural contexts of hip-hop music using background and inspiration.

Guiding Questions
- What is the hip-hop music that your students listen to?
- How does hip-hop music reflect the culture and human activity?
- How is the language in hip-hop music used to represent culture?
- How can you connect the teaching of writing and reading to hip-hop?
- How can we instill in students their cultural values, and how they can protect their cultural heritage through hip-hop music, if applicable?

- How can you help students connect with their culture through music?
- How can you be culturally responsive to your students' needs using music as one of the genres in the classroom?
- How does hip-hop music embrace and compare with other cultures in New Mexico and the United States?

Preview on the Reading

Music is a way to connect to students' interests, form relationships, and increase their engagement in the classroom. It involves all the language skills and helps students in sharing their voice, culture, and language through music. Hip-hop music supports students in integrating all the language skills and supports their social and emotional growth. Through hip-hop music, students learn about others and self. It is an engaging approach that supports students' critical learning skills.

Pre-Class Preparation Activities for Teachers
Read

Think of the tools (i.e., audiovisuals) you could use to teach a lesson on hip-hop. What topics would you cover in your teaching? What activities could you use? Please discuss them in your journal.

Read

- You are going to read about the history of hip-hop: Hip-hop between the past and the present.
  The Complete History of Hip-Hop (Milliman, n.d.) https://blog.prepscholar.com/hip-hop-history-timeline
- The components of hip-hop, focus on the last element because it is part of the activity provided.
  What Are the Four Elements of Hip-hop? (Recording Connection, n.d.) https://recordingconnection.com/blog/2022/04/28/what-are-the-four-elements-of-hip-hop/

- This article helps you learn about the language learning strategies you could use with hip-hop.

  Hip-hop Music for Language Learning (Rishma, 2021) https://www.iamhiphopmagazine.com/hip-hop-music-for-language-learning/
- Hip-hop music is "the language of global youth culture," says author and educator Carole Boston Weatherford. Hip-hop could be used as a language strategy, specifically writing, to encourage students to write and express themselves.

  The Power of Rap and Hip-Hop in the Classroom (Lee, 2020) https://www.edutopia.org/article/power-rap-and-hip-hop-classroom/
- Hip-hop music is used across the curriculum as part of the culturally responsive teaching. You will learn how this genre has been used in vocabulary development, math, and science.

  Sparking Engagement with Hip-Hop (Johnson, 2017) https://www.edutopia.org/blog/sparking-engagement-hip-hop-joquetta-johnson
- There are some vocabulary words that you need to know about hip-hop:

  Hip-hop Vocabulary (Kennedy Center, n.d.):
  https://www.kennedy-center.org/education/resources-for-educators/classroom-resources/media-and-interactives/media/hip-hop/hip-hop-a-culture-of-vision-and-voice/
- This peer-reviewed article provides an understanding of how you can connect hip-hop to the curriculum focusing on cultural-relevant pedagogy.

  Integrating Hip-Hop and Cultural Relevant Lessons into the Public School Curriculum (Ali, 2015) https://digitalcommons.uncfsu.edu/cgi/viewcontent.cgi?article=1038&context=jri

These are resources that you could use to teach your third- to fifth-grade students

Listen

- Kids Hip-hop (AmonSounds, 2017) https://www.youtube.com/watch?v=jM0e8GbkSqo
- Hand Clap Rap (Hartmann, 2019) https://www.youtube.com/watch?v=Zp5dA1FKSGI
- How to Write a Rap (How to Rap, 2020): Your First Verse in Under 11 Minutes (Step-By-Step) https://www.youtube.com/watch?v=cLUK8ob-GMQ

These are activities that you can use during instruction for teaching your students:

- Reading about hip-hop music and how it is connected to history, culture, and identity and how the history of hip-hop has changed over time (using a timeline).
- Creating a graffiti for the hip-hop music that students connect with or that they wrote. https://www.youtube.com/watch?v=60Gpi4lEOAs
- Gathering hip-hop music from different time periods through different artists in a storyline. Students add other elements not expressed that they want to include. Students will go deep on one period of hip hop.
- Students presenting the lyrics on hip-hop music they practiced writing. You can differentiate by asking students to write lyrics of different lengths.

The social studies standards for this theme focus on identifying primary and secondary sources and determining their credibility, identifying evidence that draws information from multiple perspectives, and demonstrating knowledge of family history, culture, and past contributions of people in their main identity groups.

To connect with social studies, have students

- provide context to their lyrics in terms of social, community, personal concern, and
- provide background of the hip-hop music they brought to class and research how the language use represents culture, history, and inspiration.

Thought Questions
1. In what ways do you think hip-hop music can support student learning?
2. After reading about hip-hop music and reviewing the module materials, what resonated most with you? In what way will you incorporate it in your class?
3. The module covered the Common Core Standards focusing on integrating all the language skills. How are you planning to incorporate these standards in your classroom?
4. How are you planning to teach about hip-hop in social studies using the standards provided?
5. What creativity do you hope to discover through your students' responses and reactions through your students responses?
6. Any additional thoughts? Please share!

References

Ali, S. (2015). Integrating hip-hop and cultural relevant lessons into the public school curriculum. *Journal of Research Initiatives, 1*(3), 1.

Eido1. (n.d.). *Step by step how to draw graffiti letters – Write HIP HOP in graffiti for beginners* [Video]. YouTube. https://www.youtube.com/watch?v=60Gpi4IEOAs

AmonSounds. (2017, December 7). *Rap with me kids – Mr. C lyrics* [Video]. YouTube. https://www.youtube.com/watch?v=jM0e8GbkSqo

Hartmann, J. (2019, December 1). *Hand clap rap|Jack Hartmann|Repeat after me listening skills|Clap back* [Video]. YouTube. https://www.youtube.com/watch?v=Zp5dA1FKSGI

How to Rap. (2020, May 4). *How to write a rap: Your first verse in under 11 minutes (Step-by-step)* [Video]. YouTube. https://www.youtube.com/watch?v=cLUK8ob-GMQ

Johnson, J. (2017, May 1). *Sparking engagement with hip-hop in the classroom*. Edutopia. https://www.edutopia.org/blog/sparking-engagement-hip-hop-joquetta-johnson

KennedyCenter.(n.d.).*Hip-hop:Acultureofvisionandvoice*.RetrievedFebruary 3, 2025, from https://www.kennedy-center.org/education/resources-for-educators/classroom-resources/media-and-interactives/media/hip-hop/hip-hop-a-culture-of-vision-and-voice/

Lee, L. (2020, February 7). *The power of rap and hip-hop in the classroom*. *Edutopia*. https://www.edutopia.org/article/power-rap-and-hip-hop-classroom

Milliman, H. (n.d.). *The complete history of hip hop*. PrepScholar. Retrieved January 2, 2025, from https://blog.prepscholar.com/hip-hop-history-timeline

Rishma. (2021, August 19). *Hip-hop music for language learning*. IamHipHop. https://www.iamhiphopmagazine.com/hip-hop-music-for-language-learning

Recording Connection. (n.d.). *Hip hop & beat making: Giving you the skills to puruse a career in hip hop*. Retrieved January 2, 2025, from https://recordingconnection.com/courses/hip-hop-music-school/

TESOL International Association. (2018). *Standards for initial TESOL Pre-K–12 teacher preparation programs*. https://www.tesol.org/media/v33fewo0/2018-tesol-teacher-prep-standards-final.pdf

Lesson Title: A MultiSemiotic Music Approach: Hip hop (Karkar-Esperat, 2019; National Governors Association Center for Best Practices, & Council of Chief State School Officers, 2010; New Mexico social studies Standards, 2021)

Common Core Standards for 3rd–5th Grades	Social Studies Standards for 3rd–5th Grade	Pedagogical Holistic Model of New Literacies
Third Grade	**Third Grade**	The audio mode, according to the New London Group (1996), focuses on concepts such as music as well as 'the employment of any sound effect to support student learning.' The pedagogical holistic model of new literacies uses words such as 'theater,' 'different types of audio,' 'singing,' 'dialogue,' and 'monologue' to reflect different pedagogical approaches." (Karkar-Esperat, 2019)
CCSS.ELA-LITERACY. RL.3.4 Determine the meaning of words and phrases as they are used in a text, distinguishing literal from nonliteral language.	3.4. Cite evidence that supports a response to supporting or compelling questions.	
	3.3. With support, determine the credibility of sources.	
CCSS.ELA-LITERACY. RL.3.3 Describe the relationship between a series of historical events, scientific ideas or concepts, or steps in technical procedures in a text, using language that pertains to time, sequence, and cause/effect.	3.14. Use a timeline to analyze connections among historical events, including how human settlement and movement impacted diverse groups of people.	The MultiSemiotic audio mode (Karkar-Esperat, 2025) refers to using different genres of music (hip-hop that connects with history and culture, country music, mariachi), voice, and tone (see also Mills et al., 2016; Ramjattan, 2019) and folk music (lyrics and rhyme and rhythm).
	Fourth Grade	
CCSS.ELA-LITERACY. RL.3.4 Determine the meaning of general academic and domain-specific words and phrases in a text relevant to a grade 3 topic or subject area.	4.3. Cite evidence that supports a response to supporting or compelling questions.	
	4.4. Construct responses to compelling questions using reasoning, examples, and relevant details.	

Self-Discovery Through the Audio Mode ♦ 155

CCSS.ELA-LITERACY.SL.3.5 Create engaging audio recordings of stories or poems that demonstrate fluid reading at an understandable pace; add visual displays when appropriate to emphasize or enhance certain facts or details. CCSS.ELA-LITERACY.W.3.6 With guidance and support from adults, use technology to produce and publish writing (using keyboarding skills) as well as to interact and collaborate with others. **Fourth Grade** CCSS.ELA-LITERACY.RL.4.4 Determine the meaning of words and phrases as they are used in a text, including those that allude to significant characters found in mythology (e.g., Herculean). CCSS.ELA-LITERACY.SL.4.3 Paraphrase portions of a text read aloud or information presented in diverse media and formats, including visually, quantitatively, and orally.	4.26. Explain connections among historical contexts and people's perspectives at the time. **Fifth Grade** 5.3. With support, identify primary and secondary sources and determine their credibility. 5.4. Identify evidence that draws information from multiple perspectives and sources in response to a compelling question. 5.30. Demonstrate knowledge of family history, culture, and past contributions of people in their main identity groups.

(Continued)

Common Core Standards for 3rd–5th Grades	Social Studies Standards for 3rd–5th Grade	Pedagogical Holistic Model of New Literacies
CCSS.ELA-LITERACY.SL.4.5. Add audio recordings and visual displays to presentations when appropriate to enhance the development of main ideas or themes. CCSS.ELA-LITERACY.W.4.6 With some guidance and support from adults, use technology, including the Internet, to produce and publish writing as well as to interact and collaborate with others; demonstrate sufficient command of keyboarding skills to type a minimum of one page in a single sitting. **Fifth Grade** CCSS.ELA-LITERACY.RL.5.4 Determine the meaning of words and phrases as they are used in a text, including figurative language such as metaphors and similes. CCSS.ELA-LITERACY.RI.5.3 Explain the relationships or interactions between two or more individuals, events, ideas, or concepts in a historical, scientific, or technical text based on specific information in the text.		

CCSS.ELA-LITERACY.RI.5.4
Determine the meaning of general academic and domain-specific words and phrases in a text relevant to a grade 5 topic or subject area.

CCSS.ELA-LITERACY.SL.5.5
Summarize the points a speaker makes and explain how each claim is supported by reasons and evidence.

CCSS.ELA-LITERACY.W.5.6
Include multimedia components (e.g., graphics, sound) and visual displays in presentations when appropriate to enhance the development of main ideas or themes.

References

Karkar-Esperat, T. (2019). *Assessing preservice teachers' knowledge of new literacies* [Doctoral dissertation, Texas Tech University]. Texas Tech University Archive.

Karkar-Esperat, T. M. (2025). Multiliteracies for Multilingual Learners: The MultiSemiotic Architecture Framework. *International Journal of Bilingual Education and Bilingualism. 28*(2), 117–134. https://doi.org/10.1080/13670050.2024.2409120

Mills, K. A., J. Davis-Warra, M. Sewell, and M. Anderson. (2016) "Indigenous Ways with Literacies: Transgenerational, Multimodal, Placed and Collective." *Language and Education* 30 (1): 1–21. https://doi.org/10.1080/09500782.2015.1069836

National Governors Association Center for Best Practices, & Council of Chief State School Officers. (2010). *Common Core State Standards for English language arts & literacy in history/social studies, science, and technical subjects*. Washington, DC: Authors. https://www.corestandards.org/ELA-Literacy/

New Mexico Public Education Department. (2021). *New Mexico social studies standards*. https://webnew.ped.state.nm.us/bureaus/literacy-humanities/social-studies/

New London Group (1996). "A Pedagogy of Multiliteracies: Designing Social Futures." *Harvard Educational Review 66*(1), 60–92. https://doi.org/10.17763/haer.66.1.17370n67v22j160u

Ramjattan, V. A. (2019). "Raciolinguistics and the Aesthetic Labourer." *Journal of Industrial Relations* 61 (5): 726–738. https://doi.org/10.1177/0022185618792990

Instructional Materials Used with Students
Lesson Title: A MultiSemiotic Music Approach: Hip-Hop

Language Objectives (for Students)
- To determine the meaning of words and phrases used in hip-hop to describe reality.
- To write hip-hop lyrics and produce them using technology (i.e., sound, typed lyrics, a poster to present the lyrics, a cover using graffiti for their presentation).
- To explain connections among historical and cultural contexts of hip-hop music using the artists' background and inspiration.

These are activities that you can use during instruction for teaching your students:

- Reading about hip-hop music, how it is connected to history, culture, and identity, and how hip-hop has changed over time (using a timeline).
- Creating a graffiti for the hip-hop music (Eido1, n.d.) that students connect with or that they wrote. https://www.youtube.com/watch?v=60Gpi4lEOAs
- Gathering hip-hop music from different time periods through different artists in a storyline. Students may add other elements not expressed that they want to include. Students will go deep on one period.
- Students presenting the lyrics on hip-hop music they practiced writing. You can differentiate the product by asking students to write lyrics of different lengths.

The social studies standards for this theme focus on identifying primary and secondary sources and determining their credibility, identifying evidence that draws information from multiple perspectives, and demonstrating knowledge of family history, culture, and past contributions of people in their main identity groups.

To connect with social studies, have students:

- provide context to their lyrics in terms of social, community, and personal concerns, and
- provide background of the hip-hop music they brought to class and research how the language use represents culture, history, and inspiration.
  - **Differentiation includes** vocabulary, visuals and supplementary materials, audio and visual, class discussion, drawing/visuals, modelling, online resources, and videos.

Reference

Eido1. (n.d.). *Step by step how to draw graffiti letters - Write HIP HOP in graffiti for beginners* [Video]. YouTube. https://www.youtube.com/watch?v=60Gpi4lEOAs

Modeled Lesson 3: Audio Knowledge
Lesson Title: A MultiSemiotic Music Approach: Folk Music

Lesson Overview

This lesson introduces the the MultiSemiotic audio approach: folk music. Music represents national identity and social and cultural aspects. You are going to learn how folk music is connected to cultural development and national identity (Ramadani, 2017) and how folk music is connected to poetry.

In the last module, you learned about customs and traditions and how they are significant parts of identity. You are encouraged to ask students to gather the folk music that they grew up listening to or that family members can identify with. Students are going to create a storyboard and present the information that they learned about folk music. The Common Core state standards are used to determine the meaning of words and phrases as they are used in a text. They will help interpret information presented in diverse media that reveal a human truth in rhyme and rhythm. Additionally, the standards guide you to analyze how visual and multimedia elements contribute to the meaning, tone, or beauty of a text. In this module, we use culture as a lens to explore topics.

Keep in mind this is a lesson in which you could integrate reading, listening, and speaking language skills. There are some TESOL strategies used in the module. The readings give you the how and the why for teaching folk music, and they give you good background on the teaching skills that help you introduce folk music.

The example lesson that follows is guided by the International Literacy Standards for teacher preparation in literacy, the NCTE/IRA standards for English language arts, the Common Core Standards for English language arts, and social studies standards. Following this, activities for before, during, and after the lesson are presented that you can use to teach critical literacy, translanguaging, and multiliteracies. Opportunities are also presented in the lesson to guide your third- to fifth-grade students to use this approach.

Journaling: This is a documentation of your learning journey and will be used to evaluate the effectiveness of this learning process.

Start writing about your resources, especially any material that can introduce folk music. Record your thought process as you read the modules. Consider how the information presented makes you think about your teaching of multilingual students in terms of content and teaching strategies.

Learning Outcomes for Teachers

After studying this chapter, you should be able to:

- Connect poetry to folk music.
- Create a model using a storyboard that represents the different aspects of folk music.
- Gather and organize the folk music students have brought to the classroom.
- Highlight the connection between folk music and folk culture, and humanity in general.
- Revisit the standards that focus on language in relation to folk music based on the grade level being taught.
- Provide students with texts that help them learn about folk music.
- Support students to create an understanding of how they can preserve their culture using folk music.
- Provide students with rich reading and language experiences.
- Engage in meaning-making using multiliteracies.
- Use the Multisemiotic audio approach to create a learning product for your students.
- Complete a reflection on the module.
- Scaffold your third- fifth-grade learners to complete the process.

TESOL Standards (for teachers, TESOL International Association, 2018)

- **1c.** Candidates demonstrate knowledge of language processes (e.g., interlanguage and language progressions) to facilitate and monitor ELLs' language learning in English.

- **1d.** Candidates apply knowledge of English academic language functions, learning domains, content-specific language anddiscourse structures, and vocabulary to promote ELLs' academic achievement across content areas.
- **2a.** Candidates demonstrate knowledge of how dynamic academic, personal, familial, cultural, and social contexts, including sociopolitical factors, impact the education of ELLs.
- **2b.** Candidates demonstrate knowledge of research and theories of cultural and linguistic diversity and equity that promote academic and social language learning for ELLs.
- **2c.** Candidates devise and implement methods to understand each ELL's academic characteristics, including background knowledge, educational history, and current performance data, to develop effective, individualized instructional and assessment practices for their ELLs.
- **2d.** Candidates devise and implement methods to learn about personal characteristics of the individual ELL (e.g., interests, motivations, strengths, needs) and their family (e.g., language use, literacy practices, circumstances) to develop effective instructional practices.
- **2e.** Candidates identify and describe the impact of his/her identity, role, cultural understandings, and personal biases and conscious knowledge of US culture on his/her interpretation of the educational strengths and needs of individual ELLs and ELLs in general.
- **3a.** Candidates plan for culturally and linguistically relevant, supportive environments that promote ELLs' learning. Candidates design scaffolded instruction of language and literacies to support standards and curricular objectives for ELLs in the content areas.
- **3b.** Candidates instruct ELLs using evidence-based, student-centered, developmentally appropriate interactive approaches.
- **3c.** Candidates adjust instructional decisions after critical reflection on individual ELLs' learning outcomes in both language and content.

- **3d.** Candidates plan strategies to collaborate with other educators, school personnel, and families in order to support their ELLs' learning of language and literacies in the content areas.
- **3e.** Candidates use and adapt relevant materials and resources, including digital resources, to plan lessons for ELLs, support communication with other educators, school personnel, and ELLs and to foster student learning of language and literacies in the content areas.
- **4b.** Candidates demonstrate understanding of classroom-based formative, summative, and diagnostic assessments scaffolded for both English language and content assessment. Candidates determine language and content learning goals based on assessment data.
- **5a.** Candidates demonstrate knowledge of effective collaboration strategies in order to plan ways to serve as a resource for ELL instruction, support educators and school staff, and advocate for ELLs.
- **5c.** Candidates practice self-assessment and reflection, make adjustments for self-improvement, and plan for continuous professional development in the field of English language learning and teaching.

Language Objectives (for Students)

- To analyze folk music lyrics.
- To write folk music on a storyboard.
- To state the folk music lyrics accurately.

Guiding Questions

1. What folk songs are common in your state?
2. How do folk songs reflect culture and human activity?
3. How is language used to represent culture?
4. How can you connect the teaching of poetry to folk music?
5. How can we instill in students their cultural values, and how they can protect their cultural heritage through folk music?

6. How can you help students connect with their culture through music?
7. How can you be culturally responsive to your students' needs using music?
8. How does folk music shine a light on other cultures within New Mexico and United States?

Preview the Reading

Music is a way to celebrate your students' cultures. It helps students in sharing their voice, heritage, and story through music. Folk music involves all the language skills; it supports student language development, expands vocabulary knowledge, and supports their social and emotional growth. Through folk songs, students learn about culture and history. It is an engaging approach that supports students learning.

Pre-Class Preparation Activities for Teachers
Read

- Think of the tools (i.e., audiovisuals) you have available to teach a lesson on folk music. What theme would you teach? What activities would you use? Please discuss them in your journal.
- Read an article about the history of music and how folk music was developed in different parts of the world (Belaiev, 1965): Folk Music and the History of Music. https://www.jstor.org/stable/901408
- According to Lynne Robinson of *Taos News*, "Folk Music truly is an oral tradition with its own lexicon; carrying the stories and secrets of centuries, oral histories passed down through generations." Folk music is connected to different regions and groups. Read "Ritual & Folk Music" of Northern New Mexico at MRM (Robinson, 2022). https://www.taosnews.com/tempo/music/ritual-folk-music-of-northern-new-mexico-at-mrm/article_6fcbe104-ca53-11ec-859f-2b9b82dd73c3.html

- "New Mexican folk music is regaining its traction, though it remains the least known type of the Hispano music. Not many people know that New Mexico has its own genre of music," says Lillia McEnaney. This short article gives you more background about folksongs in NM and celebrating folk music in NM. Read Celebrating the Hispano Folk Music Traditions of New Mexico (McEnaney, 2019). https://hyperallergic.com/534912/celebrating-the-hispano-folk-music-traditions-of-new-mexico/
- This article explains how folk songs are connected to language: Folk Songs as a Language Experience (Martin, 1981). How can you integrate folk songs into your curriculum? https://www.jstor.org/stable/41961304
- These are resources that you could use to teach your third- to fifth -grade students about history and culture in NM
  - Folk Songs (Songs for Teaching, n.d.) https://www.songsforteaching.com/folk/
  - Pop Goes the Weasel | Classic Folk Songs for Kids (The Secret Mountain, 2021) https://www.youtube.com/watch?v=K0gPNii3KNA
  - Introduction to Folk Songs (Music with Meg., 2021) https://www.youtube.com/watch?v=s6dOpytOfxs

These are activities that you can use during instruction for teaching your students:

- Reading about folk music.
- Creating a storyboard.
- Gathering folk music from families.
- Students presenting the folk music that they brought to class.

The social studies standards for this theme focus on students giving a background of the folk music they brought to class and researching how the language represents cultural heritage.

Thought Questions
1. How have you used any module material in your planning, and instruction?
2. How were you able to connect to your students?
3. What supported your learning?
4. What could be changed to support your learning?
5. Would you consider teaching about folk music? In what ways will you do that? Please explain and be specific.
6. What other standards would you consider using to teach a lesson on folk music/folk songs?

References

Belaiev, V. (1965). Folk music and the history of music. *Studia Musicologica Academiae Scientiarum Hungaricae, 7*(Fasc. 1/4), 19–23. https://www.jstor.org/stable/i237242

Martin, R. J. (1981). Folk songs as a language experience. *Language Arts, 58*(3), 326–329.

McEnaney, L. (2019, December 25). *Celebrating the Hispano folk music traditions of New Mexico*. Hyperallergic. https://hyperallergic.com/534912/celebrating-the-hispano-folk-music-traditions-of-new-mexico/

Music With Meg. (2021, February 8). *Introduction to folk songs!! [Video]*. YouTube. https://www.youtube.com/watch?v=s6dOpytOfxs

Ramadani, I. (2017). The Importance of Music in the Development of the Child. *International Advisory Board, 20*, 303.

Robinson, L. (2022, May 6). "Ritual & folk music" of Northern New Mexico at MRM. *Taos News*. https://www.taosnews.com/tempo/music/ritual-folk-music-of-northern-new-mexico-at-mrm/article_6fcbe104-ca53-11ec-859f-2b9b82dd73c3.html

Songs for Teaching (n.d.). *American and multicultural folk song lyrics*. https://www.songsforteaching.com/folk/

TESOL International Association. (2018). *Standards for initial TESOL Pre-K–12 teacher preparation programs*. https://www.tesol.org/media/v33fewo0/2018-tesol-teacher-prep-standards-final.pdf

The Secret Mountain. (2021, December 2). *Pop goes the weasel|Classic folk songs for kids [Video]*. YouTube. https://www.youtube.com/watch?v=K0gPNii3KNA

Lesson Title: A MultiSemiotic Music Approach: Folk Music. A MultiSemiotic Music Approach: Folk Music. A MultiSemiotic Music Approach: Folk Music (Karkar-Esperat, 2019; National Governors Association Center for Best Practices, & Council of Chief State School Officers, 2010; New Mexico Public Education Department, 2021)

Common Core Standards for 3rd–5th Grades	Social Studies Standards for 3rd–5th Grade	Pedagogical Holistic Model of New Literacies
Third Grade	**Third Grade**	The audio mode, according to the New London Group (1996), focuses on concepts such as music and "the employment of any sound effect to support student learning." The pedagogical holistic model of new literacies uses words like 'theater,' different types of audio,' 'singing,' 'dialogue,' and 'monologue' to reflect different pedagogical approaches." (Karkar-Esperat, 2019)
CCSS.ELA-LITERACY.RL.3.2 Recount stories, including fables, folktales, and myths from diverse cultures; determine the central message, lesson, or moral and explain how it is conveyed through key details in the text.	3.14. Use a timeline to analyze connections among historical events, including how human settlement and movement impacted diverse groups of people.	
CCSS.ELA-LITERACY.RL.3.4 Determine the meaning of words and phrases as they are used in a text, distinguishing literal from nonliteral language.	**Fourth Grade** 4.9. Demonstrate understanding that state symbols, holidays, traditions, and songs represent various cultural heritages, natural treasures, and the democratic values of New Mexico.	
CCSS.ELA-LITERACY.SL.3.2 Determine the main ideas and supporting details of a text read aloud or information presented in diverse media and formats, including visually, quantitatively, and orally.	**Fifth Grade** 5.30. Demonstrate knowledge of family history, culture, and past contributions of people in their main identity groups.	The MultiSemiotic audio mode (Karkar-Esperat, 2025) refers to using different genres of music (hip-hop that connects with history and culture, country music, and mariachi), voice, and tone (see also Mills et al. 2016; Ramjattan, 2019) and folk music (lyrics and rhyme and rhythm).
Fourth Grade		
CCSS.ELA-LITERACY.RL.4.4 Determine the meaning of words and phrases as they are used in a text, including those that allude to significant characters found in mythology (e.g., Herculean).		

(Continued)

Common Core Standards for 3rd–5th Grades	Social Studies Standards for 3rd–5th Grade	Pedagogical Holistic Model of New Literacies
CCSS.ELA-LITERACY.SL.4.3 Paraphrase portions of a text read aloud or information presented in diverse media and formats, including visually, quantitatively, and orally. CCSS.ELA-LITERACY.L 4.5.A. Explain the meaning of simple similes and metaphors (e.g., as pretty as a picture) in context. **Fifth Grade** CCSS.ELA-LITERACY.RL.5.4 Determine the meaning of words and phrases as they are used in a text, including figurative language such as metaphors and similes. CCSS.ELA-LITERACY.RL.5.7 Analyze how visual and multimedia elements contribute to the meaning, tone, or beauty of a text (e.g., graphic novel, multimedia presentation of fiction, folktale, myth, poem). CCSS.ELA-LITERACY.SL.5.3 Summarize the points a speaker makes and explain how each claim is supported by reason and evidence. CCSS.ELA-LITERACY.L.5.5A Interpret figurative language, including similes and metaphors, in context.		

References

Karkar-Esperat, T. (2019). *Assessing preservice teachers' knowledge of new literacies [Doctoral dissertation, Texas Tech University]*. Texas Tech University Archive.

Karkar-Esperat, T. M. (2025). Multiliteracies for multilingual learners: The multisemiotic architecture framework. *International Journal of Bilingual Education and Bilingualism. 28*(2), 117–134. https://doi.org/10.1080/13670050.2024.2409120

Mills, K. A., Davis-Warra, J., Sewell, M., & Anderson, M. (2016). Indigenous ways with literacies: Transgenerational, multimodal, placed and collective. *Language and Education 30*(1): 1–21. https://doi.org/10.1080/09500782.2015.1069836

National Governors Association Center for Best Practices, & Council of Chief State School Officers. (2010). *Common Core State Standards for English language arts & literacy in history/social studies, science, and technical subjects*. Washington, DC: Authors. https://www.corestandards.org/ELA-Literacy/

New Mexico Public Education Department. (2021). *New Mexico social studies standards*. https://webnew.ped.state.nm.us/bureaus/literacy-humanities/social-studies/

New London Group (1996). A pedagogy of multiliteracies: Designing social futures. *Harvard Educational Review 66*(1): 60–92. https://doi.org/10.17763/haer.66.1.17370n67v22j160u

Ramjattan, V. A. (2019). Raciolinguistics and the Aesthetic Labourer. *Journal of Industrial Relations 61*(5), 726–738. https://doi.org/10.1177/0022185618792990

Instructional Materials Used with Students
Lesson Title: A MultiSemiotic Music Approach: Folk Music

Language Objectives (for students)
- To analyze the folk music lyrics.
- To write the folk music on a story board.
- To perform the folk music using accurate lyrics.

These are activities that you can use during instruction for teaching your students:
- ♦ Reading about folk music.
- ♦ Creating a storyboard.
- ♦ Gathering folk music from families.
- ♦ Students presenting the folk music that they brought to class.

The social studies standards for this theme focus on students learning the background of the folk music they brought to class and researching how the language use represents cultural heritage.

Differentiation includes paraphrasing, visuals and supplementary materials, audio and visual, class discussion, drawing/visuals, online resources, and text levels.

5

Self-Discovery Through the Spatial Mode

Connecting Local to Global

VIGNETTE

My teaching philosophy stems from the notion that teaching and learning need to be meaningful and personalized to students' contexts to foster greater engagement. Without engagement, learning does not occur. Students need to know that their teachers are compassionate and empathetic by their willingness to design lessons that connect with their students' identities regardless of their backgrounds. Spatial knowledge is a well-rounded approach that supports students' identities, emphasizing their sense of belonging, where they connect to their culture by reading about their place (including its economy, historical events, symbols, and landmarks) using various resources. Students need to develop a sense of place, starting with the classroom and connecting it to their community, region, state, and country, and the rest of the world. Symbols are signs of meaning in connection to state, community, and family (such as state flowers, songs, celebrations, and birds) and are connected to place. Symbols can be used as a strategy to connect with students and connect students to their place. The teacher guides students to reflect on their learning process and social interactions while learning about their community.

As an educator with an international background, I believe that students are citizens of the world, and they have to be immersed in their culture, language, and community to connect to global experiences, as they are the future of the world. Teachers must consider the student's language, place, and culture by focusing on symbols in connection to their lives. Learning must be meaningful, starting with what the students know and connecting to and sharing that knowledge. While the teachers are expected to follow the prescribed curriculum, they need to connect it to their students by focusing on where and how they belong and accepting the world's diverse views. Then, the prescribed curriculum will begin to make sense to students as they make that connection to other cultures.

After teachers implemented the module on spatial knowledge, one conveyed: "Spatial knowledge fosters cultural identity by having students use their environment to foster learning. Although some of our environments may be similar, they will have differences that will impact each student differently." Another teacher stated, "It is important for students to learn about spatial knowledge and learn how to be resourceful when it comes to using and learning about their environment." A different teacher expressed, "Spatial knowledge should be included in the curriculum because it offers a different way for students to respond creatively. I have noticed that students struggle with imagination and thinking creatively because of technology." Another teacher concluded, "Spatial knowledge goes a long way when you allow the kids to lead the change!"

Dear teachers, parents, guardians, and students,

Spatial knowledge is an inclusive term that includes history, symbols, landmarks, culture, economy, and the industry of a place (neighborhood, city, or state). You will learn how to teach students about place while connecting them to language and culture using multiliteracies. The examples are provided in the context of New Mexico. You can follow the same structure and apply it to your own context.

This chapter will guide you in learning about spatial semiotic. Why do we need to incorporate spatial knowledge in instruction? How can we teach bilingual and multilingual learners while fostering their connection to their culture? How can we teach students language skills (speaking, reading, listening, and writing) through making connections with the place they live? How can we preserve cultural heritage by centering spatial knowledge? How can you adapt this approach in the classroom?

What Is It About?

"The spatial mode comprises the 'ecosystem and geographic meanings' and 'architectonic meanings' (New London Group 1996). Using the four pedagogical approaches, the pedagogical holistic model of new literacies added words like 'field trip,' 'artifacts from home,' and 'personalized space' (names, posters of student interests, pictures, a place other than their desk, bean bags, blanket, pillow; Karkar-Esperat 2019). The *multisemiotic spatial* mode refers to perceptions, relationships between objects (Lazutina et al. 2016), awareness of human behavior and social space (Hall 1966; see also Panos 2021), philosophy of geographic location and cultures and traditions, and spatial knowledge." (Karkar-Esperat, 2025, p. 12)

Spatial Knowledge

Spatial knowledge has impacted many different aspects of the learning environment. The physical environment can shape cultural practices, behaviors, social interactions, and language use (Li & Gleitman, 2002). Some scholars have referred to the immediate context and setting for learning as *place-based education*, connecting learning and teaching experiences with community and society (Woodhouse & Knapp, 2000). Place-based education provides students with the knowledge and experiences to participate in learning as producers, not only consumers of knowledge (McInerney et al., 2011). Within this context, more emphasis is put on social and cultural aspects of education, focusing on students learning about their local area (Harrison, 2010; Payne & Wattchow, 2008; Woodhouse & Knapp, 2000). Connecting the curriculum to students' lived experiences creates meaningful and lasting experiences and active participation (Dahlgren & Szczepanski, 1998; Robertson, 2000). Educators cultivate identity-safe classrooms by celebrating students' unique identities and bridging students' lived experiences and curricular experiences (Hernández & Darling-Hammond, 2022).

The learning space can affect how multilingual students engage with their language and culture (Buckley et al., 2018). Responsive cultural environments can also enhance students' sense of belonging and obtain a more straightforward cultural response by integrating cultural symbols. Creating a positive and comfortable environment for students to learn educational information is essential. In what Comber (2016) describes as "pedagogies of belonging," she suggests a need "to draw attention to ways of designing and negotiating curriculum that is driven by the social goal (along with academic aims) of belonging" (p. 40). By doing so, students and teachers take on the role of researchers, posing meaningful questions about place and reflecting on their understanding of themselves, their surroundings, and the development of their communities.

Language, spatial mode, and culture should be linked in almost every educational setting, especially for bilingual students. One strategy to do this is mind maps. According to Grant and Archer (2019), when teachers teach spatial modes by using mind maps, they can help students visually organize and connect information, leading to comprehension and retention. Mind maps can also incorporate language elements and cultural symbols. This will make learning more relatable and engaging for students in their classroom. Some examples of cultural symbols in mind maps can be traditional stories (Jonuzi & Selvi, 2023). Language, culture, and spatial mode work together to create a rich human experience for students in the classroom, starting at a young age (Cummins et al., 2015).

Why Do We Need To Use It?

"A focus on 'place' provides the mechanism for incorporating cultural similarities and uniqueness" (Fukuda et al., 2010, p. 119). This helps in creating a positive and comfortable environment for students. Students encounter difficulties in staying engaged in the classroom. This module assumes that connecting place to student learning increases student engagement. Knowing that literacy is a social practice (Street, 1984), spatial knowledge is critical in students making connections and using their backgrounds to build on their understanding. Kawakami and Aton (2001) indicated that successful teachers integrate experience-based, authentic activities. The design or learning space can affect how multilingual students engage with their language and culture (Buckley et al., 2018). Adopting spatial knowledge in the curricula or teaching experiences can create responsive learning opportunities that can also enhance students' sense of belonging and help them obtain connect more easily with the learning materials.

Spatial Knowledge Strategies in An Elementary Class

Spatial representations include maps, charts, aerial photographs, satellite images, graphs, and diagrams (Castellar & Juliasz, 2018). Spatial knowledge is influenced by location and culture. Teachers could use various strategies to teach students about spatial knowledge, including visual maps, mind maps, or digital storytelling. Visual maps allow for personalized learning that can be adjusted based on students' needs (Müller, 2013). Buzan and Buzan (1996) stated that visual maps are a powerful tool for spatial awareness. Mind maps support teaching language skills such as grammar and vocabulary (Vaňková et al., 2019). Mind maps combine imagination and logic (Buzan, 2007) and illustrate connections among ideas (Randall, 2012). Mind maps have been used in foreign language teaching classrooms to build on background knowledge and assist in recalling vocabulary (Casco, 2009).

Scholars such as Wang (2019) have implemented mind maps in English grammar teaching and found mind mapping enhanced students' interest in learning and improved their ability to grasp grammar knowledge efficiently. When mind mapping was used to teach vocabulary in online courses in China, Jiang (2020) found that mind mapping helped students foster a deeper understanding of the material. Other spatial knowledge strategies such as digital storytelling can be used to connect students worldwide (de Jager et al., 2017). Digital storytelling is a method that is used to provide students, especially racialized students (such as immigrants and refugees), with opportunities to represent their culture and construct meaning reflective of their lives (Nair & Yunus, 2021). Digital storytelling is beneficial in personalizing students' experiences and increasing their motivation and engagement (Nair & Yunus, 2021).

Mental maps are used to develop concepts of city and landscape. They consider three representation dimensions: the area's size, distance, and direction. These three elements help create a sense of location and the arrangement of the landscape, allowing us to identify the place. Spatial thinking is a cognitive process that enables children to reflect and compare their position in the world (Castellar & Juliasz, 2018). A mental map can be an image of a real map and help communicate spatial information (Tuan, 1975). Students also use spatial knowledge in the STEM field. They solve scientific problems using the spatial properties of objects such as location, size, and volume. Students use visualizations like diagrams, maps, and graphs to analyze spatial relationships (Gagnier et al., 2022).

Conclusion

Spatial knowledge help students process and visualize information. It is the bridge between students' culture, language, and space. Spatial knowledge allows the students to connect with the material in a multidimensional way. It supports students in building their identities and embraces their self of belonging (Comber, 2016). Spatial knowledge allows students to think critically about their environment and compare to other environments (Castellar & Juliasz, 2018) using all the language skills.

How Can We Use It?

There are three simple steps that you need to follow:

1. Read the national standards that guided these two lessons.
2. Study the learning materials, which will give you background about the chapter examples.
3. Review the instructional materials, which could be used with students in language art and social studies.

The modeled lesson is on spatial knowledge.

Guiding Table for This Chapter

Transmultiliteracies Sustaining Pedagogy Approach (Karkar-Esperat & Stickley, 2024)	♦ The use of the language arts standards and social studies standards. ♦ Applications for language arts and social studies classrooms.
The Pedagogical Holistic Model of New Literacies (Karkar-Esperat, 2019)	♦ Gathering information using various sources such as readings and interviewing community members and experts. ♦ Critically analyzing the importance of place in students' culture, heritage, people, and language. ♦ Producing a multimodal poster using text and technology (adding visuals, audio, and digital sources). ♦ Writing about a place considering the economy, migration, businesses, historical events, cultural traditions, and heritages, representing different groups that have shaped students' identity, language, and culture using mind maps. ♦ Creating mental map of local landmarks and labeling that place's cultural or historical significance.

(Continued)

The Raciosemiotic Architecture Framework (Karkar-Esperat, 2023)	♦ Learning about the place they live in by gathering information using readings and interviewing community members and experts. ♦ Recognizing local, national, or international symbols by naming, drawing, and writing about them. ♦ Comparing students' cultures, history, economy, and so forth to that of other people. ♦ Synthesizing geographic factors that influence locations and settlements and how natural resources are used to meet the basic human needs. ♦ Engaging in meaning-making using multiliteracies.
The MultiSemiotic Architecture Framework (Karkar-Esperat, 2025)	**MultiSemiotic Spatial Knowledge: Social Space** "The *multisemiotic spatial mode* refers to perceptions, relationships between objects (Lazutina et al., 2016), awareness of human behavior and social space (Hall, 1966; see also Panos 2021), philosophy of geographic location and cultures and traditions, and spatial knowledge." (Karkar-Esperat, 2025, p. 12)

References

Buckley, J., Seery, N., & Canty, D. (2018). A heuristic framework of spatial ability: A review and synthesis of spatial factor literature to support its translation into STEM education. *Educational Psychology Review, 30*(3), 947–972.

Buzan, T. (2007). *Mentální mapování*. Portál

Buzan, T., & Buzan, B. (1996). *The mind map book: how to use radiant thinking to maximize your brain's untapped potential*. Plume.

Casco, M. (2009). *The use of "mind maps" in the teaching of foreign languages*. https://wlteacher.files.wordpress.com/2013/02/mindmaps.pdf

Castellar, S. M. V., & Juliasz, P. C. S. (2018). Mental map and spatial thinking. *Proceedings of the ICA* (Vol. 1, pp. 1–6). Copernicus GmbH.

Comber, B. (2016). The relevance of composing: Children's spaces for social agency. In A. Haas Dyson, Ed., *Child cultures, schooling, and literacy* (pp. 119–132). Routledge.

Cummins, J., Hu, S., Markus, P., & Kristiina Montero, M. (2015). Identity texts and academic achievement: Connecting the dots in multilingual school contexts. *TESOL Quarterly, 49*(3), 555–581. https://doi.org/10.1002/tesq.241

Dahlgren, L-O., & Szczepanski, A. (1998). *Outdoor education – Literary education and sensory experience. An attempt at defining the identity of outdoor education.* Linköping University, Kinda Education Centre.

de Jager, A., Fogarty, A., Tewson, A., Lenette, C., & Boydell, K. M. (2017). Digital storytelling in research: A systematic review. *Qualitative Report, 22*(10), 2548–2582. https://doi.org/10.46743/2160-3715/2017.2970

Epstein, S. E. (2009). *Behind the torchlight: A teacher's journey* (2nd ed.). Peter Lang.

Fukuda, K. L., Ah Sam, A. L., & Wang, J. (2010). Place: A springboard for learning and teaching about culture and literacy. *Hūlili: Multidisciplinary Research on Hawaiian Well-Being, 6,* 117–145.

Gagnier, K. M., Holochwost, S. J., & Fisher, K. R. (2022). Spatial thinking in science, technology, engineering, and mathematics: Elementary teachers' beliefs, perceptions, and self-efficacy. *Journal of Research in Science Teaching, 59*(1), 95–126. https://doi.org/10.1002/tea.21722

Harrison, S. (2010). "Why are we here?" Taking "place" into account in UK outdoor environmental education. *Journal of Adventure and Outdoor Learning,* 10(1), 3–18. https://doi.org/10.1080/14729671003669321

Grant, T., & Archer, A. (2019). Multimodal mapping: Using mind maps to negotiate emerging professional communication practices and identity in higher education. *South African Journal of Higher Education, 33*(1), 74–91. https://hdl.handle.net/10520/EJC-15980d1bab

Hall, E. T. (1966). *The Hidden Dimension* (Vol. 609). Doubleday

Hernández, L. E., & Darling-Hammond, L. (2022, October 18). *Creating identity-safe schools and classrooms.* Learning Policy Institute. https://learningpolicyinstitute.org/product/wce-identity-safe-schools-classrooms-report

Jiang, Y. (2020). Application of the mind map in learning English vocabulary. *Open Access Library Journal, 7,* 1–4. https://doi.org/10.4236/oalib.1106484

Jonuzi, E., & Selvi, H. Z. (2023). Enhancing map comprehension via symbols: Developing symbols for thematic maps based on children's cognitive development. *Necmettin Erbakan Üniversitesi Fen ve*

Mühendislik Bilimleri Dergisi, *5*(2), 88–110. https://doi.org/10.47112/neufmbd.2023.12

Karkar-Esperat, T. (2019). Assessing preservice teachers' knowledge of new literacies [Doctoral dissertation, Texas Tech University]. Texas Tech University Archive.

Karkar-Esperat, T. (2023). *Transparency in the Classroom: The Raciosemiotic Architecture Framework for Multilingual Learners*. Semiotics Society of America 2023 Yearbook.

Karkar-Esperat, T. & Stickley, Z. (2024). Revisioning Curriculum Through the Transmulitliteracies Sustaining Pedagogy Approach. *Social Sciences & Humanities Open*, *9*, 100826.

Karkar-Esperat, T. M. (2025). Multiliteracies for Multilingual Learners: The MultiSemiotic Architecture Framework. *International Journal of Bilingual Education and Bilingualism*. *28*(2), 117–134 https://doi.org/10.1080/13670050.2024.2409120

Kawakami, A. J., & Aton, K. K. (2001). Ke aÿo Hawaiÿi/critical elements of Hawaiian learning: Perceptions of successful Hawaiian educators. *Pacific Educational Research Journal*, *11*, 53–66.

Lazutina, T. V., I. N. Pupysheva, M. N. Shcherbinin, V. N. Baksheev, and G. V. Patrakova. (2016). "Semiotics of Art: Language of Architecture as a Complex System of Signs." *International Journal of Environmental and Science Education* 11 (17): 9991–9998.

Li, P., & Gleitman, L. (2002). Turning the tables: Language and spatial reasoning. *Cognition*, *83*(3), 265–294. https://doi.org/10.1016/S0010-0277(02)00009-4

McInerney, P., Smyth, J., & Down, B. (2011). "Coming to a place near you?" The politics and possibilities of critical pedagogy of place-based education. *Asia-Pacific Journal of Teacher Education*, *39*(1), 3–16. https://doi.org/10.1080/1359866X.2010.540894

Müller, H. (2013). *Myšlenkové mapy: jak zlepšit své myšlení, paměť, koncentraci a kreativitu* [Mind maps: How to improve your thinking, memory, concentration and creativity]. Grada.

Nair, V., & Yunus, M. M. (2021). A systematic review of digital storytelling in improving speaking skills. *Sustainability*, *13*(17), 1–15. https://doi.org/10.3390/su13179829

Panos, A. (2021). "Reading About Geography and Race in the Rural Rustbelt: Mobilizing dis/Affiliation as a Practice of Whiteness."

Linguistics and Education 65: 100955. https://doi.org/10.1016/j.linged.2021.100955

Payne, P., & Wattchow, B. (2008). Slow pedagogy and placing education in post-traditional outdoor education. *Australian Journal of Outdoor Education, 12*(1), 25–38. https://doi.org/10.1007/BF03401021

Randall, T. C. (2012). *The quick and easy guide to mind map: Improve your memory, be more creative, and unleash your mind's full potential.* Thomas C Randall.

Robertson, W. H. (2000). *The critical thinking curriculum model.* The University of New Mexico

Street, B. (1984). *Literacy in theory and practice.* Cambridge University Press.

Tuan, Y. F. (1975). Images and mental maps. *Annals of the Association of American geographers, 65*(2), 205–212.

Vaňková, P., Pítrová, L., & Skoupilová, R. (2019). *Jak uspořádávat informace: Pojmové a myšlenkové mapy ve vybraných předmětech na druhém stupni základní školy* [How to organize information: Concept and mind maps in selected subjects at the second level of primary school]. Univerzita Karlova.

Wang, L. (2019). Research on the application of the mind map in English grammar teaching. *Theory and Practice in Language Studies, 9*(8), 990–995. https://doi.org/10.17507/tpls.0908.15

Woodhouse, J., & Knapp, C. (2000). *Place-based curriculum and instruction: Outdoor and environmental education approaches.* ERIC Clearinghouse on Rural Education and Small Schools.

Lesson Title: A MultiSemiotic Spatial Approach: Connecting Local to Global (Council of Chief State School Officers, 2013; International Literacy Association, 2017; National Council of Teachers of English & International Reading Association, 2012)

NCTE / IRA Standards for the English Language Arts	International Literacy Association Standards	INTASC standards
Standard #1: Students read a wide range of print and non-print texts to build an understanding of texts, of themselves, and of the cultures of the United States and the world; to acquire new information; to respond to the needs and demands of society and the workplace; and for personal fulfillment. Among these texts are fiction and nonfiction, classic and contemporary works.	Standard #1: Foundational Knowledge Candidates demonstrate knowledge of the theoretical, historical, and evidence-based foundations of literacy and language and the ways in which they interrelate and the role of literacy professionals in schools.	Standard #1: Learner Development. The teacher understands how learners grow and develop, recognizing that patterns of learning and development vary individually within and across the cognitive, linguistic, social, emotional, and physical areas, and designs and implements developmentally appropriate and challenging learning experiences.
Standard #3: Students apply a wide range of strategies to comprehend, interpret, evaluate, and appreciate texts. They draw on their prior experience, their interactions with other readers and writers, their knowledge of word meaning and of other texts, their word identification strategies, and their understanding of textual features (e.g., sound-letter correspondence, sentence structure, context, graphics).	Standard #2: Curriculum and Instruction Candidates use foundational knowledge to critique and implement literacy curricula to meet the needs of all learners and to design, implement, and evaluate evidence-based literacy instruction for all learners.	Standard #2: Learning Differences. The teacher uses understanding of individual differences and diverse cultures and communities to ensure inclusive learning environments that enable each learner to meet high standards. Standard #3: Learning Environments. The teacher works with others to create environments that support individual and collaborative learning, and that encourage positive social interaction, active engagement in learning, and self motivation.

Self-Discovery Through the Spatial Mode ◆ 183

Standard #7: Students conduct research on issues and interests by generating ideas and questions, and by posing problems. They gather, evaluate, and synthesize data from a variety of sources (e.g., print and non-print texts, artifacts, people) to communicate their discoveries in ways that suit their purpose and audience.	Standard #3: Assessment and Evaluation Candidates understand, select, and use valid, reliable, fair, and appropriate assessment tools to screen, diagnose, and measure student literacy achievement; inform instruction and evaluate interventions; participate in professional learning experiences; explain assessment results and advocate for appropriate literacy practices to relevant stakeholders.	Standard #4: Content Knowledge. The teacher understands the central concepts, tools of inquiry, and structures of the discipline(s) he or she teaches and creates learning experiences that make the discipline accessible and meaningful for learners to assure mastery of the content.
Standard #8: Students use a variety of technological and information resources (e.g., libraries, databases, computer networks, video) to gather and synthesize information and to create and communicate knowledge.	Standard #4: Diversity and Equity Candidates demonstrate knowledge of research, relevant theories, pedagogies, essential concepts of diversity and equity; demonstrate and provide opportunities for understanding all forms of diversity as central to students' identities; create classrooms and schools that are inclusive and affirming; advocate for equity at school, district, and community levels.	Standard #5: Application of Content. The teacher understands how to connect concepts and use differing perspectives to engage learners in critical thinking, creativity, and collaborative problem solving related to authentic local and global issues.
Standard #9: Students develop an understanding of and respect for diversity in language use, patterns, and dialects across cultures, ethnic groups, geographic regions, and social roles.		Standard #6: Assessment. The teacher understands and uses multiple methods of assessment to engage learners in their own growth, to monitor learner progress, and to guide the teacher's and learner's decision making.
Standard #10: Students whose first language is not English make use of their first language to develop competency in the English language arts and to develop understanding of content across the curriculum.		

(Continued)

NCTE / IRA Standards for the English Language Arts	International Literacy Association Standards	INTASC standards
Standard #11: Students participate as knowledgeable, reflective, creative, and critical members of a variety of literacy communities. Standard #12: Students use spoken, written, and visual language to accomplish their own purposes (e.g., for learning, enjoyment, persuasion, and the exchange of information).	Standard #5: Learners and the Literacy Environment Candidates meet the developmental needs of all learners and collaborate with school personnel to use a variety of print and digital materials to engage and motivate all learners; integrate digital technologies in appropriate, safe, and effective ways; foster a positive climate that supports a literacy-rich learning environment. Standard #6: Professional Learning and Leadership. Candidates recognize the importance of, participate in, and facilitate ongoing professional learning as part of career-long leadership roles and responsibilities. Standard #7: Practicum/Clinical Experiences Candidates apply theory and best practice in multiple supervised practicum/clinical experiences.	Standard #7: Planning for Instruction. The teacher plans instruction that supports every student in meeting rigorous learning goals by drawing upon knowledge of content areas, curriculum, cross-disciplinary skills, and pedagogy, as well as knowledge of learners and the community context. Standard #8: Instructional Strategies. The teacher understands and uses a variety of instructional strategies to encourage learners to develop deep understanding of content areas and their connections, and to build skills to apply knowledge in meaningful ways.

References

Council of Chief State School Officers. (2013). *InTASC model core teaching standards and learning progressions for teachers 1.0: A resource for ongoing teacher development.* https://learning.ccsso.org/intasc-model-core-teaching-standards-and-learning-progressions-for-teachers

International Literacy Association (2017). *Standards for the preparation of literacy professionals 2017.* https://www.literacyworldwide.org/get-resources/standards/standards-2017

National Council of Teachers of English & International Reading Association (1996/2012). *Standards for the English language arts (Reaffirmed 2012).* National Council of Teachers of English. https://ncte.org/resources/standards/ncte-ira-standards-for-the-english-language-arts/

Modeled Lesson: Spatial Knowledge
Social Space: Learning Module

Lesson Overview
This lesson introduces an element of MultiSemiotic spatial knowledge.

"Spatial knowledge" in this module refers to connecting language to place and to cultures. Students learn about a place in connection to its history, industry, and economy, using a cultural and multiliteracies lens. Teachers have to make curricular decisions that shape the students' identities. Our identities are shaped by people, places, and concepts. Developing a sense of place increases a sense of belonging, because "place is part of our identity—that place shapes our identity" (Epstein, 2009, p. 30). The assumption in this module is that place is connected to culture and traditions and also impacts educational decisions. The classroom is the place where the students should feel they belong, both physically and emotionally. Students need to develop a sense of place starting with the classroom and connecting it to their community, region, state, country, and the world. Symbols (such as the state flower and state bird) are connected to place and could be used as a strategy to connect with students.

Through this module, students will use mind maps to organize their thoughts, create a mental map of landmarks, and apply the module material to their place (neighborhood, city or state), then compare it to other neighborhoods, cities, states, or countries. The teacher will provide some resources and model and guide students on how they can organize the learning materials and analyze them using the guided questions. Teachers are encouraged to follow the step-by-step process provided in the instructional materials. They should encourage students to gather materials that reflect the spatial knowledge of their community before they learn about another region, state, or country.

The Common Core state standards are used to build spatial knowledge using multimedia and other resources. In this professional learning experience, we use culture as a lens to explore topics.

Keep in mind that this is a lesson in which you could integrate reading, listening, writing, and speaking language skills. There are some TESOL strategies used in the module. The readings give you the explanation on how you can teach spatial knowledge.

The example lesson below is guided by the International Literacy Standards for teacher preparation in literacy, the NCTE/ILA standards for English language arts, the Common Core Standards for English language arts and social studies standards. Following this, activities for before, during, and after your lesson are presented that you can use to teach critical literacy, translanguaging, and multiliteracies. Opportunities are also presented in the lesson to guide your third–fifth graders to use this approach.

Journaling: This is a diary that will document your learning journey and will be used to evaluate the effectiveness of this process.

Think of the tools (i.e., audiovisuals) available to teach a lesson on spatial knowledge. What topics do you want to cover in your teaching? What activities could you use? How can you connect spatial knowledge to teaching listening, speaking, reading, and writing? Please discuss them in your journal.

A) Use the guiding questions in writing your response.
B) Start writing about the resources provided in the module.

C) Record your thought processes as you read the modules.
D) Consider how the presented information makes you think about your teaching of multilingual students in terms of content and teaching strategies.

Learning Outcomes for Teachers

After studying this module, you should be able to:

- Build a lesson or a unit on spatial knowledge.
- Gather and organize information about a place that the students have introduced to the classroom.
- Guide students to reflect on their learning processes and social interaction while learning about their community, region, state, other states, their country, and the world.
- Support students to create mind maps to assist them in connecting place to language, culture, and identity.
- Provide students with rich reading language experiences.
- Guide students to use resources to create a multimodal poster of other regions or states to represent their language and culture.
- Engage in meaning-making using multiliteracies.
- Use the MultiSemiotic spatial approach to create a learning product for your students.
- Complete a reflection on the module.
- Guide learners in third through fifth grade to learn and apply their knowledge of history.

TESOL Standards (for Teachers, TESOL International Association, 2018)

- **1a**. Candidates demonstrate knowledge of English language structures in different discourse contexts to promote acquisition of reading, writing, speaking, and listening skills across content areas. Candidates serve as language models for ELLs.
- **2a**. Candidates demonstrate knowledge of how dynamic academic, personal, familial, cultural, and social contexts, including sociopolitical factors, impact the education of ELLs.

- **2d.** Candidates devise and implement methods to learn about personal characteristics of the individual ELL (e.g., interests, motivations, strengths, needs) and their family (e.g., language use, literacy practices, circumstances) to develop effective instructional practices.
- **2e.** Candidates identify and describe the impact of his/her identity, role, cultural understandings, and personal biases and conscious knowledge of US culture on his/her interpretation of the educational strengths and needs of individual ELLs and ELLs in general.
- **3a.** Candidates plan for culturally and linguistically relevant, supportive environments that promote ELLs' learning. Candidates design scaffolded instruction of language and literacies to support standards and curricular objectives for ELLs in the content areas.
- **3b.** Candidates instruct ELLs using evidence-based, student-centered, developmentally appropriate interactive approaches.
- **3c.** Candidates adjust instructional decisions after critical reflection on individual ELLs' learning outcomes in both language and content.
- **3e.** Candidates use and adapt relevant materials and resources, including digital resources, to plan lessons for ELLs, support communication with other educators, school personnel, and ELLs and to foster student learning of language and literacies in the content areas.
- **5a.** Candidates demonstrate knowledge of effective collaboration strategies in order to plan ways to serve as a resource for ELL instruction, support educators and school staff, and advocate for ELLs.

Language Objectives (for Students)
1. To read about the place (community, region, state, other states, and the world), economy, migration, historical events, symbols, and landmarks using various resources.
2. To create a mental map of landmarks in Roswell and New Mexico at large and label that place's cultural or historical significance.

3. To recognize local, national, or international symbols by naming, drawing, and writing about them.
4. To gather information using various sources such as readings and interviewing community members and experts.
5. To write about a place considering the economy, migration, businesses, historical events, cultural traditions, and heritage representing different groups in shaping their identity, language, and culture using mind maps.
6. To produce a multimodal poster using text and technology (adding visuals, audio, and digital sources).
7. To present the project to other students.

Guiding Questions
1. How can we teach students about place while connecting them to culture? What topics and materials would you use?
2. How can we preserve historical landmarks and cultural heritage through teaching students about community, region, city, or state as well as its economy, centering spatial knowledge?
3. How can we teach students language skills (speaking, reading, listening, and writing) through connecting with the place and people?
4. What resources are provided in the classroom that support students learning about their surroundings?
5. How do these connections support multilingual and bilingual student learning?
6. How do industrial and economic changes affect the area students live in?
7. How can students in New Mexico connect to people around the country or outside the United States?
8. How is space connected to culture and traditions?
9. What activities could be used to understand how identity is shaped by land and space?
10. How can you be culturally responsive to your students' needs, focusing on spatial knowledge in the classroom?

Preview the Reading
The readings cover different aspects of spatial knowledge by first considering how to build a safe and inclusive classroom. Some

readings provide background information on Roswell, farming, industry, and landmarks. Place-based learning occurs as teachers assist students in the construction of spatial knowledge. A variety of strategies are provided to help students create a multimodal poster.

Pre-Class Preparation Activities for Teachers
Read

1. Readings about Roswell and its spatial community: Historically Speaking: Early Roswell farming and ranching industry (Stock, 2021) https://www.rdrnews.com/arts_and_entertainment/vision/historically-speaking-early-roswell-farming-and-ranching-industry/article_0ff0d3e8-0f56-5cd7-bc78-d0f5f593bb71.html
   - Encyclopedia of the Great Plains: Roswell New Mexico (Wishart, n.d.):
     https://plainshumanities.unl.edu/encyclopedia/doc/egp.ct.044.html
2. Roswell landmarks (Tripadvisor, n.d.):
   - https://www.tripadvisor.com/Attractions-g47182-Activities-c47Roswell_New_Mexico.html
   - https://www.touropia.com/best-things-to-do-in-roswell-nm/ (Gambetta, 2024)
3. "Drawing on the work of Jean Piaget, Gandy (2007) suggests that children begin developing their sense of place during early childhood. Equipped with curiosity and their five senses, young children explore and manipulate materials in their environment to understand the world around them (Brillante & Mankiw, 2015, p. 2)."
   - A Sense of place: Human Geography in the early childhood classroom (Brillante & Mankiw, 2015) https://www.naeyc.org/resources/pubs/yc/jul2015/sense-of-place-human-geography
4. Identity-safe classrooms are integral to the students' success and allow them to develop a sense of spatial knowledge.

- Creating Identity-Safe Schools and Classrooms (Hernandez & Darling-Hammond, 2022) https://learningpolicyinstitute.org/product/wce-identity-safe-schools-classrooms-report

Listen

- Creating a mind map after gathering information to plan the poster presentation
  Step-by-step directions for creating a mind map (MooMooMath and Science, 2017): https://www.youtube.com/watch?v=oY4sUQzXJ1g
- Creating meaningful experiences using place-based learning: Place-Based Learning: Using Your Location as a Classroom (Edutopia, 2015) https://www.edutopia.org/video/place-based-learning-using-your-location-classroom/
- A song that can be used with kindergarteners that focuses on land:
  This Land Is Your Land Children's Book by Woody Guthrie | Read Aloud Singalong Music for Kids (Paper Begg Band, 2023) https://www.youtube.com/watch?v=8Dn4XZqRAck

Multimodal posters: How to Create a Multimodal Poster
- Multimodal posters and alternative assignments (University of Alabama-Birmingham, 2023): https://guides.library.uab.edu/multimodal/posters
- Basics of multimodal posters (Purdue University, n.d.): https://www.cla.purdue.edu/academic/english/icap/techmentor/icap-technology-pages/multimodal-projects.html
- Glogster (Sheilaopsal, n.d.): https://www.livebinders.com/play/play?id=30957

Children's Books That Foster a Sense of Place
- *Alphabet City* (1999), by Stephen T. Johnson
- *Around the Pond: Who's Been Here?* (1996), by Lindsay Barrett George

- *Buenas Noches Luna* (2006), by Margaret Wise Brown, illus. by Clement Hurd (Spanish language version of *Goodnight Moon*)
- *Come On, Rain!* (1999), by Karen Hesse, illus. by Jan J. Muth
- *Flower Garden* (2000), by Eve Bunting, illus. by Kathryn Hewitt
- *In the Woods: Who's Been Here?* (1998), by Lindsay Barrett George
- *Listen to the City* (2001), by Rachel Isadora Nana in the City (2014) by Lauren Castillo
- *Sam and Dave Dig a Hole* (2014) by Mac Barnett, illus. by Jon Klassen
- *Tap Tap Boom Boom* (2014) by Elizabeth Bluemie, illus. by G. Brian Karas
- *Tar Beach* (1996), by Faith Ringold
- *The Bus for Us* (2013), by Suzanne Bloom
- *The Green Line* (2014), by Polly Farquharson
- *The Listening Walk* (1993), by Paul Showers, illus. by Aliki
- *The Snowy Day* (1976), by Ezra Jack Keats
- *Wave* (2008) by Suzy Lee

These Are Activities That You Can Use During Instruction For Teaching Your Students

- **Home**: Students think of a place they would like to go to. Ask them to create a mental map and provide details about what makes this place special.
- Students examine the cultural significance of that place and how it could be connected to a community, region, state, other states, and the world.
- **Local**: Students gather information about New Mexico or any other state using various resources.
- Students learn about the place they live in by gathering information using readings and interviewing community members and experts. Topics could be Roswell dairy farming, economy, migration, businesses, historical events, cultural traditions, and heritage. Students reflect on how the information gathered has shaped their identity, language, and culture.

- **Local to Global**: Students gather information about local, national, or international symbols by naming, drawing, and writing about their cultural and historical significance.
- Students choose a country, state, or region using a US or world map or an almanac to learn about the place's economy, migration, businesses, historical events, cultural traditions, heritage, and the national or international symbols representing different groups in shaping their identity, language, and culture, applying the same steps mentioned above to learn about the new place.
- Students compare their cultures, history, economy, etc., to other people's using a Venn diagram.
- Students create a mental map to identify landmarks (social space) in regions, their state, neighboring states, or the world.
- Students read about geographic factors that influence locations and settlements and the ways that people use natural resources to meet their basic human needs.
- Students critically analyze the importance of place in their culture, heritage, people, and language by providing them with guiding questions.
- Students use mind maps to organize ideas about a topic they want to explore (history, culture, landmarks, economy, and industry).
- Students describe New Mexico's culture, language, and history and make connections to their identity.

The social studies standards for this theme focus on migration, exploring history and describing people groups' contributions to New Mexico cultures, and demonstrating knowledge of family history and culture and the past contributions of people in their main identity groups.

- To connect with social studies, have students provide knowledge through a multimodal poster about culture, industries, holidays, traditions, and environmental factors in New Mexico, specifically Roswell. This lesson could also be applied in national and international context.

Thought Questions
1. Why do you think spatial knowledge should be included in the curriculum?
2. How does learning about spatial knowledge foster cultural identity?
3. In what ways do you think researching spatial knowledge supports student learning?
4. After reading about spatial knowledge and reviewing the module materials, what resonated most with you? In what way will you incorporate the materials in your class?
5. The module covered the Common Core Standards focusing on all the language skills. How are you planning to incorporate them in your classroom?
6. How are you planning to teach about spatial knowledge in social studies using the standards provided?
7. What kinds of creativity (think about the modes of meanings that could be used) do you hope to discover through your students' responses and reactions?
8. Do you see any challenges in implementing this approach into your classrooms? Explain.
9. Any additional thoughts? Please share!

References

Brillante, P., & Mankiw, S. (2015, July). *A sense of place: Human geography in the early childhood classroom.* NAEYC. https://www.naeyc.org/resources/pubs/yc/jul2015/sense-of-place-human-geography

Edutopia. (2015, November 10). *Place-based learning: Using your location as a classroom* [Video]. YouTube. https://www.youtube.com/watch?v=Q3ij_dFpZgw

Epstein, S. E. (2009). *Behind the torchlight: A teacher's journey* (2nd ed.). Peter Lang.

Gambetta, J. (2024, May 4). *12 best things to do in Roswell, NM*. Touropia. https://www.touropia.com/best-things-to-do-in-roswell-nm/

Hernandez, L. E., & Darling-Hammond, L. (2022, October 18). *Creating identity-safe schools and classrooms*. Learning Policy Institute. https://learningpolicyinstitute.org/product/wce-identity-safe-schools-classrooms-report

Karkar-Esperat, T. (2019). Assessing preservice teachers' knowledge of new literacies [Doctoral dissertation, Texas Tech University]. Texas Tech University Archive.

Karkar-Esperat, T. M. (2025). Multiliteracies for Multilingual Learners: The MultiSemiotic Architecture Framework. *International Journal of Bilingual Education and Bilingualism. 28*(2), 117–134 doi.org/10.1080/13670050.2024.2409120

MooMooMath and Science. (2017, February 16). *Step by step directions for creating a mind map [Video]*. YouTube. https://www.youtube.com/watch?v=oY4sUQzXJ1g

Purdue University (n.d.) *Multimodal projects & digital composition tools*. Retrieved February 12, 2025, from https://www.cla.purdue.edu/academic/english/icap/techmentor/icap-technology-pages/multimodal-projects.html

Paper Bagg Band. (2023, October 6). *This land is your land children's book + song by Woody Guthrie | Read aloud singalong music for kids* [Video]. YouTube. https://www.youtube.com/watch?v=8Dn4XZqRAck

Robertson, W. H. (2000). *The critical thinking curriculum model*. The University of New Mexico.

Sheilaopsal. (n.d.). *Glogster – Your online poster maker*. LiveBinders. Retrieved February 13, 2025, from https://www.livebinders.com/play/play?id=30957

Stock, C. (2021, July 26). Historically speaking: Early Roswell farming and ranching industry. *Roswell Daily Record*. https://www.rdrnews.com/arts_and_entertainment/vision/historically-speaking-early-roswell-farming-and-ranching-industry/article_0fhttps://www.rdrnews.com/arts_and_entertainment/vision/historically-speaking-early-roswell-farming-and-ranching-industry/article_0ff0d3e8-0f56-5cd7-bc78-d0f5f593bb71.htmlf0d3e8-0f56-5cd7-bc78-d0f5f593bb71.html

Tripadvisor. (n.d.). *The best Roswell Sights & historical landmarks to visit (2024)*. Retrieved February 13, 2025, from https://www.tripadvisor.com/Attractions-g47182-Activities-c47-Roswell_New_Mexico.html

TESOL International Association. (2018). *Standards for initial TESOL Pre-K–12 teacher preparation programs*. https://www.tesol.org/media/v33fewo0/2018-tesol-teacher-prep-standards-final.pdf

University of Alabama-Birmingham. (2023, March 23). *Multimodal and alternative assignments: Tools: Posters*. https://guides.library.uab.edu/multimodal/posters

Wishart, D. J. (Ed.). (n.d.). Roswell, New Mexico. In *Encyclopedia of the Great Plains*. University of Nebraska–Lincoln. http://plainshumanities.unl.edu/encyclopedia/doc/egp.ct.044

Lesson Title: A MultiSemiotic Spatial Knowledge: Social Space (Karkar-Esperat, 2019, National Governors Association Center for Best Practices, & Council of Chief State School Officers, 2010; New Mexico Public Education Department, 2021).

Common Core Standards for 3rd–5th Grades	Social Studies Standards for 3rd–5th Grade	Pedagogical Holistic Model of New Literacies
Third Grade	**Third Grade**	"The spatial mode comprises the 'ecosystem and geographic meanings' and 'architectonic meanings' (New London Group 1996). Using the four pedagogical approaches, the pedagogical holistic model of new literacies added words like 'field trip,' 'artifacts from home,' and 'personalized space' (names, posters of student interests, pictures, a place other than their desk, bean bags, blanket, pillow; Karkar-Esperat 2019). The *multisemiotic spatial mode* refers to perceptions, relationships between objects (Lazutina et al. 2016), awareness of human behavior and social space (Hall, 1966; see also Panos 2021), philosophy of geographic location and cultures and traditions, and spatial knowledge." (Karkar-Esperat, 2025, p. 12)
CCSS.ELA-LITERACY. RI.3.7 Use information gained from illustrations (e.g., maps, photographs) and the words in a text to demonstrate understanding of the text (e.g., where, when, why, and how key events occur).	3.2. Use supporting questions to help answer the compelling question in an inquiry.	
	3.23. Identify and use a variety of digital and analog mapping tools to locate places.	
CCSS.ELA-LITERACY. SL.3.5 Create engaging audio recordings of stories or poems that demonstrate fluid reading at an understandable pace; add visual displays when appropriate to emphasize or enhance certain facts or details.	**Fourth Grade**	
	4.4. Construct responses to compelling questions using reasoning, examples, and relevant details.	
CCSS.ELA-LITERACY. W.3.8 Recall information from experiences or gather information from print and digital sources; take brief notes on sources and sort evidence into provided categories.	4.9. Demonstrate understanding that state symbols, holidays, traditions, and songs represent various cultural heritages, natural treasures, and the democratic values of New Mexico.	
CCSS.ELA-LITERACY. W.3.6 With guidance and support from adults, use technology to produce and publish writing (using keyboarding skills) as well as to interact and collaborate with others.		

(*Continued*)

Common Core Standards for 3rd–5th Grades	Social Studies Standards for 3rd–5th Grade	Pedagogical Holistic Model of New Literacies
Fourth Grade CCSS.ELA-LITERACY.RI.4.3 Explain events, procedures, ideas, or concepts in a historical, scientific, or technical text, including what happened and why, based on specific information in the text. CCSS.ELA-LITERACY.SL.4.5 Add audio recordings and visual displays to presentations when appropriate to enhance the development of main ideas or themes. CCSS.ELA-LITERACY.W.4.8 Recall relevant information from experiences or gather relevant information from print and digital sources; take notes and categorize information, and provide a list of sources. CCSS.ELA-LITERACY.W.4.7 With some guidance and support from adults, use technology, including the Internet, to produce and publish writing as well as to interact and collaborate with others; demonstrate sufficient command of keyboarding skills to type a minimum of one page in a single sitting.	**Fifth Grade** 5.2. Use supporting questions to help answer the compelling question in an inquiry. 5.27. Using a map, identify and locate the 50 states in the United States and know the capitals of each state along with the surrounding US territories.	

Fifth Grade

CCSS.ELA-LITERACY.RI.5.3
Explain the relationships or interactions between two or more individuals, events, ideas, or concepts in a historical, scientific, or technical text based on specific information in the text.

CCSS.ELA-LITERACY.SL.5.5
Explain the relationships or interactions between two or more individuals, events, ideas, or concepts in a historical, scientific, or technical text based on specific information in the text.

CCSS.ELA-LITERACY.W.5.8
Recall relevant information from experiences or gather relevant information from print and digital sources; summarize or paraphrase information in notes and finished work, and provide a list of sources.

CCSS.ELA-LITERACY.W.5.6
With some guidance and support from adults, use technology, including the Internet, to produce and publish writing as well as to interact and collaborate with others; demonstrate sufficient command of keyboarding skills to type a minimum of two pages in a single sitting.

References

Hall, E. T. 1966. *The Hidden Dimension* (Vol. 609). Doubleday.

Karkar-Esperat, T. (2019). Assessing preservice teachers' knowledge of new literacies [Doctoral dissertation, Texas Tech University]. Texas Tech University Archive.

Karkar-Esperat, T. M. (2025). Multiliteracies for Multilingual Learners: The MultiSemiotic Architecture Framework. *International Journal of Bilingual Education and Bilingualism. 28*(2), 117–134 doi.org/10.1080/13670050.2024.2409120

Lazutina, T. V., I. N. Pupysheva, M. N. Shcherbinin, V. N. Baksheev, & G. V. Patrakova. (2016). Semiotics of art: Language of architecture as a complex system of signs. *International Journal of Environmental and Science Education 11*(17), 9991–9998.

Panos, A. (2021). Reading about geography and race in the rural rust-belt: Mobilizing dis/affiliation as a practice of whiteness. *Linguistics and Education, 65*, 100955. https://doi.org/10.1016/j.linged.2021.100955

National Governors Association Center for Best Practices, & Council of Chief State School Officers. (2010). *Common Core State Standards for English language arts & literacy in history/social studies, science, and technical subjects.* Washington, DC: Authors. https://www.corestandards.org/ELA-Literacy/

New Mexico Public Education Department. (2021). *New Mexico social studies standards.* https://webnew.ped.state.nm.us/bureaus/literacy-humanities/social-studies/

New London Group (1996). "A Pedagogy of Multiliteracies: Designing Social Futures." *Harvard Educational Review 66*(1), 60–92. https://doi.org/10.17763/haer.66.1.17370n67v22j160u

Instructional Materials Used with Students

Lesson Title—A MultiSemiotic Spatial Approach: Social Space

Language Objectives (for students)

To read about a place (community, region, state, other states, and the world) and its economy, migration, historical events, symbols, and landmarks using various resources.

1. To create a mental map of landmarks in Roswell or New Mexico in general and label that place's cultural or historical significance.
2. To recognize local, national, or international symbols by naming, drawing, and writing about them.
3. To gather information using various sources such as readings and interviewing community members and experts.
4. To write about a place considering the ways its economy, migration, businesses, historical events, and cultural traditions, and the heritage of its different groups has shaped people's identity, language, and culture using mind maps.
5. To produce a multimodal poster using text and technology (adding visuals, audio, and digital sources).
6. To present the project to other students.

During instruction, these are activities that you can use for teaching your students:

- **Home:** Students think of a place they would like to go to, and they create a mental map and provide details about this place and what makes it special.
- Students examine the cultural significance of that place and how it is connected to a community, region, state, other states, and the world.
- **Local:** Students gather information about New Mexico or any other state using various resources.
- Students learn about the place they live in by gathering information using readings and interviewing community members and experts. Topics could be Roswell's dairy farming, economy, migration, businesses, historical events, cultural traditions, and heritage. Students reflect on how the information gathered shaped their identity, language, and culture.
- **Local to Global:** Students gather information about local, national, or international symbols by naming, drawing, and writing about their cultural and historical significance.

- Students choose a country, state, or region using a US or world map and learn about the place's economy, migration, businesses, historical events, cultural traditions, and heritage, and the national or international symbols representing different groups in shaping their identity, language, and culture, applying the same steps mentioned above to learn about the new place.
- Students compare their cultures, history, economy, and so forth to that of other people using a Venn diagram.
- Students create a mental map to identify landmarks (social space) in regions, states, neighboring states, or the world.
- Students read about geographic factors that influence locations and settlements and the ways that people use natural resources to meet their basic human needs.
- Students critically analyze the importance of place in their culture, heritage, people, and language.
- Students use mind maps to organize ideas about a topic they want to explore (history, culture, landmarks, economy, and industry).
- Students describe New Mexico (culture, language, and history) and make connections to their identity.

Aligning with the social studies standards (for students)

- Students demonstrate knowledge through a multimodal poster about the culture, industries, holidays, traditions, and environment of New Mexico. Their work could focus specifically on Roswell or could be applied in national and international context.
- Students will express a positive view of themselves while demonstrating respect and empathy for others.
- Students present the multimodal poster representing a state and country.

Differentiation includes the use of leveled text, visuals and supplementary materials, audio and visual supports, class discussion, drawings and visuals, online resources, and videos.

6

Self-Discovery Through the Gestural Mode

Examining Gestures in the Classroom

> **VIGNETTE**
>
> *Gestures describe personal identity. In our early years, we learned gestures before we learned language, responding to our parents' signals. As we got older, we understood that these gestures played a role in family dynamics, expressing emotions and strengthening connections. In the classroom, there are many different symbolic gestures that both the students and teachers bring to class. The teachers' body language is critical in the classroom—it may cue excitement for a new concept or intensity as the class digs further into a familiar topic. Gesture becomes a sentence without words. This term is often referred to as nonverbal communication, a term that I will be using.*
>
> *Gesture is further exploration for all students, especially multilingual classes, because it becomes a language on its own for all students. So why don't we incorporate gestures into the curriculum? As a bilingual teacher, I understood the value of connection across language, culture, and gestures. It becomes the universal language for all students at the same time. Gestures help the*

teacher to connect with students and their background knowledge. Our goal as teachers should be encouraging creativity and self-discovery through learning. Allowing students to explore gestures in various activities guides them to explore cultures, find themselves, and express themselves. It's a holistic approach that brings togetherness.

One of the in-service teachers who implemented this module shared, "I have found that adding gestures or movement when teaching helps me as I explain/teach and also helps my students remember information." Another teacher added, "It [gestural knowledge] opens the world to them [students] and gives them a heads up that just because we don't do something or act a certain way, doesn't mean that is what they grew up seeing—it teaches acceptance. Another teacher conveyed that gestural knowledge helped her: "We begin to understand the dynamics within families and appreciate the differences we see, and also, it helps us to see different perspectives and where certain gestures come from and how they can mean completely different things in certain cultures [other] than our own." A different teacher expressed, "It [spatial knowledge] helps kids understand and accept differences within families, cultures, and our world." Another teacher stated, "I believe that learning about gestural knowledge helps with cultural identity by providing insight on what gestures can be offensive to other cultures and learning the meanings behind them." Finally, a teacher noted, "This module was interesting for me and my class. We looked at the gestures we use and how they are the same and different depending on where they are being used. We talked about gestures, what they mean, and how they are used in Roswell and New Mexico."

Let's take learning to a different level!

Dear teachers, parents, guardians, and students,

Gestural knowledge in this module refers to nonverbal communication, which includes signs, logos, ads, exercises, expression, collaboration, and unity to support students' learning. Gestures are used to express meaning through body language. You will learn how to teach students about gestures while connecting the gestures to language and culture using multiliteracies. The examples are provided in the context of New Mexico, but you can follow the same structure and apply it to your own context.

This chapter will guide you in learning about gestural semiotics. Why do we need to incorporate gestural knowledge in instruction? What gestures are used in teaching students' languages and cultures? How can we teach students language skills (speaking, reading, listening, and writing) through connecting with gestures? How does the teacher's use of gestures support students' learning?

What Is It About?

"The gestural mode refers to behavior, physical movement, gestures, sensuality, feelings and effects, in addition to kinesics and proxematics (the New London Group, 1996). The pedagogical holistic model of new literacies used the four pedagogies and focused on words like 'body movements,' 'theater,' 'five senses,' 'eye contact,' and 'role play,' based on discussions with New Literacies experts (Karkar-Esperat, 2019). The *multisemiotic gestural* mode focuses on hand movement in connection to culture, history, and religion to refer to racial and religion equity, #BlackLivesMatter gestures, anti-/racism gestures, or gestures that convey diversity and inclusion, racial equality and social justice, and beliefs about racial discrimination (see Lemke et al., 2015), and gestural knowledge." (Karkar-Esperat, 2025, p. 11)

Gestural Knowledge

Gestures have been defined as body movements that communicate action or motion (Adler & Rodman, 2006; McNeil, 2005). They are nonverbal communication (McNeill, 1992) and are connected to spoken language (Antes, 1996). Gestures have been classified as emblems (symbols) and sign language (McNeil, 2005). Teachers use them frequently (Annisah, 2013). Teaching and learning in the classrooms require using gestures to communicate ideas. Gestures convey messages to explain how a symbol is connected to a concept (Flevares & Perry, 2001). They are cultural, and knowing the nonverbal cues across cultures is important. For instance, in the United States, nodding denotes agreement, and shaking one's head is associated with negativity. However, in the Bulgarian culture, nodding means no, and shaking your head means yes (Andonova & Taylor, 2012). Teachers use facial expressions, pointing, and nodding to allocate turns (Mortensen, 2006; Watanabe, 2016). They are an important part of the student–teacher relationship (Richmond, 2002) and increase the students' commitment level (Witt & Wheeless, 1999). Teachers who use body language enhance students' understanding, retention, and motivation (Hanif et al., 2014). There are many gestures within a culture that share a common meaning, which Peltier and McCafferty (2010) referred to as "gestures of identity." Such gestures are critical in "languaculture" (McCafferty & Rosborough, 2014) and are connected, nonverbal forms of communication.

A teacher uses various types of gestures, including (1) deictic gestures, which involve pointing to give directions or capture attention, pointing to content on the blackboard, pointing to the front of the classroom to refer to space, or pointing to students; (2) representational gestures, which imitate the shape or movement of an object, such as using your fingers to show a circle; (3) metaphoric gestures, which illustrate abstract ideas; (4) emblematic gestures, which are conventional gestures understood within a specific community or culture, such as waving hi; (5) beat gestures, which are repetitive movements used to emphasize a point, such as repeatedly tightening fist to indicate struggle (Liu et al., 2022; McNeill, 1992; Wang et al., 2004); (6) emotional gestures, which express emotions, such as happiness, anger, and puzzlement; and (7) evaluative gestures, which give feedback, indicate praise, or criticize (Liu et al., 2022).

Examples of How Gestures Have Been Used in the Classroom

In the L2 online classroom, teachers use gestures to prompt students' responses. One study found that the teacher provided explanations and created learning opportunities that were accessible to the entire class, particularly because the teacher's approach involved using hand gestures, such as thumbs up or thumbs down, to encourage student participation in responding to questions. They were mindful of adjusting the gestures based on the nature of the questions (Şimşek Tontuş & Kuru Gönen, 2025). In a study by Malabarba et al. (2022), gestures were used to establish an interactional space, supporting student participation and managing turn-taking during tutoring sessions.

Gestures serve as a mediating tool in L2 learning and development (Smotrova & Lantolf, 2013). In their study, teachers employed metaphoric and iconic gestures to support learners' visuals in the context of the words. McCafferty (2002) demonstrated that gestures improve comprehension in social interactions between native and non-native English speakers. McCafferty (2004) also discovered that various types of gestures, including representational gestures (such as iconic and deictic gestures) and beats, were used to encourage students to verbalize a vocabulary word when they hesitated. Similarly, Matsumoto and Dobs (2017) studied the effects of gestures on L2 learners' development of grammar concepts. Teachers used deictic and metaphoric gestures to make abstract concepts of the present tense concrete. Similarly, Tai and Khabbazbashi (2019) used metaphoric gestures to teach adverbs and found that metaphoric gestures in particular helped express time.

Gestural Strategies in an Elementary Class

Teachers use gestures to enhance students' learning experiences and participation. They strategically use gestures to highlight certain mathematic contributions (Alibali et al., 2019). In their teaching practices, teachers may imitate students' gestures (Arzarello et al., 2008) or modify them (Flood, 2018). Afdaliah (2022) studied teachers' gestures in EFL classrooms, noting that the teacher used hand gestures for management (pointing, clapping hands, knocking on the table, hitting the whiteboard), regulations (beckoning/inviting, pointing), instruction (numbering, nodding), and input (shaking head, holding out a hand when giving an example or illustrating). Teachers also used gestures accompanied with a smile to show affection and reward students. Other teachers used gestures to emphasize, complement, and repeat words. The goal of using gestures was to support students' learning (Afdaliah, 2022). A teacher may use gestures to facilitate turn-taking by pointing. Teachers also use gestures to enhance comprehension (Dargue & Sweller, 2018; Macoun & Sweller, 2016), assist with the recall of story events (Cook et al., 2010; Igualada et al., 2017; Zimmer et al., 2000), and support vocabulary acquisition (Mavilidi et al., 2015; Toumpaniara et al., 2015).

Conclusion

Gestures support multilingual classrooms. Teachers use gestures to support their instruction and the learning process. Gestures mediate L2 learning and development. L2 learners use gestural resources to facilitate their language development (Matsumoto & Dobs, 2017). Teachers can use different head and hand gestures in their teaching, such as pointing, illustrating, numbering, and beckoning. Gestures are used with all students to teach vocabulary, emphasize recalling information, and increase reading comprehension. Teachers should be mindful of the gestures they use with their students to ensure they are understood correctly and help build positive relationships.

How Can We Use It?

There are three simple steps that you need to follow:

1. Read the national standards that guided these two lessons.
2. Study the learning materials, which will give you background about the chapter examples.
3. Review the instructional materials, which could be used with students in language art and social studies.

The modeled lesson covers gestural knowledge.

Guiding Table for This Chapter the Modeled Lesson Uses the Gestural Approach

Transmultiliteracies Sustaining Pedagogy Approach	♦ The use of the language arts standards and social studies standards. ♦ Applications for language arts and social studies classrooms.
The Pedagogical Holistic Model of New Literacies(Karkar-Esperat, 2019)	♦ Reading about the topic using various resources. ♦ Using critical thinking skills to analyze a scene or character. ♦ Creating a poster of a local sign that represents a segment of a student's place/culture and interpreting the sign using the cultural and historical background of the sign. ♦ Choosing an activity that could include a cheerleading dance movement, line or square dance movement, or a type of exercise, and exploring the cultural and historical background associated with it. ♦ Explaining movements represented in the posters that calls for collaboration and group participation and expresses an idea
The Raciosemiotic Architecture Framework (Karkar-Esperat, 2023)	♦ Analyzing the power of words under the sign. ♦ Connecting gestures with students' identities considering the message and background. ♦ Gathering pictorial representations using various gestures that represent collaboration and unity. ♦ Discussing a logo, pictures, or illustrations considering context, time, culture, and gestures. ♦ Engaging in meaning-making using multiliteracies.
The MultiSemiotic Architecture Framework (Karkar-Esperat, 2025)	**A MultiSemiotic Gestural Mode: Examining Gestures in the Classroom** "The *multisemiotic gestural mode* focuses on hand movement in connection to culture, history, and religion to refer to racial and religion equity, #BlackLivesMatter gestures, anti-/racism gestures, or gestures that convey diversity and inclusion, racial equality and social justice, and beliefs about racial discrimination (see Lemke et al., 2015)" (Karkar-Esperat, 2025, p. 12).

References

Adler, R. B., & Rodman, G. (2006). *Understanding human communication*. Oxford University Press.

Alibali, M. W., Nathan, M. J., Boncoddo, R., & Pier, E. (2019). Managing common ground in the classroom: Teachers use gestures to support students' contributions to classroom discourse. *ZDM, 51*, 347–360. https://doi.org/10.1007/s11858-019-01043-x

Afdaliah, N. (2022). Teachers' gestures in EFL classroom. *Al-Lisan: Jurnal Bahasa (e-Journal), 7*(2), 182–197.

Andonova, E., & Taylor, H. A. (2012). Nodding in dis/agreement: A tale of two cultures. *Cognitive Processing, 13*(1), 79–82. https://doi.org/10.1007/s10339-012-0472-x

Annisah. (2013). *The analysis of nonverbal communication used by teacher in the classroom activities*. State University of Makassar.

Antes, T. A. (1996). Kinesics: The value of gesture in language and in the language classroom. *Foreign Language Annals, 29*(3), 311–320. https://doi.org/10.1111/j.1944-9720.1996.tb01255.x

Arzarello, F., Paola, D., Robutti, O., & Sabena, C. (2008). Gestures as semiotic resources in the mathematics classroom. *Educational Studies in Mathematics, 70*, 97–109. https://doi.org/10.1007/s10649-008-9163-z

Cook, S., Yip, T., & Goldin-Meadow, S. (2010). Gesturing makes memories that last. *Journal of Memory and Language, 63*(4), 465–475. https://doi.org/10.1016/j.jml.2010.07.002

Dargue, N., & Sweller, N. (2018). Not all gestures are created equal: The effects of typical and atypical iconic gestures on narrative comprehension. *Journal of Nonverbal Behavior, 42*, 327–345. https://doi.org/10.1007/s10919-018-0278-3

Flevares, L. M., & Perry, M. (2001). How many do you see? The use of non-spoken representations in first-grade mathematics lessons. *Journal of Educational Psychology, 93*(2), 330–345. https://doi.org/10.1037//0022-0663.93.2.330

Flood, V. J. (2018). Multimodal revoicing as an interactional mechanism for connecting scientific and everyday concepts. *Human Development, 61*, 145–173. https://doi.org/10.1159/000489493

Haneef, M., Faisal, M. A., Alvi, A. K., & Zulfiqar, M. (2014). The role of nonverbal communication in teaching practice. *Science International, 26*(1).

Igualada, A., Esteve-Gibert, N., & Prieto, P. (2017). Beat gestures improve word recall in 3- and 5-year-old children. *Journal of Experimental Child Psychology, 156*, 99–112. https://doi.org/10.1016/j.jecp.2016.11.017

Karkar-Esperat, T. (2019). Assessing preservice teachers' knowledge of new literacies [Doctoral dissertation, Texas Tech University]. Texas Tech University Archive.

Karkar-Esperat, T. (2023). Transparency in the Classroom: The Raciosemiotic Architecture Framework for Multilingual Learners. Semiotics Society of America 2023 Yearbook.

Karkar-Esperat, Tala Michelle. (Invited, 2024). "Multiliteracies in Teacher Education." In George Noblit (Ed.), *Oxford Research Encyclopedia of Education*. New York: Oxford University Press. doi:10.1093/acrefore/9780190264093.013.1890

Karkar-Esperat, T. M. (2025). Multiliteracies for Multilingual Learners: The MultiSemiotic Architecture Framework. *International Journal of Bilingual Education and Bilingualism. 28*(2), 117–134 doi.org/10.1080/13670050.2024.2409120

Lemke, J., Lecusay, R., Cole, M., & Michalchick, V. (2015). *Documenting and assessing learning in media-rich environments*. MIT Press and MacArthur Foundation.

Liu, Q., Zhang, N., Chen, W., Wang, Q., Yuan, Y., & Xie, K. (2022). Categorizing teachers' gestures in classroom teaching: From the perspective of multiple representations. *Social Semiotics, 32*(2), 184–204. https://doi.org/10.1080/10350330.2020.1722368

Macoun, A., & Sweller, N. (2016). Listening and watching: The effects of observing gesture on preschoolers' narrative comprehension. *Cognitive Development, 40*, 68–81. https://doi.org/10.1016/j.cogdev.2016.08.005

McNeill, D. (1992). *Hand and mind: What gestures reveal about thought*. University of Chicago Press.

Malabarba, T., Mendes, A. C. O., & De Souza, J. (2022). Multimodal resolution of overlapping talk in video-mediated L2 instruction. *Languages, 7*(2), 154. https://doi.org/10.3390/languages7020154

Matsumoto, Y., & Dobs, A. M. (2017). Pedagogical gestures as interactional resources for teaching and learning tense and aspect in the

ESL grammar classroom. *Language Learning, 67*(1), 7–42. https://doi.org/10.1111/lang.12181

Mavilidi, M.-F., Okely, A. D., Chandler, P., Cliff, D. P., & Paas, F. (2015). Effects of integrated physical exercises and gestures on preschool children's foreign language vocabulary learning. *Educational Psychology Review, 27*, 413–426. https://doi.org/10.1007/s10648-015-9337-z

McCafferty, S. G. (2002). Gesture and creating zones of proximal development for second language learning. *The Modern Language Journal, 86*(2), 192–203. https://psycnet.apa.org/doi/10.1111/1540-4781.00144

McCafferty, S. G. (2004). Space for cognition: Gesture and second language learning. *International Journal of Applied Linguistics, 14*(1), 148–165. https://doi.org/10.1111/j.1473-4192.2004.0057m.x

McCafferty, S. G., & Rosborough, A. (2014). Gesture as a private form of communication during lessons in an ESL-designated elementary classroom: A sociocultural perspective. *TESOL Journal, 5*(2), 225–246.

McNeill, D. (2005). *Gesture and thought*. University of Chicago Press.

Mortenson, S. T. (2006). Cultural differences and similarities in seeking social support as a response to academic failure: A comparison of American and Chinese college students. *Communication Education, 55*(2), 127–146.

New London Group (1996). "A Pedagogy of Multiliteracies: Designing Social Futures." *Harvard Educational Review* 66(1): 60–92. https://doi.org/10.17763/haer.66.1.17370n67v22j160u

Peltier, I. N., & McCafferty, S. G. (2010). Gesture and identity in the teaching and learning of Italian. *Mind, Culture, and Activity, 17*(4), 331–349.

Richmond, V. P. (2002). Teaching nonverbal immediacy. In J. L. Chesebro (Ed.), *Communication for teachers* (pp. 230). Allyn & Bacon.

Şimşek Tontuş, A., & Kuru Gönen, S. İ. (2025). Teachers' gestures in synchronous online language classrooms: Embodied elicitation strategies for student participation. *Social Semiotics*, 1–23. https://doi.org/10.1080/10350330.2024.2448007

Smotrova, T., & Lantolf, J. P. (2013). The function of gesture in lexically focused L2 instructional conversations. *The Modern Language Journal, 97*(2), 397–416. https://doi.org/10.1111/j.1540-4781.2013.12008.x

Tai, K. W. H., & Khabbazbashi, N. (2019). The mediation and organisation of gestures in vocabulary instructions: A microgenetic analysis of interactions in a beginning-level adult ESOL classroom. *Language and Education*, *33*(5), 445–468. https://doi.org/10.1080/09500782.2019.1596122

Toumpaniara, K., Loyens, S., Mavilidi, M., & Paas, F. (2015). Preschool children's foreign language vocabulary learning by embodying words through physical activity and gesturing. *Educational Psychology Review*, *27*, 445–456. https://doi.org/10.1007/s10648-015-9316-4

Wang, X. L., Bernas, R., & Eberhard, P. (2004). Engaging ADHD students in tasks with hand gestures: A pedagogical possibility for teachers. *Educational Studies*, *30*(3), 217–229. https://doi.org/10.1080/0305569042000224189

Witt, P. L., & Wheeless, L. R. (1999). Nonverbal communication expectancies about teacher and enrollment behavior in distance learning. *Communication Education*, *48*(2), 149–154. https://doi.org/10.1080/03634529909379162

Zimmer, H. D., Helstrup, T., & Engelkamp, J. (2000). Pop-out into memory: A retrieval mechanism that is enhanced with the recall of subject-performed tasks. *Journal of Experimental Psychology: Learning, Memory, and Cognition*, *26*(3), 658–670. https://doi.org/10.1037/0278-7393.26.3.658

Lesson Title: A MultiSemiotic Gestural Approach: Examining Gestures in the Classroom (Council of Chief State School Officers, 2013; International Literacy Association, 2017; National Council of Teachers of English & International Reading Association, 2012)

NCTE/IRA Standards for the English Language Arts	International Literacy Association Standards	INTASC standards
Standard #1: Students read a wide range of print and non-print texts to build an understanding of texts, of themselves, and of the cultures of the United States and the world; to acquire new information; to respond to the needs and demands of society and the workplace; and for personal fulfillment. Among these texts are fiction and nonfiction, classic and contemporary works.	Standard #1: Foundational Knowledge Candidates demonstrate knowledge of the theoretical, historical, and evidence-based foundations of literacy and language and the ways in which they interrelate and the role of literacy professionals in schools.	Standard #1: Learner Development. The teacher understands how learners grow and develop, recognizing that patterns of learning and development vary individually within and across the cognitive, linguistic, social, emotional, and physical areas and designs and implements developmentally appropriate and challenging learning experiences.
	Standard #2: Curriculum and Instruction Candidates use foundational knowledge to critique and implement literacy curricula to meet the needs of all learners and to design, implement, and evaluate evidence-based literacy instruction for all learners.	Standard #2: Learning Differences. The teacher uses understanding of individual differences and diverse cultures and communities to ensure inclusive learning environments that enable each learner to meet high standards.
Standard #3: Students apply a wide range of strategies to comprehend, interpret, evaluate, and appreciate texts. They draw on their prior experience, their interactions with other readers and writers, their knowledge of word meaning and of other texts, their word identification strategies, and their understanding of textual features (e.g., sound-letter correspondence, sentence structure, context, graphics).	Standard #3: Assessment and Evaluation Candidates understand, select, and use valid, reliable, fair, and appropriate assessment tools to screen, diagnose, and measure student literacy achievement; inform instruction and evaluate interventions; participate in professional learning experiences; explain assessment results and advocate for appropriate literacy practices to relevant stakeholders.	Standard #3: Learning Environments. The teacher works with others to create environments that support individual and collaborative learning, and that encourage positive social interaction, active engagement in learning, and self-motivation.

Standard #8: Students use a variety of technological and information resources (e.g., libraries, databases, computer networks, video) to gather and synthesize information and to create and communicate knowledge.

Standard #9: Students develop an understanding of and respect for diversity in language use, patterns, and dialects across cultures, ethnic groups, geographic regions, and social roles.

Standard #10: Students whose first language is not English make use of their first language to develop competency in the English language arts and to develop understanding of content across the curriculum.

Standard #11: Students participate as knowledgeable, reflective, creative, and critical members of a variety of literacy communities.

Standard #4: Diversity and Equity
Candidates demonstrate knowledge of research, relevant theories, pedagogies, essential concepts of diversity and equity; demonstrate and provide opportunities for understanding all forms of diversity as central to students' identities; create classrooms and schools that are inclusive and affirming; and advocate for equity at school, district, and community levels.

Standard #5: Learners and the Literacy Environment
Candidates meet the developmental needs of all learners and collaborate with school personnel to use a variety of print and digital materials to engage and motivate all learners; integrate digital technologies in appropriate, safe, and effective ways; and foster a positive climate that supports a literacy-rich learning environment.

Standard #4: Content Knowledge. The teacher understands the central concepts, tools of inquiry, and structures of the discipline(s) he or she teaches and creates learning experiences that make the discipline accessible and meaningful for learners to assure mastery of the content.

Standard #5: Application of Content. The teacher understands how to connect concepts and use differing perspectives to engage learners in critical thinking, creativity, and collaborative problem solving related to authentic local and global issues.

Standard #6: Assessment. The teacher understands and uses multiple methods of assessment to engage learners in their own growth, to monitor learner progress, and to guide the teacher's and learner's decision making.

(*Continued*)

NCTE/IRA Standards for the English Language Arts	International Literacy Association Standards	INTASC standards
Standard #12: Students use spoken, written, and visual language to accomplish their own purposes (e.g., for learning, enjoyment, persuasion, and the exchange of information).	Standard #6: Professional Learning and Leadership. Candidates recognize the importance of, participate in, and facilitate ongoing professional learning as part of career-long leadership roles and responsibilities Standard #7: Practicum/Clinical Experiences Candidates apply theory and best practice in multiple supervised practicum/clinical experiences.	Standard #7: Planning for Instruction. The teacher plans instruction that supports every student in meeting rigorous learning goals by drawing upon knowledge of content areas, curriculum, cross-disciplinary skills, and pedagogy, as well as knowledge of learners and the community context. Standard #8: Instructional Strategies. The teacher understands and uses a variety of instructional strategies to encourage learners to develop deep understanding of content areas and their connections and to build skills to apply knowledge in meaningful ways.

References

Council of Chief State School Officers. (2013). *InTASC model core teaching standards and learning progressions for teachers 1.0: A resource for ongoing teacher development.* https://learning.ccsso.org/intasc-model-core-teaching-standards-and-learning-progressions-for-teachers

International Literacy Association. (2017). *Standards for the preparation of literacy professionals 2017.* https://www.literacyworldwide.org/get-resources/standards/standards-2017

National Council of Teachers of English & International Reading Association. (1996/2012). *Standards for the English language arts (Reaffirmed 2012).* National Council of Teachers of English. https://ncte.org/resources/standards/ncte-ira-standards-for-the-english-language-arts/

Modeled Lesson: Gestural Knowledge
Gestural Knowledge: Learning Module

Lesson Overview
This lesson introduces an element of the MultiSemiotic gestural approach (Karkar-Esperat, 2025).

Gestural knowledge in this module refers to discovery through signs, logos, ads, exercise, expression, collaboration, and unity to support students' learning. Teachers use their hidden curriculum actively to support students. Nunan (1989) defined hidden curriculum as the verbal and nonverbal messages that convey messages about the teachers' attitudes and values beyond the curriculum. This chapter refers to the *Hidden Curriculum* for communication through body language and interactions.

Gestures are a tool to support students with nonverbal cues, for example, by teaching vocabulary through role play. Teachers need to be aware of the cultural values that could be attached to some signs. Gestures are also used in addition to sign language to support students. They are consciously used to express meaning, but body language exposes the inner being.

Teachers are encouraged to follow the step-by-step process provided in the instructional materials. They should encourage students to gather materials that reflect their community's gestural knowledge and the use of gestures around the world.

The Common Core state standards are used to build gestural knowledge using multimedia and other resources. In this professional learning experience, we use culture as a lens to explore topics.

Keep in mind that this is a lesson in which you could integrate reading, listening, writing, and speaking language skills. There are some TESOL strategies used in the module. The readings give you an explanation of how you can teach gestural knowledge.

The example lesson that follows is guided by the International Literacy Standards for teacher preparation in literacy, the NCTE/ILA standards for English language arts, the Common Core Standards for English language arts and social studies standards. Following this, activities for before, during, and after the lesson are presented that you can use to teach critical literacy, translanguaging, and multiliteracies. Opportunities are also presented in the lesson to guide students in third–fifth grade to use this approach.

Journaling: This is a diary that will document your learning journey and will be used to evaluate the effectiveness of this process.

Think of the tools (i.e., audio visuals) to teach a lesson on gestural knowledge. What topics will you cover in your teaching? What activities can you use to teach students about gestures (movies, picture books, silent movies)? How can you connect gestural knowledge to teaching language (listening, speaking, reading, and writing)?

Please discuss them in your journal.

A) Use the guiding questions in writing your response.
B) Start writing about the resources provided in the module.
C) Record your thought processes as you read the modules.
D) Consider how the presented information makes you think about your teaching of multilingual students in terms of content and teaching strategies.

Learning Outcomes for Teachers

After studying this module, you should be able to:

- Build a lesson or a unit on gestural knowledge.
- Guide students in making connections with using the pictures in the books you are teaching or in using separate mime gestures.
- Develop students' writing skills using ideas, which is a writing trait.
- Guide students in using their critical thinking skills to analyze a scene or character.
- Connect gestures with students' identities considering the gesture's message and background.
- Provide students with opportunities to collect and distinguish between words and gestures, including signs, logos, and ads.
- Encourage students to analyze the power of words in signage.
- Guide students to use resources to create a poster to represent their theme or idea.
- Engage in meaning-making using multiliteracies.
- Use the MultiSemiotic gestural approach to create a learning product for your students.
- Complete a reflection on the module.

TESOL Standards (for Teachers, TESOL International Association, 2018)

- **2a.** Candidates demonstrate knowledge of how dynamic academic, personal, familial, cultural, and social contexts, including sociopolitical factors, impact the education of ELLs.
- **3a.** Candidates plan for culturally and linguistically relevant, supportive environments that promote ELLs' learning. Candidates design scaffolded instruction of language and literacies to support standards and curricular objectives for ELLs in the content areas.

- **3b.** Candidates instruct ELLs using evidence-based, student-centered, developmentally appropriate interactive approaches.
- **3e.** Candidates use and adapt relevant materials and resources, including digital resources, to plan lessons for ELLs, support communication with other educators, school personnel, and ELLs and to foster student learning of language and literacies in the content areas.
- **5a.** Candidates demonstrate knowledge of effective collaboration strategies in order to plan ways to serve as a resource for ELL instruction, support educators and school staff, and advocate for ELLs.

Language Objectives (for Students)
1. To read about gestures.
2. To reflect on gestures and discuss their interpretations.
3. To write how gestures represent language.
4. To gather information using various pictures of gestures that represent collaboration and unity.
5. To discuss a logo, considering time, culture, and gestures.
6. To produce a poster that includes pictures of gestures to other students.

Guiding Questions
1. How do you use gestures in teaching? How do you connect those gestures to the curriculum?
2. What gestures are used in teaching students about language and culture?
3. How can gestures be cultural?
4. How do costumes play a role in understanding gestures and body language?
5. How can we teach students language skills (speaking, reading, listening, and writing) by connecting with gestures?
6. What resources are provided in the classroom that support students in learning about gestures?
7. How do these connections support multilingual and bilingual student learning?

8. How can students in New Mexico connect to people around the country or outside the United States through gestures?
9. How are gestures connected to culture and traditions?
10. What methods are being used to connect gestures on topics such as unity and social justice?
11. How can you be culturally responsive to your students' needs, focusing on gestural knowledge in the classroom?

Pre-Class Preparation Activities for Teachers
Gestures Use in the Classroom

- ♦ Todd Finley discusses how gestures support students' retention of information, facilitate communication with students, and explain vocabulary words (Finley, 2022):

    Tips for Using Hand Gestures to Support Learning https://www.edutopia.org/article/tips-using-hand-gestures-support-learning/

- ♦ Gestures allow all students to participate and increase their engagement, fostering equitable opportunities. They are a valuable tool because they allow teachers to gauge students' understanding of a concept, enabling teachers to adjust instruction to meet students' needs. You will learn about how to incorporate gestures into small and large groups:

    "Making Classroom Participation More Equitable with Hand Gestures (Collier, 2023)." https://www.edutopia.org/article/using-hand-gestures-classroom-participation/

How Gestures Connect with Culture

You will learn from this article how body language can be a universal form of nonverbal communication and culture. Detailed examples are provided regarding facial expressions and head movements, hand gestures, greetings, silence, posture, and personal space:

- ♦ Body Language in Different Cultures Around the World Zucchet (2023): A Top Guide https://www.berlitz.com/blog/body-language-different-cultures-around-world

Gesture and Language
John Haviland explains gestures, recent approaches, what is and is not considered a gesture, and different forms of gestures and their meaning:

- ♦ Gesture as cultural and linguistic practice (Haviland, n.d.) https://pages.ucsd.edu/~jhaviland/Publications/GestureCultLingPractice.htm

Body Language and Teaching
Hidden Curriculum
- ♦ This article provides insights on the importance of teachers paying attention to our body language and considering students' cultures in the classroom to ensure a positive environment: The Importance of Positive Body Language in the Classroom (Mednick, 2022) https://www.nea.org/advocating-for-change/new-from-nea/bring-positive-body-language-classroom
- ♦ Brittany Williamson reminds us of the critical role of body language in teaching and provides six ways to "empower and engage students": The Importance of Body Language in Teaching (Williamson, 2023) https://everfi.com/blog/k-12/the-importance-of-body-language-in-teaching/
- ♦ This resource provides a summary of using gestures in learning and teaching. For instance, teachers use gestures to guide students' attention and emphasize a point, and students use gestures to problem-solve. The summary addresses how digital tools such as AI help teachers interact with the content and make inferences:
Gestures in Learning and Teaching (Lindgren et al., n.d.) https://www.isls.org/research-topics/gestures-learning-teaching/

Gestures and Culture
- ♦ This article provides cultural awareness of using gestures: Gestures and Culture (Humintell, 2013) https://www.humintell.com/2013/06/gestures-and-culture/

- This article highlights the results of examining the gestural differences among cultures, such as American and Chinese cultures:

  Researchers Study Influence of Cultural Factors on Gesture Design (Hallman, 2020) https://www.psu.edu/news/research/story/researchers-study-influence-cultural-factors-gesture-design
- You will learn about gestures of solidarity in African American culture.

  Gestures of Solidarity in African American Culture (National Museum of African American History and Culture, 2020) https://nmaahc.si.edu/explore/stories/gestures-solidarity-african-american-culture

Gestures Supporting Students

- You will learn about the six types of gestures and their meanings (Perry, 2021):

  https://www.betterup.com/blog/types-of-gestures
- This podcast addresses incorporating purposeful movement into instruction:

  How Movement and Gestures Can Improve Student Learning (Kris, 2023) https://www.kqed.org/mindshift/58051/how-movement-and-gestures-can-improve-student-learning
- There are seven reasons to integrate gestures with your ESL students. Gestures are handy (Roger, 2020) https://edu.rsc.org/feature/using-gestures-in-the-classroom/4012415.article:
  - Lending a Hand: 7 Reasons to Use Gestures in the ESL Classroom (Busy Teacher, 2018) https://m.busyteacher.org/21593-gestures-7-reasons-to-use-esl-class.html

Thought Questions

1. Why do you think gestural knowledge should be included in the curriculum?
2. How does learning about gestural knowledge foster cultural identity?
3. In what ways do you think researching gestural knowledge would support student learning?

4. After reading about gestural knowledge and reviewing the module materials, what resonated most with you? In what way will you incorporate it in your class?
5. The module covered the Common Core Standards focusing on all the language skills. How are you planning to incorporate language skills in your classroom?
6. How are you planning to teach about gestural knowledge in social studies using the standards provided?
7. Do you foresee any challenges in implementing this approach into your classrooms? Explain.
8. Any additional thoughts? Please share!

References

Busy Teacher. (2018). *Lending a hand: 7 reasons to use gestures in your ESL classroom.* https://m.busyteacher.org/21593-gestures-7-reasons-to-use-esl-class.html

Collier, K. (2023, December 11). *Making classroom participation more equitable with hand gestures.* Edutopia. https://www.edutopia.org/article/using-hand-gestures-classroom-participation/

Finley, T. (2022, October 13). *Tips for using hand gestures to support learning.* Edutopia. https://www.edutopia.org/article/tips-using-hand-gestures-support-learning/

Hallman, J. (2020, November 30). *Researchers study influence of cultural factors on gesture design.* Penn State University. https://www.psu.edu/news/research/story/researchers-study-influence-cultural-factors-gesture-design/

Haviland, J. B. (n.d.). Gesture as cultural and linguistic practice. https://pages.ucsd.edu/~jhaviland/Publications/GestureCultLingPractice.htm

Humintell, A. (2013, June). *Gestures and culture.* Humintell.com. https://www.humintell.com/2013/06/gestures-and-culture/

Karkar-Esperat, T. M. (2025). Multiliteracies for Multilingual Learners: The MultiSemiotic Architecture Framework. *International Journal of Bilingual Education and Bilingualism. 28*(2), 117–134 doi.org/10.1080/13670050.2024.2409120

Kris, D. F. (2023, November 21). How movement and gestures can improve student learning [Audio podcast episode]. In *Mindshift Podcast.*

KQED. https://www.kqed.org/mindshift/58051/how-movement-and-gestures-can-improve-student-learning

Lindgren, R., Perry, M., Beilstein, S., & Alibali, M. (n.d.). *Gestures in learning & teaching – ISLS*. Gestures in Learning & Teaching. https://www.isls.org/research-topics/gestures-learning-teaching/

Mednick, J. (2022, August 24). *The importance of positive body language in the classroom*. NEAToday. https://www.nea.org/advocating-for-change/new-from-nea/bring-positive-body-language-classroom

National Museum of African American History and Culture. (2020, June 13). *Gestures of solidarity in African American culture*. https://nmaahc.si.edu/explore/stories/gestures-solidarity-african-american-culture

Perry, E. (2021, November 15). *Learn types of gestures and how they impact communication*. BetterUp. https://www.betterup.com/blog/types-of-gestures/

Nunan, D. (1989). Hidden agendas: The role of the learner in programme implementation. In R. K. Johnson (Ed.), *The second language curriculum*. Cambridge University Press

Rogers, B. (2020, September 21). *Using gestures in the classroom*. RSC Education. https://edu.rsc.org/feature/using-gestures-in-the-classroom/4012415.article

TESOL International Association. (2018). *Standards for initial TESOL Pre-K–12 teacher preparation programs*. https://www.tesol.org/media/v33fewo0/2018-tesol-teacher-prep-standards-final.pdf

Williamson, B. (2023, December 11). *The importance of body language in teaching*. EVERFI. https://everfi.com/blog/k-12/the-importance-of-body-language-in-teaching/

Zucchet, E. (2023, August 21). *Body language in different cultures around the world: A top guide*. Berlitz. https://www.berlitz.com/blog/body-language-different-cultures-around-world

Lesson Title: A MultiSemiotic Gestural Knowledge (Karkar-Esperat, 2019, National Governors Association Center for Best Practices, & Council of Chief State School Officers, 2010; New Mexico Public Education Department, 2021)

Common Core Standards for 3rd–5th Grades	Social Studies Standards for 3rd–5th Grade	Pedagogical Holistic Model of New Literacies
Third Grade CCSS.ELA-LITERACY. RI.3.7 Use information gained from illustrations (e.g., maps, photographs) and the words in a text to demonstrate understanding of the text (e.g., where, when, why, and how key events occur). CCSS.ELA-LITERACY. SL.3.1A Come to discussions prepared, having read or studied required material; explicitly draw on that preparation and other information known about the topic to explore ideas under discussion. CCSS.ELA-LITERACY. SL.3.1C Ask questions to check understanding of information presented, stay on topic, and link their comments to the remarks of others. CCSS.ELA-LITERACY. SL.3.4 Report on a topic or text, tell a story, or recount an experience with appropriate facts and relevant, descriptive details, speaking clearly at an understandable pace.	**Third Grade** 3.2. Use supporting questions to help answer the compelling question in an inquiry. 3.27. Compare and contrast their cultural identity with other people and groups. **Fourth Grade** 4.4. Construct responses to compelling questions using reasoning, examples, and relevant details. 4.9. Demonstrate understanding that state symbols, holidays, traditions, and songs represent various cultural heritages, natural treasures, and the democratic values of New Mexico.	The gestural mode refers to behavior, physical movement, gestures, sensuality, feelings, and effects, in addition to kinesics and proxemics (the New London Group,1996). The pedagogical holistic model of new literacies used the four pedagogies and focused on words like "body movements," "theater," "five senses," "eye contact," and "role play," based on discussions with New Literacies experts (Karkar-Esperat, 2019). The *MultiSemiotic gestural mode* focuses on hand movement in connection to culture, history, and religion to refer to racial and religion equity, #BlackLivesMatter gestures, anti-/racism gestures, or gestures that convey diversity and inclusion, racial equality and social justice, and beliefs about racial discrimination (see Lemke et al., 2015)" (Karkar-Esperat, 2025, p.11).

Self-Discovery Through the Gestural Mode ♦ 227

CCSS.ELA-LITERACY. W.3.1B
Provide reasons that support the opinion.

CCSS.ELA-LITERACY. W.3.2B
Develop the topic with facts, definitions, and details.

CCSS.ELA-LITERACY. W.3.6
With guidance and support from adults, use technology to produce and publish writing (using keyboarding skills) as well as to interact and collaborate with others.

Fourth Grade

CCSS.ELA-LITERACY.RI.4.7
Interpret information presented visually, orally, or quantitatively (e.g., in charts, graphs, diagrams, timelines, animations, or interactive elements on Web pages) and explain how the information contributes to an understanding of the text in which it appears.

CCSS.ELA-LITERACY.RI.4.7
Integrate information from two texts on the same topic in order to write or speak about the subject knowledgeably.

CCSS.ELA-LITERACY.SL.4.5
Add audio recordings and visual displays to presentations when appropriate to enhance the development of main ideas or themes.

Fifth Grade

5.2. Use supporting questions to help answer the compelling question in an inquiry.

5.5. Construct responses to compelling questions supported by reasoning and evidence.

(Continued)

Common Core Standards for 3rd–5th Grades	Social Studies Standards for 3rd–5th Grade	Pedagogical Holistic Model of New Literacies
CCSS.ELA-LITERACY.SL.4.4 Report on a topic or text, tell a story, or recount an experience in an organized manner, using appropriate facts and relevant, descriptive details to support main ideas or themes; speak clearly at an understandable pace. CCSS.ELA-LITERACY.W.4.1A Introduce a topic or text clearly, state an opinion, and create an organizational structure in which related ideas are grouped to support the writer's purpose. CCSS.ELA-LITERACY.W.4.3D Use concrete words and phrases and sensory details to convey experiences and events precisely. CCSS.ELA-LITERACY.W.4.7 Conduct short research projects that build knowledge through investigation of different aspects of a topic. **Fifth Grade** CCSS.ELA-LITERACY.RI.5.7 Draw on information from multiple print or digital sources, demonstrating the ability to locate an answer to a question quickly or to solve a problem efficiently. CCSS.ELA-LITERACY.RI.5.9 Integrate information from several texts on the same topic in order to write or speak about the subject knowledgeably.		

CCSS.ELA-LITERACY.SL.5.1A
Come to discussions prepared, having read or studied required material; explicitly draw on that preparation and other information known about the topic to explore ideas under discussion.

CCSS.ELA-LITERACY.SL.5.4
Report on a topic or text or present an opinion, sequencing ideas logically and using appropriate facts and relevant, descriptive details to support main ideas or themes; speak clearly at an understandable pace.

CCSS.ELA-LITERACY.SL.5.5
Include multimedia components (e.g., graphics, sound) and visual displays in presentations when appropriate to enhance the development of main ideas or themes.

CCSS.ELA-LITERACY.W.5.1A
Introduce a topic or text clearly, state an opinion, and create an organizational structure in which ideas are logically grouped to support the writer's purpose.

CCSS.ELA-LITERACY.W.5.3D
Use concrete words and phrases and sensory details to convey experiences and events precisely.

CCSS.ELA-LITERACY.W.5.7
Conduct short research projects that use several sources to build knowledge through investigation of different aspects of a topic.

(Continued)

References

Karkar-Esperat, T. (2019). Assessing preservice teachers' knowledge of new literacies [Doctoral dissertation, Texas Tech University]. Texas Tech University Archive.

Karkar-Esperat, T. M. (2025). Multiliteracies for Multilingual Learners: The MultiSemiotic Architecture Framework. *International Journal of Bilingual Education and Bilingualism. 28*(2), 117–134 doi.org/10.1080/13670050.2024.2409120

Lemke, J., Lecusay, R., Cole, M., & Michalchick, V. (2015). *Documenting and assessing learning in media-rich environments*. Cambridge, MA: MIT Press and MacArthur Foundation.

National Governors Association Center for Best Practices, & Council of Chief State School Officers. (2010). *Common Core State Standards for English language arts & literacy in history/social studies, science, and technical subjects*. Washington, DC: Authors. https://www.corestandards.org/ELA-Literacy/

New Mexico Public Education Department. (2021). *New Mexico social studies standards*. https://webnew.ped.state.nm.us/bureaus/literacy-humanities/social-studies/

New London Group (1996). "A Pedagogy of Multiliteracies: Designing Social Futures." *Harvard Educational Review* 66 (1): 60–92. https://doi.org/10.17763/haer.66.1.17370n67v22j160u

Instructional Materials Used with Students

Lesson Title—A MultiSemiotic Gestural Approach: Gestural Knowledge

Language Objectives (for Students)

- To read about gestures.
- To identify gestures and discuss interpretations.
- To write how gestures represent language.
- To gather pictorial representations using various gestures that represent collaboration and unity.
- To discuss gestures across development stages (age groups 3–6 years, 7–10 years old)
- To discuss a logo/picture/illustration considering its context, time, culture, and gestures

♦ To produce a poster that include pictures of gestures to present to other students.

During instruction, these are activities that you can use for teaching your students

Home: The students create a poster of a local sign that represents a segment of their place or culture and interpret the sign using the cultural and historical background of the sign. The student will answer the thought questions: What do you see in the photo? Describe the gestures being used. Find out the history or background of this sign. Does it resemble a group? Culture? Please explain.
State: Students will choose an activity, which could include a cheerleading dance movement, line or square dance movement, or a type of exercise, and they will explore the cultural and historical background associated with the activity. Students are encouraged to discuss the music associated with it if applicable. Discuss unity representation if applicable.
World: Students will represent movements through pictures on a poster or using technology. That way this lesson doesn't have to use as much posterboard and explain the movements represented in the posters. This activity calls for collaboration and group participation and builds students' ability to express an idea.

Aligning with the social studies standards (for students)

♦ Students will inquire about an object they chose by asking question and finding resources that will give them information about the background of that object.
♦ **Differentiation includes** leveled texts, visuals, and supplementary materials and the use of audiovisuals, class discussion, drawings and illustrations, and online resources.

7

Self-Discovery Through the Synesthesia Mode

Examining Culture Through Local Historical Figures

> **VIGNETTE**
>
> *As teachers, we promote self-discovery in the early grades by asking students to draw family members to decorate a tree, allowing them to express themselves. As they progress, in later grades, we ask them to inquire about their family history through storytelling, letters, holiday cards, and family projects. We encourage them to reflect on where they see themselves in their culture and place using language as a tool. Students start to design their own identity through their family perceptions. As teachers, we may overlook how students perceive their identity and miss opportunities to help them understand it through the teaching and learning experiences we design. However, if our elementary classrooms lack a self-discovery approach, we will not present students the chance to learn about their own cultures through language. We must delve deeper into the content we teach and when we teach it.*

Students learn about World War I and World War II but don't have the opportunity to learn about their own place, family, community, and future. The national curriculum standards emphasize an inquiry approach, but it is seldom used and modeled to students to explore familial cultures.

Topics covered in the classroom need to be relevant and current. For instance, students need to learn about the history of their place, the legendary people in their community, and topics that connect to being productive citizens. It's time to revise the curriculum and explore how to connect it meaningfully to students' identities so that students can find their place within their community and find ways to support the community. Self-discovery through one's own place, family, and culture is a critical way to engage students in reading.

Teachers shared their experiences implementing the knowledge they gained and the activities guided by this chapter:

> *Researching local historical figures would support students' learning by giving them a topic to research. As I have mentioned, they could write a biography of one of the local historical figures. We have several writing standards that we can work on as students research these historical figures. They could also write an opinion piece about their local historical figure. Do they think this person is a good person why or why not and use facts to support their answer. I think most students would be engaged and interested in learning more about their community.*

Another teacher educator expressed, "Just the feeling of belonging! I want them to take pride and care for our great state, and to know they are a continuing part of where things are going to go as a state!" Another teacher indicated, "This has been my favorite lesson so far, and my kids got really involved. I will be using this and things like this is a lot of my lessons from now on." A teacher shared, "I have done the cemetery scavenger hunt and learned so much about Roswell that I didn't know. I would

> *love for this activity to be a field trip. I think this would be the only challenge in implementing this approach. I think this module would be easy enough to do 5–10 minutes once a week." A teacher stated, "Researching is always a good starting point to get students engage in learning new skills or acquiring new knowledge."*

Dear teachers, parents, guardians, and students,

The synesthesia approach refers to using more than one mode to support and scaffold students' learning experiences. It includes integrating the visual, linguistic, audio, spatial, and/or gestural modes. You will understand how you can connect students' learning experiences to their community and the curriculum using language and culture. The examples are provided in the context of New Mexico. You can follow the same structure and apply it to your own context.

This chapter will guide you in learning about synesthesia semiotics. It highlights educators' critical role in teaching inquiry skills and designing and implementing activities for learners to have well-rounded experiences. Some questions to consider are: How can we teach critical literacy, translanguaging, and multiliteracies through a synesthesia approach? How can we connect oral and personalized history to our teaching and learning content? How does this approach assist in reflecting critically in writing or speaking, connecting to culture and identity? What multimodal activities can we plan in order to engage students in inquiry using primary and secondary sources? How can we promote self-discovery through the classroom and community?

What Is It About?

"The synesthesia mode describes moving towards using different modes (New London Group 1996). The pedagogical holistic model of new literacies included terms such as 'different texts (graphic novels, digital stories, primary source documents, advertisements, or electronic texts) and used visuals,' 'sound effects,' 'music,' and 'language or body language' (Karkar-Esperat 2019). The MultiSemiotic synesthesia mode includes the use of audio-visuals, memoirs, historical and cultural documen- taries, dancing, fiction, poetry, and animations. The gestural visual mode, for example, could reflect expressions in magazines and gestures in photos (Cloonan 2008). The visual gestural linguistic can consist of book characters, and the audiovisual might include music visuals or interplay (Cloonan 2008; see also Mills and Unsworth, 2018).Using the MultiSemiotic architecture allows teachers and educators to extend on their pedagogical practices using multiliteracies and new literacies in ways that center culture and bring justice to all learners" (Karkar-Esperat, 2025, p. 12).

Synesthesia Knowledge

The term *synesthesia knowledge* refers to using and moving from one mode to another (body movement, visuals), and using multiple modes to support students' learning and scaffold content and language learning (Smith et al., 2021). Students draw on different modalities when engaging in a learning activity. They could negotiate meaning through linguistic resources, sounds, and visuals. Incorporating multiple modalities can support student writing experiences (Smith et al., 2021) and reading abilities (Hasselbring & Goin, 1994). Yi et al. (2019) concluded that using multimodal composition in bilingual classrooms provides students with authentic writing opportunities and develops English language proficiency. Another review conducted by Rajendram (2015) confirmed that adopting multimodal composing can increase student engagement and collaboration. Cummins et al. (2015) suggested using multiple modalities to create identity texts. Considering "the context shapes [students'] meaning, [and] these meanings are also shaped by culture and history" (Smith et al., 2021, p. 3). Bilingual and multilingual learners can utilize various modes of multiliteracies, including audio, visual, gestural, and linguistic modes, to demonstrate their reading and writing abilities (Hasselbring & Goin, 1994; Karkar-Esperat, 2024).

Why Do We Need to Use It?

This chapter uses synesthesia in the context of place-based learning (Bransford et al., 2004). This approach focuses on using local experiences as the foundation for students' learning processes, which in this chapter is framed within the context of teaching history through the stories of legendary people. With this learning experience, teachers and students reflect on history, using history lessons as an opportunity to instill profound values. Historical awareness skills involve understanding and analyzing historical facts and interpreting the value of past areas, linking the past, present, and future (Mulyani et al., 2024). Students learning about their heritage and local history facilitate their understanding of historical concepts, which builds on the understanding of three pillars of history education: history, memory, and identity (Magro et al., 2014). The use of teaching and learning about history supports students in developing their national identities. It also assists them in conveying past narratives about relationships between community groups, regions, and ethnicities, contributing to the formation of shared identity by examining historical materials to find connections between groups. This allows diverse students to foster stronger links between them (Yefterson et al., 2020).

Some critical skills used in learning about history are reading using various resources, like textbooks and online historical documents, and referencing them. Learners also use writing skills to write stories based on interviews (Mulyani et al., 2024). Application activities for learning about history that require using multiple modes include timelines, storyboards, videography, infographics, comics, photos, documentaries, sound recordings, posters, vlogs, concept maps, and mock-ups (Mulyani et al., 2024). These activities allow students to provide facts, engage in critical discussion, and develop knowledge independently using various sources (Hasan, 2019). Some technological resources used in teaching history are smartphones, Google Earth, and the Active Track software (Magro et al., 2014). Teachers will use digital and nondigital resources in teaching history. These synesthesia forms are used to differentiate products and support students' learning styles and needs.

Synesthesia Strategies In An Elementary Class

Teachers need to make learning accessible and suited to the content to support learners (Gee, 1989; New London Group, 1996). Digital tools are not necessary for multimodal learning, but they are significant in supporting students' access to more modes of learning (Tricamo, 2021). In social studies, teachers could use historical photographs, oral histories, portrait studies, political cartoons, graphic novels, and music to design interactive activities (Tricamo, 2021). The nature of the social studies discipline is inquiry. Inquiry-based learning can be used to improve students' educational experiences (Al-Hazza & Lucking, 2017; Miller et al., 2018). Art- and project-based learning can work together to make meaning from historical narratives (Chisholm & Whitmore, 2016). Teachers can use multimodal texts that include audio, spatial, gestural, linguistic, and visual elements (New London Group, 1996). In social studies class, using the spatial mode means using maps and the positioning of historical figures; using the gestural mode can include debates, role-play, and theatre. Using the audio mode could mean speeches, oral histories, lectures, and videos. Using the visual mode could include transcripts, books, newspaper articles, advertisements, and elements of rhetoric including text features and word choice, especially in debates (Tricamo, 2021).

Tricamo (2021) suggested some curriculum activities such as argumentative writing, where students use primary and secondary document sources to synthesize ideas and identifying perspectives and bias, using multiple modes for students to learn the content so that they can understand the writing structure and create their historical writing. Teachers can use digital sources to engage students in text-coding activities and in examining photographs in this inquiry process. Another activity is engaging students in interpreting speeches through different modes such as the speech transcript or the audio or video recording, depending on the historical era and technology availability. Tricamo (2021) recommended using digital inquiry stations where the station activities provide students with a variety of resources including websites, images, blueprints, videos, and so on to inquire about a topic and make conclusions. Students could work on the stations independently or with a partner, and each station would be organized on Google Slides with inquiry packets. Other activities could include interactive mapping projects via Google Maps. In this chapter you will learn about other activities you can design for your students such as timelines, conceptual maps, cemetery scavenger hunt, and memoirs.

Conclusion

Using primary and secondary sources, teachers and students can use the synesthesia mode to inquire about any topic. The sources can reflect different modes and students' interests and needs. Teachers can use different leveled materials and differentiate products. They need to consider self-paced assignments, clear instructions, time, access, and students' languages and cultures to practice mindfulness, support students' success, and achieve the goals set.

How Can We Use It?

There are three simple steps that you need to follow:

1. Read the national standards that guided these two lessons.
2. Study the learning materials, which will give you background about the chapter examples.
3. Review the instructional materials, which could be used with students in language art and social studies.

The modeled lesson uses the synesthesia approach.

Guiding Table for This Chapter

Transmultiliteracies Sustaining Pedagogy Approach (Karkar-Esperat & Stickely, 2024)	◆ The use of the language arts standards and social studies standards. ◆ Applications for language arts and social studies classrooms.
The Pedagogical Holistic Model of New Literacies (Karkar-Esperat, 2019)	◆ Gathering information using various sources such as readings and interviewing community members and experts. ◆ Making a visual timeline to represent the major events throughout a historical figure's life or throughout the student's life. ◆ Writing a memoir that represents their history, culture, and identity that captures important memories of the student's family, culture, and literacy experiences. ◆ Producing a multimodal identity project using text and technology (adding visuals, audios, and digital sources). ◆ Presenting the project to other students and learning about other students' lived experiences. ◆ Role-playing a historical figure.
The Raciosemiotic Architecture Framework (Karkar-Esperat, 2023)	◆ Gathering information about legendary locals from different areas through various stories in books. ◆ Reading about legendary locals and how their stories are connected to local history, culture, and identity. ◆ Expressing a positive view of themselves while demonstrating respect and empathy for others. ◆ Engaging in meaning-making using multiliteracies.
The MultiSemiotic Architecture Framework (Karkar-Esperat, 2025)	**MultiSemiotic Spatial Knowledge: Social Space** "The *multisemiotic spatial mode* refers to perceptions and relationships between objects (Lazutina et al., 2016), awareness of human behavior and social space (Hall, 1966), philosophy of geographic location and cultures and traditions, and spatial knowledge." (Karkar-Esperat, 2025, p. 12)

References

Al-Hazza, T. C., & Lucking, R. (2017). An examination of preservice teachers' view of multiliteracies: Habits, perceptions, demographics and slippery slopes. *Reading Improvement*, *54*(1), 32–43.

Bransford, J. D., Brown, A. L., & Cocking, R. R. (Eds.). (2004). *How people learn: Brain, mind, experience, and school* (Expanded ed.). National Research Council, National Academy Press.

Chisholm, J. S., & Whitmore, K. F. (2016). Bodies in space/bodies in motion/bodies in character: Adolescents bear witness to Anne Frank. *International Journal of Education & the Arts*, *17*(5), 1–31.

Cloonan, A. (2008). Multimodality pedagogies: A multiliteracies approach. *International Journal of Learning*, *15*(9), 159–168. https://doi.org/10.18848/1447-9494/CGP/v15i09/45952

Cummins, J., Hu, S., Markus, P., & Montero, M.K. (2015). Identity texts and academic achievement: Connecting the dots in multilingual school contexts. *TESOL Quarterly*, *49*(3), 555–581. https://doi.org/10.1002/tesq.241

Gee, J. P. (1989). What is literacy? *Journal of Education*, *171*(1), 18–25. https://doi.org/10.1177/002205748917100102

Hall, E. T. (1966). *The Hidden Dimension* (Vol. 609). Doubleday.

Hasan, S. H. (2019). Pendidikan sejarah untuk kehidupan abad ke-21 [History education for 21st-century life]. *Historia*, *2*(2), 61–72.

Hasselbring, T. S., & Goin, L. (1994). *Advanced Institute: Anchored instruction multimedia for enhancing teacher education*. Vanderbilt University.

Karkar-Esperat, T. (2019). *Assessing preservice teachers' knowledge of new literacies* [Doctoral dissertation, Texas Tech University]. Texas Tech University Archive.

Karkar-Esperat, T. (2023). Transparency in the Classroom: The Raciosemiotic Architecture Framework for Multilingual Learners. Semiotics Society of America 2023 Yearbook.

Karkar-Esperat, T. & Stickley, Z. (2024). Revisioning Curriculum Through the Transmulitliteracies Sustaining Pedagogy Approach. *Social Sciences & Humanities Open*, *9*, 239.

Karkar-Esperat, T. M. (2025). Multiliteracies for Multilingual Learners: The MultiSemiotic Architecture Framework. *International Journal of Bilingual Education and Bilingualism*. *28*(2), 117–134 https://doi.org/10.1080/13670050.2024.2409120.

Karkar-Esperat, Tala Michelle. (Invited, 2024). "Multiliteracies in Teacher Education." In George Noblit (Ed.), *Oxford Research Encyclopedia of Education*. New York: Oxford University Press. https://doi.org/10.1093/acrefore/9780190264093.013.1890

Lazutina, T. V., I. N. Pupysheva, M. N. Shcherbinin, V. N. Baksheev, and G. V. Patrakova. (2016). "Semiotics of Art: Language of Architecture as a Complex System of Signs." *International Journal of Environmental and Science Education* 11 (17): 9991–9998.

Magro, G., De Carvalho, J. R., & Marcelino, M. J. (2014). *Improving history learning through cultural heritage, local history and technology*. International Association for the Development of the Information Society.

Miller, D. M., Scott, C. E., & McTigue, E. M. (2018). Writing in the secondary-level disciplines: A systematic review of context, cognition, and content. *Educational Psychology Review*, *30*(1), 83–120. https://doi.org/10.1007/s10648-016-9393-z

Mills, K. A., & Unsworth, L. (2018). *Multimodal literacy*. Oxford University Press.

Mulyani, F. F., Syahriani, F., & Dos Santos, M. (2024). Analysis of history subject teaching modules in high school: A review based on the Merdeka Curriculum. *ALMAARIEF*, *6*, 23–37.

New London Group. (1996). A pedagogy of multiliteracies: Designing social futures. *Harvard Educational Review*, *66*(1), 60–92. https://doi.org/10.17763/haer.66.1.17370n67v22j160u

Rajendram, S. (2015). Potentials of the multiliteracies pedagogy for teaching English language learners (ELLs): A review of the literature. *Critical Intersections in Education*, *3*, 1–18.

Smith, B. E., Pacheco, M. B., & Khorosheva, M. (2021). Emergent bilingual students and digital multimodal composition: A systematic review of research in secondary classrooms. *Reading Research Quarterly*, *56*(1), 33–52.

Tricamo, L. (2021). Multiliteracies, multimodalities, and social studies education. *Proceedings of GREAT Day*, *2020*(1), 21.

Yefterson, R. B., Naldi, H., Erniwati, E., Lionar, U., & Syafrina, Y. (2020). The relevance of local historical events in building national identities: Identification in the history learning curriculum in Indonesia. *International Journal of Progressive Sciences and Technologies*, *23*(1), 500–504.

Yi, Y., Shin, D., & Cimasko, T. (2019). Multimodal literacies in teaching and learning in and out of school. In L. C. de Oliveira (Ed.), *Handbook of TESOL in K–12* (pp. 163–177). John Wiley & Sons.

Lesson Title: A MultiSemiotic Synesthesia Approach: Historical Figures (Council of Chief State School Officers, 2013; International Literacy Association, 2017; National Council of Teachers of English & International Reading Association, 2012)

NCTE / IRA Standards for the English Language Arts	International Literacy Association Standards	INTASC Standards
Standard #1: Students read a wide range of print and non-print texts to build an understanding of texts, of themselves, and of the cultures of the United States and the world; to acquire new information; to respond to the needs and demands of society and the workplace; and for personal fulfillment. Among these texts are fiction and nonfiction, classic and contemporary works.	Standard #1: Foundational Knowledge. Candidates demonstrate knowledge of the theoretical, historical, and evidence-based foundations of literacy and language and the ways in which they interrelate and the role of literacy professionals in schools.	Standard #1: Learner Development. The teacher understands how learners grow and develop, recognizing that patterns of learning and development vary individually within and across the cognitive, linguistic, social, emotional, and physical areas and designs and implements developmentally appropriate and challenging learning experiences.
Standard #2: Students read a wide range of literature from many periods in many genres to build an understanding of the many dimensions (e.g., philosophical, ethical, aesthetic) of human experience.	Standard #2: Curriculum and Instruction. Candidates use foundational knowledge to critique and implement literacy curricula to meet the needs of all learners and to design, implement, and evaluate evidence-based literacy instruction for all learners.	Standard #2: Learning Differences. The teacher uses understanding of individual differences and diverse cultures and communities to ensure inclusive learning environments that enable each learner to meet high standards.

Standard #3: Students apply a wide range of strategies to comprehend, interpret, evaluate, and appreciate texts. They draw on their prior experience, their interactions with other readers and writers, their knowledge of word meaning and of other texts, their word identification strategies, and their understanding of textual features (e.g., sound-letter correspondence, sentence structure, context, graphics).

Standard #4: Students adjust their use of spoken, written, and visual language (e.g., conventions, style, vocabulary) to communicate effectively with a variety of audiences and for different purposes.

Standard #5: Students employ a wide range of strategies as they write and use different writing process elements appropriately to communicate with different audiences for a variety of purposes.

Standard #7: Students conduct research on issues and interests by generating ideas and questions, and by posing problems. They gather, evaluate, and synthesize data from a variety of sources (e.g., print and non-print texts, artifacts, people) to communicate their discoveries in ways that suit their purpose and audience.

Standard #3: Assessment and Evaluation. Candidates understand, select, and use valid, reliable, fair, and appropriate assessment tools to screen, diagnose, and measure student literacy achievement; inform instruction and evaluate interventions; participate in professional learning experiences; explain assessment results and advocate for appropriate literacy practices to relevant stakeholders.

Standard #4: Diversity and Equity. Candidates demonstrate knowledge of research, relevant theories, pedagogies, and essential concepts of diversity and equity; demonstrate and provide opportunities for understanding all forms of diversity as central to students' identities; create classrooms and schools that are inclusive and affirming; advocate for equity at school, district, and community levels.

Standard #3: Learning Environments. The teacher works with others to create environments that support individual and collaborative learning, and that encourage positive social interaction, active engagement in learning, and self motivation.

Standard #4: Content Knowledge. The teacher understands the central concepts, tools of inquiry, and structures of the discipline(s) he or she teaches and creates learning experiences that make the discipline accessible and meaningful for learners to assure mastery of the content.

Standard #5: Application of Content. The teacher understands how to connect concepts and use differing perspectives to engage learners in critical thinking, creativity, and collaborative problem solving related to authentic local and global issues.

(Continued)

NCTE / IRA Standards for the English Language Arts	International Literacy Association Standards	INTASC Standards
Standard #8: Students use a variety of technological and information resources (e.g., libraries, databases, computer networks, video) to gather and synthesize information and to create and communicate knowledge. Standard #9: Students develop an understanding of and respect for diversity in language use, patterns, and dialects across cultures, ethnic groups, geographic regions, and social roles. Standard #10: Students whose first language is not English make use of their first language to develop competency in the English language arts and to develop understanding of content across the curriculum. Standard #11: Students participate as knowledgeable, reflective, creative, and critical members of a variety of literacy communities. Standard #12: Students use spoken, written, and visual language to accomplish their own purposes (e.g., for learning, enjoyment, persuasion, and the exchange of information).	Standard #5: Learners and the Literacy Environment. Candidates meet the developmental needs of all learners and collaborate with school personnel to use a variety of print and digital materials to engage and motivate all learners; integrate digital technologies in appropriate, safe, and effective ways; foster a positive climate that supports a literacy-rich learning environment. Standard #6: Professional Learning and Leadership. Candidates recognize the importance of, participate in, and facilitate ongoing professional learning as part of career-long leadership roles and responsibilities Standard #7: Practicum/Clinical Experiences. Candidates apply theory and best practice in multiple supervised practicum/clinical experiences.	Standard #6: Assessment. The teacher understands and uses multiple methods of assessment to engage learners in their own growth, to monitor learner progress, and to guide the teacher's and learner's decision making. Standard #7: Planning for Instruction. The teacher plans instruction that supports every student in meeting rigorous learning goals by drawing upon knowledge of content areas, curriculum, cross-disciplinary skills, and pedagogy, as well as knowledge of learners and the community context. Standard #8: Instructional Strategies. The teacher understands and uses a variety of instructional strategies to encourage learners to develop deep understanding of content areas and their connections and to build skills to apply knowledge in meaningful ways.

References

Council of Chief State School Officers. (2013). *InTASC model core teaching standards and learning progressions for teachers 1.0: A resource for ongoing teacher development.* https://learning.ccsso.org/intasc-model-core-teaching-standards-and-learning-progressions-for-teachers

International Literacy Association. (2017). *Standards for the preparation of literacy professionals 2017.* https://www.literacyworldwide.org/get-resources/standards/standards-2017

National Council of Teachers of English & International Reading Association. (1996/2012). *Standards for the English language arts (Reaffirmed 2012).* National Council of Teachers of English. https://ncte.org/resources/standards/ncte-ira-standards-for-the-english-language-arts/

Modeled Lesson: Synesthesia

Synesthesia Approach: Historical Figures

Lesson Overview

This lesson introduces an element of the MultiSemiotic Synesthesia Approach: Historical Figures. Students will read about the legendary people in Roswell to connect with their culture and identity.

History is "a fluid continuum" that is the present we live in; it's the future for the past and the past for the future (Ellis, 2010, p. 317). Students need to know about the local history to learn about their inheritance and traditions. History helps us understand people and societies. It is important in our lives and is essential for good citizenship. History contributes to moral understanding and provides identity (Ellis, 2010).

Through this module, students will learn about the important local figures that contributed to Roswell. They will connect their contributions to culture and historical aspects. In teaching history, it is key to implement primary resources (Ellis, 2010) to make a more meaningful learning experience for students. To create these meaningful experiences, we must connect oral history and personalized history and intertwine them into the content we are learning. Timelines are an important factor in history that create a clear understanding of chronological events that have taken place prior to our existence.

In this module, students are encouraged to create timelines, role-play historical figures, and share their memoirs and cardboard displays to present the information that they have learned. Videos provided in the module will help you complete these activities. You are expected to help your students reflect critically in writing or speaking about how this genre connects to culture and identity. This genre develops all the language skills.

The Common Core state standards are used to build knowledge of history using multimedia and different resources. Additionally, the standards guide you to use research to learn about how you can implement this unit in the classroom. In this professional learning experience, we use culture as a lens to explore topics.

Keep in mind that this is a lesson in which you can integrate reading, listening, writing and speaking language skills. There are some TESOL strategies used in the module. The readings give you an explanation on how you can teach historical figures.

The following example lesson is guided by the International Literacy Standards for teacher preparation in literacy, the NCTE/IRA standards for English language arts, the Common Core standards for English language arts, and social studies standards. Following this, pre-, during- and post-lesson activities are presented that you can use to teach critical literacy, translanguaging, and multiliteracies. Opportunities are also presented in the lesson to guide your third- to fifth-grade students to use this approach.

Journaling: As you are learning about this module, use a diary to document your learning journey and to evaluate the effectiveness of this process.

 A). Use the guiding questions in writing your response.
 B). Start writing about the resources provided in the module that can introduce legendary people of Roswell.
 C). Record your thought processes as you read this chapter.
 D). Consider how the presented information and reflect on your teaching of multilingual students in terms of content, and teaching strategies.

Learning Outcomes for Teachers

After studying this module, you should be able to:

- Connect history to culture and language using primary and secondary sources.
- Share history through storytelling with young students.
- Gather and organize the information students have brought to the classroom about a legendary figure.
- Guide students to reflect on their learning processes and social interaction while learning about history in Roswell.
- Highlight the power of storytelling as history
- Support students to create their own memoirs to represent their cultural identities.
- Provide students with rich reading language experiences.
- Guide students to use the mentor texts provided on the legendary figures to write their memoirs.
- Engage in meaning-making using multiliteracies.
- Use the MultiSemiotic synesthesia approach to guide your students to create a learning product.
- Complete a reflection on the module.
- Guide third- to fifth-grade learners to learn and apply their knowledge of history.

TESOL Standards (for Teachers, TESOL International Association, 2018)

- **2a:** Candidates demonstrate knowledge of how dynamic academic, personal, familial, cultural, and social contexts, including sociopolitical factors, impact the education of ELLs.
- **2d:** Candidates devise and implement methods to learn about personal characteristics of the individual ELL (e.g., interests, motivations, strengths, needs) and their family (e.g., language use, literacy practices, circumstances) to develop effective instructional practices.
- **2e:** Candidates identify and describe the impact of his/her identity, role, cultural understandings, and personal biases and conscious knowledge of US culture on his/her

interpretation of the educational strengths and needs of individual ELLs and ELLs in general.

- **3a**: Candidates plan for culturally and linguistically relevant, supportive environments that promote ELLs' learning. Candidates design scaffolded instruction of language and literacies to support standards and curricular objectives for ELLs in the content areas.
- **3b**: Candidates instruct ELLs using evidence-based, student-centered, developmentally appropriate interactive approaches.
- **3c**: Candidates adjust instructional decisions after critical reflection on individual ELLs' learning outcomes in both language and content.
- **3e**: Candidates use and adapt relevant materials and resources, including digital resources, to plan lessons for ELLs, support communication with other educators, school personnel, and ELLs and to foster student learning of language and literacies in the content areas.
- **5a**: Candidates demonstrate knowledge of effective collaboration strategies in order to plan ways to serve as a resource for ELL instruction, support educators and school staff, and advocate for ELLs.
- **5c**: Candidates practice self-assessment and reflection, make adjustments for self- improvement, and plan for continuous professional development in the field of English language learning and teaching.
- **5d**: Candidates engage in supervised teaching to apply and develop their professional practices using self-reflection and feedback from their cooperating teachers and supervising faculty.

Language Objectives (for Students)

1. To read about two legendary people in Roswell. (Teachers make sure that students do not choose the same figure.)
2. To make a visual timeline to represent major events throughout the historical figure's life or throughout the student's life.
3. To write a memoir that represents the student's history, culture, and identity and that captures important

memories of the student's family, culture, and literacy experiences.
4. To produce a multimodal identity project using text and technology (adding visuals, audios, digital sources).
5. To present the project to other students and learn about other students' lived experiences.

Guiding Questions
1. Why is using primary sources to teach social studies more beneficial than secondary ones?
2. How do we, as educators, create experiences that allow students to connect to the past?
3. How can we incorporate oral history into our daily teaching strategies?
4. How can we clear the confusion for young learners regarding timelines?
5. How can you connect the teaching of writing and reading to history?
6. How can we instill in students their cultural values, and how can they protect their cultural heritage through personal and local history?
7. How can you help students connect with their culture through history?
8. How can you be culturally responsive to your students' needs using memoirs as one of the genres in the classroom?
9. How does local history represent diverse cultures in New Mexico and the United States?

Preview On the Reading
Most curricula for social studies are grounded in a scope and sequence. Decisions will be made by the district and state as to what comprises history. Your own professional judgment needs to come into play. The most common resource for learning history in elementary is the social studies textbook, but students should also use their families as a critical source of history. This module focuses on collecting information about the history of Roswell. Students will learn about using primary sources

(texts, images, and artifacts produced at the same time the events being recorded took places) and secondary sources.

Pre-Class preparation Activities for Teachers
Read

- You are going to read about local heroes in *Legendary Locals of Roswell* by John Lemay and Roger K. Burnett (Lemay & Burnett, 2012).
- You will read about local New Mexico history in *South Park Cemetery: Exploring Roswell's Roots*, a book that was published by 7th and 8th grade students and their teachers, Heidi Huckabee and Valarie Grant (Huckabee & Grant, n.d.).

Listen

- Dr. Christian Knudsen explains the differences between primary and secondary sources in history in this short video.
  What's the difference between primary and secondary sources in history? (The Medieval Historian, 2021) https://www.youtube.com/watch?v=XU0fAhss-yg
- Sara shares six storytelling activities: story cubes, act it out, prompts in a jar, spin for a story, draw a picture, and story in a box.
  Storytelling Activities Elementary https://www.youtube.com/watch?v=wQEeukEe2vE
- Amanda Werner discusses the differences between memoirs and personal narratives:
  What's the difference between memoirs and personal narratives? (Amanda, 2019) https://www.youtube.com/watch?v=SWuGrqNzqho
- Learn Bright provides an explanation of using timelines (Learn Bright, 2017) A comprehensive overview of timelines for K–6 students https://www.youtube.com/watch?v=o50HA6QTxj0

Thought Questions
1. Why do you think local historical figures should be included in the curriculum?
2. How does learning about local legendary figures represent cultural identity?
3. In what ways do you think researching historical figures supports student learning?
4. After reading about historical figures and reviewing the module materials, what resonated most with you? In what way will you incorporate that in your class?
5. The module covered the Common Core Standards focusing on all the language skills. How are you planning to incorporate the standards in your classroom?
6. How are you planning to teach about historical figures in social studies using the standards provided?
7. What kinds of creativity (thinking about the modes of meanings that could be used) do you hope to discover through your students' responses and reactions?
8. Do you see any challenges in implementing this approach in your classrooms? Explain.

References

Amanda, W. (2019, August 31). *What's the difference between memoirs and personal narratives* [Video]. YouTube. https://www.youtube.com/watch?v=SWuGrqNzqho

The Colorful Apple. (2021, January 23). *Story telling games for kids|Storytelling Activities Elementary* [Video]. YouTube. https://www.youtube.com/watch?v=wQEeukEe2vE

Ellis, A. K. (2010). *Teaching and learning elementary social studies* (9th ed.). Pearson/Allyn & Bacon. ISBN 978-0137039494.

Huckabee, H., Grant, V., & 7th and 8th Grade Students. (n.d.). *South Park Cemetery: Exploring Roswell's roots* [Class project, Berrendo Middle School].

Learn Bright. (2017, July 29). *Timelines for kids – A comprehensive overview of timelines for k-6 students* [Video]. YouTube. https://www.youtube.com/watch?v=o50HA6QTxj0

LeMay, J., & Burnett, R. K. (2012). *Legendary locals of Roswell*. Arcadia Publishing.

Storytelling with Ritu. (2022, September 6). *STORY TELLING GAMES FOR KIDS | Storytelling Activities Elementary* [Video]. YouTube. https://www.youtube.com/watch?v=wQEeukEe2vE

TESOL International Association. (2018). *Standards for initial TESOL Pre-K–12 teacher preparation programs.* https://www.tesol.org/media/v33fewo0/2018-tesol-teacher-prep-standards-final.pdf

The Medieval Historian. (2021, December 20). *What's the difference between primary and secondary sources in history?* [Video]. YouTube. https://www.youtube.com/watch?v=XU0fAhss-yg

Lesson Title: A MultiSemiotic Synesthesia Approach: Historical Figure (Karkar-Esperat, 2019, National Governors Association Center for Best Practices, & Council of Chief State School Officers, 2010; New Mexico Public Education Department, 2021)

Common Core Standards for 3rd–5th Grades	Social Studies Standards for 3rd–5th Grade	Pedagogical Holistic Model of New Literacies
Third Grade	**Third Grade**	"The synesthesia mode describes moving toward using different modes (New London Group, 1996). The pedagogical holistic model of new literacies included terms such as "different texts (graphic novels, digital stories, primary source documents, advertisements, or electronic texts)" and used terms such as "visuals," "sound effects," "music," and "language or body language" (Karkar-Esperat, 2019).
CCSS.ELA-LITERACY. RI.3.3 Describe the relationship between a series of historical events, scientific ideas or concepts, or steps in technical procedures in a text, using language that pertains to time, sequence, and cause/effect.	3.26. Express a positive view of themselves while demonstrating respect and empathy for others.	
CCSS.ELA-LITERACY. SL.3.5 Create engaging audio recordings of stories or poems that demonstrate fluid reading at an understandable pace; add visual displays when appropriate to emphasize or enhance certain facts or details.	3.27. Compare and contrast their cultural identity with other people and groups.	
CCSS.ELA-LITERACY. W.3.8 Recall information from experiences or gather information from print and digital sources; take brief notes on sources and sort evidence into provided categories.	**Fourth Grade** 4.25. Participate in inquiry of other people's lives and experiences while demonstrating respect and empathy for others.	
CCSS.ELA-LITERACY. W.3.6 With guidance and support from adults, use technology to produce and publish writing (using keyboarding skills) as well as to interact and collaborate with others.		

(Continued)

Common Core Standards for 3rd–5th Grades	Social Studies Standards for 3rd–5th Grade	Pedagogical Holistic Model of New Literacies
Fourth Grade CCSS.ELA-LITERACY.RI.4.3 Explain events, procedures, ideas, or concepts in a historical, scientific, or technical text, including what happened and why, based on specific information in the text. CCSS.ELA-LITERACY.SL.4.5 Add audio recordings and visual displays to presentations when appropriate to enhance the development of main ideas or themes. CCSS.ELA-LITERACY.W.4.8 Recall relevant information from experiences or gather relevant information from print and digital sources; take notes and categorize information, and provide a list of sources. CCSS.ELA-LITERACY.W.4.7 With some guidance and support from adults, use technology, including the Internet, to produce and publish writing as well as to interact and collaborate with others; demonstrate sufficient command of keyboarding skills to type a minimum of one page in a single sitting. **Fifth Grade** CCSS.ELA-LITERACY.RI.5.3 Explain the relationships or interactions between two or more individuals, events, ideas, or concepts in a historical, scientific, or technical text based on specific information in the text.	**Fifth Grade** 5.13. Examine history from the perspectives of the participants using a variety of narratives. 5.30. Demonstrate knowledge of family history, culture, and past contributions of people in their main identity groups.	"The MultiSemiotic synesthesia mode includes the use of audiovisuals, memoirs, historical and cultural documentaries, dancing, fiction, poetry, and animations. The gestural visual mode, for example, could reflect expressions in magazines and gestures in photos (Cloonan 2008). The visual gestural linguistic can consist of book characters, and the audiovisual might include music visuals or interplay (Cloonan 2008; see also Mills and Unsworth 2018)." (Karkar-Esperat, 2025, p. 12)

CCSS.ELA-LITERACY.SL.5.5
Explain the relationships or interactions between two or more individuals, events, ideas, or concepts in a historical, scientific, or technical text based on specific information in the text. CCSS.ELA-LITERACY.W.5.8
Recall relevant information from experiences or gather relevant information from print and digital sources; summarize or paraphrase information in notes and finished work, and provide a list of sources.

CCSS.ELA-LITERACY.W.5.6
With some guidance and support from adults, use technology, including the Internet, to produce and publish writing as well as to interact and collaborate with others; demonstrate sufficient command of keyboarding skills to type a minimum of two pages in a single sitting.

References

Cloonan, A. (2008). Multimodality pedagogies: A multiliteracies approach. *International Journal of Learning*, *15*(9), 159–168. https://doi.org/10.18848/1447-9494/CGP/v15i09/45952

Ellis, A. K. (2010). *Teaching and Learning Elementary Social Studies* (9th ed.). Pearson/Allyn & Bacon. ISBN 978-0137039494.

Karkar-Esperat, T. (2019). Assessing preservice teachers' knowledge of new literacies [Doctoral dissertation, Texas Tech University]. Texas Tech University Archive.

Karkar-Esperat, T. M. (2025). Multiliteracies for Multilingual Learners: The MultiSemiotics Architecture. Framework. *International Journal of Bilingual Education and Bilingualism*. https://doi.org/10.1080/13670050.2024.2409120

Karkar-Esperat, Tala Michelle. (2024). Multiliteracies in Teacher Education. In George Noblit (Ed.), *Oxford Research Encyclopedia of Education*. Oxford University Press. https://doi.org/10.1093/acrefore/9780190264093.013.1890

Lazutina, T. V., Pupysheva, I. N., Shcherbinin, M. N., Baksheev, V. N., & Patrakova, G. V. (2016). Semiotics of art: Language of architecture as a complex system of signs. *International Journal of Environmental and Science Education*, *11*(17), 9991–9998.

Mills, K. A., & Unsworth, L. (2018). The multimodal construction of race: A review of critical race theory research. *Language and Education*, *32*(4), 313–332.

National Governors Association Center for Best Practices, & Council of Chief State School Officers. (2010). *Common Core State Standards for English language arts & literacy in history/social studies, science, and technical subjects*. Authors. https://www.corestandards.org/ELA-Literacy/

New London Group (1996). A Pedagogy of Multiliteracies: Designing Social Futures. *Harvard Educational Review*, *66*(1), 60–92. https://doi.org/10.17763/haer.66.1.17370n67v22j160u

New Mexico Public Education Department. (2021). *New Mexico social studies standards*. https://webnew.ped.state.nm.us/bureaus/literacy-humanities/social-studies/

Panos, A. (2021). Reading about geography and race in the rural Rustbelt: Mobilizing dis/affiliation as a practice of whiteness. *Linguistics and Education*, *65*, 100955. https://doi.org/10.1016/j.linged.2021.100955

Instructional Materials Used with Students

Lesson Title—A MultiSemiotic Synesthesia Approach: Historical

Language Objectives (for Students)
- To read about legendary people in Roswell.
- To make a visual timeline to represent the major events throughout the historical figure's life or student's life.
- To write a memoir that represents the student's history, culture, and identity and that captures important memories of the student's family, culture, and literacy experiences.
- To produce a multimodal identity project using text and technology (adding visuals, audios, digital sources).
- To present the project to other students and learn about other students' lived experiences.

During instruction, these are activities that you can use for teaching your students:

- Students read about legendary locals and how they are connected to history, culture, and identity (visual map).
- Students gather information about legendary locals from different areas through various stories in books.
- Students use a visual map or a timeline to think in a more concrete way.
- Students describe legendary locals and their contributions to Roswell.
- Students compare their cultural identity with other people in their community.
- Students gather data by conducting interviews with family members or members of another ethnic group to learn about family history or local events.
- Students use the mentor texts provided to write their memoir.
- Students create a personal timeline to record one or two significant events from each year of their life (differentiation).

Aligning with the social studies standards (For students)

- Students provide knowledge through multimodal expressions of history, culture, and past contributions of people in Roswell.
- Students will express a positive view of themselves while demonstrating respect and empathy for others.
- Students role-play a historical figure.

Differentiation includes using leveled text, visuals and supplementary materials, audio and visual materials, class discussion, drawing/visuals, online resources, videos, and storytelling.

Postscript

This guide centers students' language and culture by recognizing and harnessing students' assets through semiotics (the study of signs using multiliteracies) and self-discovery. This guide enhances relationships between families, students, and teachers. It will assist teachers in embracing joy in the curriculum using a variety of strategies that involve students' assets, languages, and cultures to engage in discovery. It promotes compassionate education, fostering empathy and connection to students' identities in response to the known problem of student disengagement and the challenges in teaching reading and writing. I consider this guide as an atlas that provides a worldwide, timeless collection of methods that have been used and continue to be used, focusing on students pursuing lifelong learning experiences, enlightening teachers to have open minds toward learning with and from their students and embracing the ways every generation creates their own culture as we move through their world.

A last word about your students: Celebrate with them what they can be. Enjoy their enjoyment in their self-discovery. Be there for all their steps and encourage them to continue living and learning. Remember that their future is also yours—and it is future of the world.

Embracing students' identity through language and culture should be the New Day of Awakening and Self-Discovery.

I am eager to learn about your story, methods, and new approaches using this guide as a teacher, a parent, or a student; please share your ideas, successes, and challenges!

Your always listening and faithful educator,
Tala Michelle Karkar-Esperat
selfdiscoverythroughsemiotics@gmail.com

For Product Safety Concerns and Information please contact our EU
representative GPSR@taylorandfrancis.com
Taylor & Francis Verlag GmbH, Kaufingerstraße 24, 80331 München, Germany

www.ingramcontent.com/pod-product-compliance
Lightning Source LLC
Chambersburg PA
CBHW070243230426
43664CB00014B/2393